Public Protection and the Criminal Justice Process

Public Protection and the Criminal Justice Process

Mike Nash

OXFORD
UNIVERSITY PRESS

OXFORD
UNIVERSITY PRESS

Great Clarendon Street, Oxford OX2 6DP

Oxford University Press is a department of the University of Oxford.
It furthers the University's objective of excellence in research, scholarship,
and education by publishing worldwide in

Oxford New York

Auckland Cape Town Dar es Salaam Hong Kong Karachi
Kuala Lumpur Madrid Melbourne Mexico City Nairobi
New Delhi Shanghai Taipei Toronto

With offices in

Argentina Austria Brazil Chile Czech Republic France Greece
Guatemala Hungary Italy Japan Poland Portugal Singapore
South Korea Switzerland Thailand Turkey Ukraine Vietnam

Oxford is a registered trademark of Oxford University Press
in the UK and in certain other countries

Published in the United States
by Oxford University Press Inc., New York

British Library Cataloguing in Publication Data

Data available

Library of Congress Cataloging in Publication Data
Nash, Mike.
    Public protection and the criminal justice process / Mike Nash.
        p. cm.
    Includes bibliographical references and index.
    ISBN-13: 978-0-19-928943-1
    ISBN-10: 0-19-928943-3
1.   Criminal justice, Administration of–Great Britain. 2.   Criminal behavior,
Prediction of–Great Britain. 3.   Violent offenders–Government policy–Great Britain.
4.   Mentally ill offenders–Government policy–Great Britain. 5.   Danger (Law)–Great
Britain. 6.   Criminals–Civil rights–Great Britain.   I. Title.
    HV9960.G7N37 2006
    364.6'5—dc22

                                                                        2006009078

Typeset by Laserwords Private Limited, Chennai, India
Printed in Great Britain
on acid-free paper by
Ashford Colour Press Ltd, Gosport, Hampshire

ISBN 978-0-19-928943-1

10 9 8 7 6 5 4 3

For
Karen, Will and Linz
As ever

Contents

Abbreviations

ACOP	Association of Chief Officers of Probation
ACPO	Association of Chief Police Officers
ASBO	Anti-Social Behaviour Order
CJCSA	Criminal Justice and Court Services Act 2000
CJPOA	Criminal Justice and Public Order Act 1994
CSA	Crime (Sentences) Act 1997
DSPD	Dangerous Severe Personality Disorder
HMIP	Her Majesty's Inspectorate of Probation
IWF	Internet Watch Foundation
MAPP	Multi-Agency Public Protection
MAPPA	Multi-Agency Public Protection Arrangements
NCIS	National Criminal Intelligence Service
NOMS	National Offender Management Service
OASys	Offender Assessment System
PCL–R	Psychopathy Check List—Revised
PDO	Potentially Dangerous Offender
PITO	Police Information Technology Organisation
PNC	Police National Computer
POLIT	Paedophile On Line Investigation Team
RRASOR	Rapid Risk Assessment for Sex Offender Recidivism
RSHO	Risk of Sexual Harm Order
SACJ	Structured Anchored Clinical Judgement
SARA	Spousal Assault Risk Assessment Guide
SOA	Sex Offenders Act
SOO	Sex Offender Order
SOR	Sex Offender Register
SPOC	Single Point of Contact
SVP	Sexually Violent Predator
VGT	Virtual Global Taskforce
VISOR	Violent and Sex Offender Register
VORAG	Violent Offences Risk Appraisal Guide

Foreword

Can any subject be more important than public protection? It is unlikely. Yet, these two words cover a minefield of issues ranging from ethical to economic.

The early twentieth century saw the emergence of the Probation Service, with a mission enshrined in law to assist, advise, and befriend offenders. Almost one hundred years later, that mission has been changed to law enforcement and public protection. This change reflects the importance of probation as well as changing priorities for criminal justice, but there have been consequences, largely unforeseen, for policy, practice, resourcing, and inter-agency working, let alone public understanding and confidence.

Public protection challenges us emotionally, spiritually, and professionally. In six years serving the Parole Board for England and Wales, I came to realize, even more strongly than as a probation officer and manager, that the capacity of human beings to inflict pain, abuse, and terror was at the very margins of belief and, although the most appalling behaviours are rare, I had constantly to adjust what I believed human beings at their worst were capable of doing.

Together with the shocking impact of much violent and sexual crime, there is often a longer-term corrosive effect. Like many colleagues in the field, I have interviewed men convicted of serious sexual offences against children who have claimed that the years of abuse they inflicted caused no lasting damage. In contrast, I have read victim statements written many years after these same original offences which bear bitter testimony to the personal legacy of profound harm and violation still being experienced long into adulthood.

More recently, those of us with responsibility for staff (and indeed offenders under supervision) have needed to protect them from the public. Sometimes the targets have been offenders living legitimately in the community, for example those resident in probation hostels or attending specialist sex offender programmes. At other times, the targets have been public servants such as probation staff vilified in the media for their legitimate role in risk assessing and managing high-profile cases.

In spite of major improvements to public protection—such as strengthened professional assessment tools, legislation, and the much closer relationships forged between prison, probation, and police—much of the media in this country remains obsessed with notorious crimes. It is this media obsession, rather than considered debate, that Mike Nash fears is driving politicians of all parties to react in a way that is counter-productive, and does not create safer communities. Does the demonization of dangerous offenders by the tabloid press, for example, confuse and distract from the fact that so many incidents of sexual and domestic abuse are committed by persons known to their victims? More generally, does it inform or undermine effective work with dangerous offenders?

Mike Nash and I started our careers together as probation officers in Hampshire in the early 1980s. Since then our careers have followed different, but related, paths. Mike Nash has become a distinguished academic, and it is from this position—in touch with, but not part of, criminal justice (not just probation) practice—that he has written this timely and important book. The literature about public protection has been strengthened considerably by his experience, intellectual grasp, humanity, and courage in confronting issues that many choose to overlook or find too difficult to discuss.

It is Mike Nash's wish that the 'runaway train' of public protection be slowed sufficiently to allow for mature reflection and informed debate. It may not be possible to affect the speed of the train, but if his book helps to improve the signalling and the track on which the train runs it will have made a very substantial contribution to really protecting the public.

David Scott
Chief Officer London Probation
London, January 2006

Introduction

From emerging to established agendas

Six years ago, *Police, Probation and Protecting the Public* (Nash, 1999a) described an emerging agenda on two levels. The first was the increasing dominance of public protection issues across the criminal justice and the wider 'care' sector. The second was the developing multi-agency approach to dangerousness and more specifically, the emerging collaboration between the police and probation services at the heart of public protection in the United Kingdom. Indeed, in this embryonic form it was more of a dual approach. Since describing what was emerging in 1999, it has now clearly 'emerged' and has also become a defining feature of criminal justice practice. Public protection has also become a major political issue, fuelled and fanned by a number of high profile crimes with children as the primary victims. Successive Labour governments have not flinched from introducing strengthened legislation aimed at potentially dangerous offenders. This legislation has seen longer sentences, mandatory minimum sentences, severe constraints on the freedoms of those who have been released, and of course the likelihood of no release. Although the British government has introduced its first ever Human Rights Act (1998), it has in many respects disregarded rights when they are vested in potentially dangerous individuals. They have followed the view of Floud (1982), who suggested that the commission of very harmful behaviour once, removes the presumption of harmlessness and therefore justifies the removal of the offender's rights. In other words, the right of the public to be protected outweigh those of the offender.

The aim of the earlier book was to describe and critique an unfolding process. The widespread assumption in government was that existing processes were inadequate to protect the public effectively, although perhaps in private they were more inclined to think in terms of management of risk rather than risk reduction. Not only would legislation have to be strengthened but also agency practices changed, with risk assessment and management becoming the heart not only of probation work but that of the police service also. This meant a new role for police officers, becoming much more involved in the assessment of risk and the management of potentially dangerous offenders in the community.

Tasks that were once predominantly the preserve of probation officers and medical personnel were increasingly shared among a community of professionals all serving as members of multi-agency public protection panels (MAPPPs). In 1999, these panels were beginning to spread across the country in an ad hoc and voluntary fashion, but by 2000 the Criminal Justice and Court Services Act required their establishment by law.

Of course, as the machinery of public protection has grown, so has the number of cases considered. Public protection is now a huge industry; in 2003–4 alone 39,492 cases were considered by MAPPPs across the country, with 2,152 assessed as constituting the very highest risk, the so-called 'critical few'. The Sex Offenders Register, established by the Sex Offenders Act 1997, now has nearly 25,000 names on it—an increase of 15% over the previous year, although the other multi-agency public protection arrangements (MAPPA) numbers represented a significant fall. Due to concerns about future risk of harm, widespread concerns with sex offenders and an increasing number of 'eligible' offences, it is highly likely that the sex offender register will continue to grow, with current forecasts topping out at 125,000. Any increase in the length of the registration period (as presently unfolding in the USA), will instantly increase the numbers registered. Regular strengthening of the register's provisions and requirements has added significantly to the workload of the police service, usually without additional resources and at the expense of other tasks.

For the probation service, public protection and risk assessment and management has now become its most important function. The bureaucracy of the task, however, determined by its multi-agency nature, has meant that it too has had to reconsider the work it is able to undertake. The emergence of the National Probation Service in 2001 has seen its work increasingly prescribed by national agendas with constant calls from leading probation figures that the service should stop working with low and possibly medium risk offenders. Much of the traditional probation intervention may yet again return to agencies outside of the statutory framework or at least no longer be conducted by trained probation officers. Indeed proposals announced by the government in October 2005 suggested that all of the functions covered by probation boards could be put out to tenders from a range of private, independent, and public providers. It will be extremely interesting to see if the very sensitive area of public protection also treads the same path. Public protection has then changed the nature of police and probation work. It also impacts increasingly upon the works of other agencies, the prison service in particular but also housing services for example, which are seen as key partners in the multi-agency public protection arrangements (MAPPA).

From once being something more or less carried on behind closed doors, public protection has now spread its tentacles across the public sector and is a much more open process. This in itself may have the effect of increasing not only awareness but also fear and anxiety. Yet, the evidence for such massive change and resource diversion remains at best sketchy. Incidents of dangerous behaviour have remained rare and indeed it is more an increase in *potential* rather than *actual* dangerousness that is driving the agenda. This, of course, becomes something of a self-fulfilling prophecy, as the 'potential for dangerousness' categories expand, and then more people are found who meet the criteria. What happened to these people before the establishment of elaborate public protection machinery? Were there fewer incidents of extreme violence or sexual offending by those known to the police and probation services? Have we become a more dangerous society? Are we sure that the problem has grown sufficiently to justify significant erosion of individual rights and freedoms (Tonry, 2004)? Indeed, are we happy that the risks posed by lower level but much more numerous offenders, those most likely to impact upon a greater percentage of the population, are not as significant as the rare and unusual individuals who now consume so much time and energy? In terms of the perception of crime, these 'everyday' offenders will shape people's experience, yet are increasingly regarded as almost peripheral to routine criminal justice interventions.

Numerous authors have testified to a fundamental change in recent years, variously described as 'post-modern' society, 'late modern' society, or, more aptly for this book, 'risk' society (see, for example, Giddens, 1990, Beck, 1992 and 2000). Among many strands emerging from these depictions are a greater awareness and fear of numerous risks and a loss of faith in experts to deal with them. In other words, uncertainties appear to have increased when technological advances suggest that we should have greater control. For criminal justice practitioners, this brave new world opens up a parallel universe of worry and potential catastrophe. In attempting to control the future by managing these serious criminal risks, police and probation officers in particular are in an almost no-win situation. As we shall see in Chapters 1 and 5, identifying and predicting future dangerousness is a notoriously difficult task in itself. Attempting to manage and reduce risk of serious harm is even more difficult. Yet, in demanding that agencies engage in complex bureaucratic processes that are regarded as the only way to be effective, governments build expectations of success in the minds of the public. By seemingly conflating the problem of dangerousness, public fears are increased and evermore-draconian measures are taken. Within this whole agenda the notion of individual offender rights is subsumed beneath those rights of the public to be protected. This may be fine when there is evidence of clear and vivid danger (Dworkin, 1977), when extreme measures need to be taken to protect human life. Yet, the nature of the beast is that it is not those offenders presenting this extreme and imminent risk who are solely the recipients of this agenda. They are but a sub-group of a much larger number who are deemed to pose potential risks—but of course may never do so.

Understanding dangerousness—shaping the agenda

The next four chapters examine behaviour that may be framing and driving the dangerousness debate, in popular and policy terms. Chapters 2, 3, and 4 examine behaviour that may both fuel public concern and fear, or, is perhaps behaviour traditionally regarded as on the periphery of dangerousness, but could be considered more mainstream. Specific types of offences, and the more extreme variants of those offences have shaped the public's mind concerning dangerousness. Sexual offences undoubtedly come near the top of this category. However, other crimes, such as those tagged with the label of 'hate', may not regularly be included in the dangerousness category, even though serious assaults or death may be the outcome. Racist and homophobic attacks may come into that class of offences where, despite the seriousness of outcomes, even public concern is lessened by the seemingly less deserving status of the victim. As unpleasant a reality as this may be, it is probably the case that the media will be less interested in black or homosexual victims than in white and 'straight' victims. The public perception of dangerousness is therefore skewed and this undoubtedly will have some impact upon the professionals involved—to greater or lesser degree.

The issue with sex offending is essentially how, despite its relative rarity, it has managed to drive the agenda. Sex offenders have, almost universally, been given the label of sexual pariahs or predators. Little distinction is made between their offending patterns as all are effectively regarded as the same. This is unfortunate because the risks posed by this disparate group vary considerably. Yet by generalizing their behaviour their risk is also generalized—at least in the public mind—and any form of response to their offending other than a harsh, punitive one will not be tolerated. This unitary notion of sex offender risk itself presents a danger to society, as an ever-growing pool of undifferentiated worry clouds real and imminent dangers. The public obsession with sex offenders also tends to mask dangers posed by offences that are either less well known or, at least on the surface, are not so threatening. However, their persistence, in repeated familial sexual abuse for example, can be equally as harmful as more 'public' displays of sexual aggression, especially for the victim.

Enduring associations

There has long been a view that dangerousness and madness are linked. Despite the clear lack of evidence to support this notion it remains embedded in the public consciousness. It appears as if anyone who doesn't behave as others, who is different, is at the very least capable of harmful behaviour. This otherness taps into a deep well of public disquiet and fear. The Guardian (27 October 2005) carried a report indicating that the Metropolitan Police admitted that they too readily adopted the association between mental illness and violence and had, by their practice, done much to perpetuate those myths. The public and the media generally support measures proposed by governments to tackle this group, no matter how draconian. Chapter 4 will consider how a newly prominent group, those suffering from dangerous severe personality disorder (DSPD), have been targeted for a range of measures that completely overrides their human and civil rights. Indeed, they have been deemed as worthy of detention without committing a crime in certain circumstances—a clear sign of how effective the public protection agenda is at sweeping all before it. Although we know that the most pervasive forms of danger occur in the most familiar of settings, it appears as if we continue to want to label it as different and abnormal, thus a ready association of dangerousness with people suffering from mental health problems is made and reaffirmed on a daily basis.

Scientific prediction—or a shot in the dark?

The assessment and prediction of the risk of serious harm from known offenders lies at the heart of the dangerousness debate. Hugely important choices are made based upon judgements as to the likelihood that a person will, in the future, pose a high risk of serious harm to a known or unknown victim(s). Chapter 5 will examine what has become an enduring debate concerning assessment methods, in particular, the relative merits of clinical or actuarially based judgement. Just as the notion of risk has largely supplanted notions of dangerousness, so have actuarial methods increasingly replaced clinical judgement. These two factors should not be viewed in isolation. Dangerousness has a large degree of uncertainty attached to it—in essence the serious event may or may not happen. Traditionally, clinical judgement has been regarded as having little more than an even chance in making the correct judgement call. The application of more scientific methods, based upon aggregating huge data sets and identifying a number of predictive factors, carries an impression of greater certainty. This is why it sits better with the notion of risk, as this is said to be measurable in terms of both its seriousness and its imminence. Risk can also be graduated, in effect from 0 to 100 and therefore appears to offer the prospect of assessing the degree and range of interventions necessary to protect the public. For example, the distinction between 'serious harm' and 'very serious harm' will make a considerable difference to resources deployed, whether or not the community is to be notified about an offender, the range of agencies involved and so on.

Has risk supplanted dangerousness because it can supposedly be more effectively measured and predicted? Or is it, because of the burgeoning scale of the public protection problem, that assessment methods could be developed for use by a range of non-clinical practitioners, operating across the criminal justice sector? Formulaic assessment tools are more easily used by and transported across professional groups. Yet, certainly at the more extreme and serious end of criminal behaviour, base rates are thankfully very low. It is therefore very difficult to extrapolate a range of common features and predictive factors from what is often a small and uniquely contextualized group of offenders. All decisions concerning dangerousness and risk, from sentencing, to release and supervision in the community, are determined as much by risk assessment as they are by the instant offence. At the same time, the safety of the public is also in part determined by these same decisions. It is therefore unsurprising that professionals may wish to exercise caution and rely upon scientifically generated tools rather than professional judgement. At least if a situation does go badly wrong, the practitioner can blame his or her tools. Yet the use of these tools should never be a substitute for professional skill and judgement, if for no other reason than the protection of the worker involved, even before moving on to protect the public.

Dealing with dangerous and high risk offenders

Chapters 6 and 7 examine the legislative agenda that has unfolded since the Criminal Justice Act 1991. A decade and a half has witnessed a huge battery of powers to be deployed against the potentially dangerous offender. These powers entail both a considerable increase in sentencing dispositions and in constraining measures for offenders released back into the community—what may prove to be an increasingly remote possibility for many. A number of linked themes emerge from the programme of legislation. Among the most prominent would be a focus on sexual and violent offenders in particular, with the former very broadly drawn. In some cases these developments reflect changes in offending behaviour, for example the use of the Internet to facilitate the commission of a range of sexual offences. Others reflect more a process of generalizing certain offending into the potentially dangerous behaviour category. This has led to what Garland (2000:350) describes as 'penal marking' for life for sex offenders, but that labelled existence may not reflect the actual risk they pose—many, if not the majority, are constructed as posing a greater risk than they actually do.

Public expectation, fuelled by an undifferentiated understanding of actual risks, is, however, tolerant of the measures and unconcerned with the loss of rights for those who make them afraid. The Criminal Justice Act 1991 had seen the start of a process by which certain categories of offenders would be singled out for 'special attention'. An act premised upon the idea of proportionality in sentencing, saw this principle undercut by notions of risk and future harms allegedly posed by certain offenders. Once identified these offenders could be given 'longer than desert' sentences up to the maximum available in law—even if the instant offence did not warrant it. Since 1991, sentences for potentially dangerous offenders have gone through phases such as mandatory minimum or mandatory life sentences for certain second time offenders, to the most recent development of protective sentences and the notion of long term incarceration even if a crime has not been committed (civil detention). The focus on sexual and violent crime has been relentless, although increasingly a category known as 'other' has come into prominence. This is something of a 'catch-all' group that will include offenders who cause concern due to their alleged risk. It is not difficult to see how elastic the boundaries of this group could become.

At the other end of the sentencing process, release itself has become increasingly difficult for many offenders. Once again, developments in North America have led the way. There, offenders at the end of the lawful period of custody have been released, only to be further detained under civil mental health procedures. They are then moved to closed psychiatric facilities, many with little prospect of eventual release. Similar restraints upon release are emerging in the United Kingdom. Even if released, offenders falling into certain categories will face pre- and post-release assessments of their potential risks, and then find themselves subject to a range of community interventions determined by that assessment. All of these arrangements are on an increasingly large and intrusive scale, as the pool of potential risk shows no signs of becoming smaller. This process acts as something of a self-fulfilling prophecy, with the growth in the public protection machinery seemingly fuelling public fear and anxiety—demanding in turn more punitive and controlling measures.

It is not difficult to see the problems in these policies. Longer sentences and restricted release opportunities will quickly overburden the prison system. The growing number of criminal behaviours featuring in lists carrying longer and potentially protective sentences will not help this scenario. The long term and potentially dangerous offender prison population must surely therefore grow very quickly. At the same time, those who are released into a climate of fear, anxiety and blame avoidance, will find themselves under restrictive and intrusive supervision. How long agencies will be able to cope effectively with this growing number of cases remains to be seen. However, just as periodically the prison system is reduced by introducing a new measure to monitor them in the community (and to avoid greater overcrowding), so it is likely that potentially dangerous offenders will be regraded as a lower risk, simply because insufficient resources are available. This is a real time bomb waiting to explode.

A problem shared is a problem halved!

If assessment and prediction is at the heart of the public protection process, then the body is the multi-agency public protection panel (MAPPP). From embryonic beginnings in the early to mid-1990s, these collaborative arrangements have grown and are now defined by statute in the Criminal Justice and Court Services Act 2000 (s. 67). From tentative agreements between police and probation services, the public protection family has now grown to include the prison service as another responsible authority (Criminal Justice Act, 2003, s. 325), and also sees health, housing, victim services, mental health, social services, and other providers included and involved on an 'as required' basis. These meetings and the risk management plans generated by them (and their lower tiers), demand huge professional resources. For the probation service they have accelerated the move away from dealing with lower risk offenders, leaving a temporary vacuum that once the probation service itself moved in to fill. As noted below, changes to professional cultures may be a significant aspect of the public protection agenda and could certainly hasten the demise of the probation service 'as was'. It is as if a discrete public protection agency is on the brink of formation, with unified aims and purpose. A range of research has already hinted at how easy this step could be taken (Nash, 1999a, Nash, 1999b, Kemshall and Maguire, 2001, Kemshall, 2002, Lieb, 2003) as the boundaries between police and probation services in particular, and also prisons with the development of the national offender management service (NOMS), become increasingly blurred.

Making real decisions

In Chapter 9, four cases that are loosely based on real life incidents, are provided for the reader to work through a number of the issues raised in this book. Despite governments periodically reasserting that safety cannot be guaranteed, their continued escalation of the legislative agenda does suggest to the public that the situation can be managed (although for the public this may mean solved). It is doing this by lengthening sentences, making release less likely for certain offenders, by increasing surveillance and controls in the community and even locking up people who may not have committed a crime. Such an agenda almost suggests that devising risk management plans is easy because the goal is to protect the public and issues concerning the rights of the offender are very much secondary. Perhaps by examining these four cases, the tensions involved in the debate come to the fore a little more prominently. Managing potential dangerousness in the community is a difficult and fraught task that not only requires effective systems management but also professional skill and experience. By definition, the offenders under consideration and supervision are very difficult and many are adept at manipulation. In such cases, there cannot really be any substitution for a good working knowledge of and relationship with the offender. Prison and probation services can develop programmes to tackle a range of offending behaviours but on the day that the offender chooses to reveal his darkest thoughts before acting, he will want someone to talk to whom he believes he can trust. This is where the professional relationship will be essential.

Rights in a climate of fear

It would be surprising in such a climate if the issue of offender rights were high on the political or public agenda. Public sympathy is necessary to a certain extent if offenders are to be shown a more tolerant attitude, which is geared towards their integration back into society once punishment has been served. Yet, we have already seen that such forgiveness is not forthcoming for these types of offender and that their potential risks are generalized to include all those convicted, or indeed even suspected, of certain crimes. This widespread public attitude, reflected in or driven by the media, is reciprocated by government policy. There is, however, another, somewhat unseen, outcome to this generally very public process. This general change in attitude towards some offenders, with knock-on effects for many more, has significant consequences for those agencies dealing with offenders, notably the probation service. Having owed its very existence to a late Victorian desire to save lost souls, it had emerged as a professional organization concerned with the rehabilitation of offenders. Its language was one that stressed the opportunity for offenders to change, that challenged offenders but tempered this by an acceptance that others would have found difficult, and by a belief that many offenders could move on from their offending past. These beliefs and values are, to a large extent, absent from the language of public protection. Another language, shared in common with the police service, talks of surveillance, monitoring and risk management. Change and rehabilitation would be a valuable bonus, but does probably remain a bonus rather than the primary purpose of intervention. Once again, this philosophy may be justified for those posing the greater and more certain risk, but as noted, it is all too easy for it to spread to the probation service's dealings with all offenders. This cultural shift in the probation service, and to a lesser extent within the police service also, may be one of the unforeseen consequences of public protection work.

Chapter 10 therefore discusses the issue of rights, and whether or not high risk and dangerous offenders should have any at all. It is towards the end of the book because, symbolically, that seems to be the most appropriate place. Human and civil rights for offenders are in many respects losing their place on the criminal justice agenda, and for dangerous offenders it is as if they never had any to begin with. Yet it could equally be argued that this chapter should have come first. The issue of rights should underpin every criminal justice process yet, in the context of potential dangerousness, other more deserving rights have won the competition. If we adopt Floud and Young's (1981) terminology, there has been a competition between the public and dangerous offender rights, and the public have won. Many people may find the decision to place one set of rights above another an entirely appropriate one, especially when one party appears, because of their behaviour, to be so undeserving. Yet it has been the case that democracies have prided themselves on their defence of rights for all. Making such choices threatens to isolate a significant number of people for long periods of time, if not for life. It is also much easier, once this process has been set in train, to abrogate the rights of other groups who are deemed to threaten the social or moral order. It is a slippery slope and that may be the really dangerous choice.

Reading this book

It has not been the author's intention to produce a guide or handbook that purports to inform readers, and especially practitioners, how to deal with potentially dangerous offenders. Such an idea could be problematic in that it might suggest one way of working over another, one degree of risk over another, once choice of offence or offender over another based on formulaic, generalized assumptions. True dangerousness remains rare and distinctive but there is a prospect of its replacement by graduated risk calculations enlarging this problem until it becomes unmanageable. Because risk is pervasive then so has dangerousness become an assumed widespread problem, the two are inextricably linked even though risk has been developed in many ways to supplant notions of dangerousness. The pervasiveness of risk, closely linked with the huge growth in the risk assessment and management machinery, by default persuades the public of unseen dangers everywhere. Dangerousness has therefore, to a certain extent, become devalued by risk, as it assumes a commonality way beyond its real extent in the community.

Public protection increasingly resembles a runaway train and as it careers forward, it gathers up more people, resources, and fears, making stopping it increasingly difficult. The highly politicized nature of managing risks to the public ensures that opposition to any measure remains at best muted, so that each new incident automatically triggers a hardening of the punitive response. The intention in this book is to step off the train and consider the issues in a critical and constructive manner—one step removed from the daily grind of policy and practice and outsole of the political pressures faced by those charged with the increasingly onerous job of protecting the public.

1

Trying to Understand Dangerousness

Introduction

Dangerous people and dangerous behaviour appear to be at the top of everyone's agenda. Lurid and sensationalized stories sporadically fill the pages of national newspapers and, as a result, governments are seemingly compelled to introduce ever-tougher measures to combat the problem and reassure the public. Yet these stories frequently not only fail to distinguish between types of risk and danger, but in effect distort the true picture concerning where danger really lies. In this chapter there will be an attempt to define and conceptualize dangerousness so that readers can cut through some of the hype that traditionally surrounds this subject.

Dangerous and seriousness—trying to understand the difference

With the publication of the 2003–4 annual reports of the multi-agency public protection arrangements (MAPPA), Paul Goggins, the Minister for Correctional Services, boldly claimed that 'Public protection from dangerous offenders was better than ever.' This claim was based upon a reoffending rate of 1% for those subject to the MAPPA. The MAPPA system will be reviewed in Chapter 8, but at this point it is perhaps interesting to think a little about Goggins' claim. As we shall consider in this chapter, dangerousness is a future event—it is very much about something that might happen, but equally might not. Success in this instance, therefore, is about what has not happened rather than what already has. We cannot know if any of the offenders subject to MAPPA would have offended if they had not been so—and therein lies the really problematic nature of dangerousness. Not only is it difficult to agree upon which behaviour actually should be considered potentially or actually dangerous, but it is probably much more difficult to predict *if* it will happen again, *when* and *how seriously*. It is for this reason perhaps that the notion of risk, and its management, has superseded potential dangerousness in the everyday language of criminal justice practition-ers. Risk is, at least on paper, a more tangible concept in that it can potentially be measured along a scale of seriousness. If it can be measured then there is every opportunity to put in place methods to manage and possibly reduce the risk, and to deploy appropriate measures against the perceived level of harm. With potential dangerousness the concept is much more ephemeral. Its imprecise and uncertain nature makes planning difficult. Therefore, in an era where fears are out of control and risks dominate the public agenda, it is easier to reconfigure the problem into one that appears to be both manageable and containable.

When the Criminal Justice Act 1991 came into force (October 1992), offence seriousness gained a prominent and more public place in criminal justice (the notion of just deserts). Although it may have been felt by most people that offence seriousness would normally determine sentence severity, this was clearly not so, with a range of other factors having influence (ie age, race, gender, class, employment status, etc.). However, with the newfound prom-inence came a lack of clear advice on assessing offence seriousness. The lack of guidelines for sentencers to evaluate and differentiate levels of seriousness suggested that it was 'obvious', and therefore detailed guidance was unneces-sary. Indeed, early indications were that an 'ordinary' person on the proverbial Clapham Omnibus would instantly recognize a serious offence, and the image of an elephant was conjured up as something that everyone, everywhere would recognize. This simplistic—and undoubtedly oversimplistic—notion of serious-ness can also be linked with perceptions of dangerousness.

Many people are clear in their minds what constitutes dangerous behaviour. For most people it would be an image of a man (invariably) who commits very serious sexual (usually) and violent offences against (predictably) vulnerable individuals with whom they have not had previous knowledge—in other words the classic 'stranger predator'. This image is extremely powerful and draws upon very significant personal fears and worries. It thus constructs a perception of dangerousness that is reinforced by media reporting of particularly notorious cases. Petrunik (2003) utilizes Durkheim's notion of the sacred and the profane to make this point. He argues that the more sacred, pure, or innocent the vic-tim, the more profane or unclean the assault and the person committing it are considered to be. This results in a scale of revulsion, which in turn becomes associated with perceptions of dangerousness. The obverse of this would be that less repulsive behaviour, with victims considered to be less 'innocent', would find itself pushed down the scale of potential dangerousness. This notion suggests a hierarchy of victims, with innocent children at the top and then moving through a series of victim categories who may become increasingly less deserving of care, concern, or protection. This may be an unpalatable proposition. Yet consider reactions to sexual assaults against prostitutes compared with those against 'ordinary' women. Or indeed consider the reaction to crimes against the elderly to those against young people, white victims compared with ethnic minorities, and 'straight' victims against gays. Our perceptions are closely linked with how we feel about certain activities, and how at risk we believe our family and friends might be. In a sense this says something about crime coming 'close to home' in that it is a concern with becoming a victim. Yet, as we know, the constructions of danger referred to above are extremely rare, and the vast majority of sexual abuse and severe violence occurs within a domestic context. If, however, you ask your friends or colleagues to describe dangerous people and behaviour, it is likely to be the stranger you do not know rather than someone that you do know, who will be identified.

Dangerousness in essence therefore speaks of the 'quality' of the behaviour, its seriousness and predictability. Dangers are to be avoided, as are dangerous individuals. The criminal justice system is involved with these people for predominantly one simple reason, to institute measures to prevent them acting in a dangerous way in the future—to prevent another person falling victim to their criminal behaviour. Dangerous criminal behaviour is, therefore, for many people, somewhat out of the ordinary, bizarre or unnatural. It is certainly not behaviour that 'we' could or would do—it is something done by 'others'. The more 'ordinary' the behaviour, the less likely the perpetrator will be regarded as dangerous, even if the outcome of their actions is very serious. These shadowy 'others' become the repository for our fears and worries, for our condemnation and revulsion. It is easy to understand why mental illness becomes associated with dangerous behaviour—an association lacking in substantial empirical evidence as an across the board explanation. The sense of unpredictability and lack of control, too readily associated with mental illness, becomes a convenient hook upon which to hang the label of dangerous. Behaviour that is different becomes, by default, behaviour that poses a threat. The 'mad or bad' debate is not new and is built upon a popular myth linking mental illness with the devil. However, even in a technologically driven scientific world, these associations have not disappeared. Indeed, in 2005, a psychiatrist from Columbia University in New York has resurrected the notion of evil in considering the behaviour of certain very serious offenders (The Sunday Times, 13 February 2005). Michael Stone claimed that the behaviour of some of the worst serial murderers and mass killers could best be described as evil. He believed that their behaviour was not explained by mental illness but rather as a rational choice based upon the pleasure they derived from their activities. He cited notorious British murderers such as Fred West and Ian Brady but did not include Myra Hindley, as he believed Brady had led her to some extent. These associations would resonate with many people who describe much serious behaviour as having been committed by 'nutters'.

Cases that personify dangerousness

A case reported early in 2005 gives graphic illustration to the demonization of dangerous behaviour. Peter Bryan was given two life sentences on 15 March 2005 for two separate murders—nothing particularly newsworthy until the circumstances of the murders is understood (The Guardian, 16 and 17 March and The Observer, 20 March 2005). The notoriety of this case was twofold. The first instance of concern was that having been committed to a secure hospital following the murder of a shop assistant in 1994, by 2000 (and in a chilling reminder of the Graham Young case described below), he was adjudged as stable and moved to hostel in London following review by a tribunal. He was assessed as not presenting 'any major risk' by his mental health social worker and by 2004 was transferred to an open psychiatric ward. There he was described as calm and jovial and was given the freedom to come and go as he wished—and he killed within 24 hours. It is here that the second notorious aspect of the case arises. Bryan killed and dismembered a 43-year-old man and, at the time of his arrest, was found by police to be eating his victim's brains having fried them in margarine. He then subsequently killed again, eight weeks later, whilst on remand in a medium secure ward at Broadmoor. He had allegedly told staff there that he wanted to eat someone's nose and also, at a later date, attacked staff.

As indicated above, and in similar circumstances to the Graham Young case, a life sentence has now been passed following another killing subsequent to a mental health release, altering the future consideration of future release plans towards the parole board rather than the mental health tribunal. This case therefore offers us some of the classic examples of 'dangerousness' issues. We have a man released as 'safe', a brutal and bizarre second killing, and a third murder supposedly in a safe environment and one which might be interpreted as preventable. Predictably the tabloids leapt on the case with The Sun (16 March 2005) demanding to know 'Who let out the cannibal killer?' and wanting their identities made public, 'The government should name them—then sack them.' It is perhaps therefore easy to understand the public linkage of mental illness and dangerousness with Bryan diagnosed as a paranoid schizophrenic with a personality disorder. Yet, as The Observer reported (20 March 2005), out of approximately 900 murders committed each year (itself an inflated figure due to the activities of the serial killer Dr Harold Shipman, see below), only 30–50 can be attributed to the severely mentally ill, a figure that has remained stable since records began.

A case fitting the classic dangerous/evil profile appeared in The Guardian (22 February 1992). The case in many respects ticks all the boxes in terms of public conceptions of dangerousness, and is manna from heaven for the media. A 37-year-old man was convicted of murdering his wife following a row over her relationship with another man, he claimed to have been provoked by her infidelity, and argued that he acted out of diminished responsibility. He had strangled his wife and then placed her in an 80-litre vat full of hydrochloric acid.

He had purchased this a week earlier, tried it for size by sitting in it himself, and taken out a £51,000 insurance policy on her life. However, she was not dead when she was put into the vat (her husband claimed he had only locked her in the garage and she had stumbled into it). Her screams alerted passers-by but she later died in hospital. The case contained many classic dangerousness associations. The defendant claimed he was provoked beyond reason by his wife's allegations of his sexual inadequacy compared with her new lover. The defendant was said to have been engulfed by the 'green-eyed monster of jealousy'—a passion that Scott (1977) notes as being notoriously dangerous and one which is difficult to move away from or overcome. The judge described the defendant as arrogant in not checking his wife's pulse before putting her into the acid vat, saying that she 'recovered consciousness only to die a most horrible death'. In summing up, the Judge described the husband as, 'a very dangerous man with an enormous capacity for evil', describing his crime as, 'one of the most horrific it is possible to imagine'. The defendant was sentenced to life imprisonment with a recommendation that he serve a minimum of 18 years. In terms of profiling behaviour, it is interesting to note that this defendant had previously been sentenced to two years' imprisonment for imprisoning a previous girlfriend and beating her up when she threatened to leave him—another stark reminder that behind what may be regarded as just another 'domestic', extreme danger may lurk.

Cases such as this feed the stereotype of dangerousness, supporting the notion of 'extraordinary' beings in our midst. The brother of the 'Yorkshire Ripper' Peter Sutcliffe, responsible for the murder of 13 women and young girls, said that he believed the man responsible would be 'an ugly hunchback with boils all over his face' (The Guardian, 18 February 2005). These powerful, almost primal images and feelings are therefore commonplace and undoubtedly exist, to a greater or lesser extent, in the consciousness of criminal justice practitioners. No matter the extent of professional training, it is difficult to completely eradicate such powerful feelings from one's everyday professional practice. Yet, the real danger here is the possibility of overlooking the more obvious signs of potential dangerousness, in behaviour that may be regarded as 'everyday', or relatively normal. Dangerousness is not only about the extreme forms of violence and sexual assault, but the possibility of serious harm recurring in any situation. The effect of dangerous behaviour on the victim does not have to be physical, as long term trauma may have an equally negative impact.

These powerful and deeply embedded feelings concerning dangerous people are very much based on the notion of the 'other', a person unlike the 'rest of us'—a person who would do what we would not and therefore deserve no sympathy or forgiveness. Undoubtedly, the 'other' person is invariably cast as the stranger, or even the bogeyman in the case of children. The bogeyman will not only come and take you away, he is also the type of person to be avoided—he is not one of us. Yet much of the evidence on homicide for example negates this image. In her detailed work on the subject, Brookman (2005:40) reviews the homicide index for 1995–2001 to show that 31.5% of homicides in that period were domestic (1,742 cases), with a further 18% (1,013) being classified as acquaintance and 6.4% (367) committed by a friend. In other words there appeared to be evidence of a relationship in over 56% of all homicides. Only 15% (824) of all homicides were classed as having been committed by a stranger during this period. In 23% of cases there was no victim or no suspect.

Similarly, the notion of safe space is somewhat shot through by the fact that over 52% of all homicides were located in the home environment. Safe spaces and safe people contradict the image of the dangerous predator and it is in this simple misconception, fuelled all too readily by media and politicians, where the real danger lies. The relatively static homicide rate in England and Wales (between 500–600 per year) was heavily skewed in 2002 by the conviction of Dr Harold Shipman, a family general practitioner who was, it emerged, a mass murderer, responsible for in excess of 230 deaths over a period of 24 years. This man represented most people's idea of safety and security, a GP, a local man, a trusted man, and an older man. Danger comes in many forms but, with a few notable exceptions, it is not expected to reside in the family doctor. In many ways Shipman's horrendous activities demonstrate the constant need for potential dangerousness not to be pigeonholed into the stranger–predator category. Although his behaviour did not present as being of someone who was engaged in fatal activity and was not detectable or even regarded as problematic (other than by the occasional pharmacist or undertaker), he does show that a suspicious nature is necessary in dealings with offenders, even if they appear not to meet the classic model of the predator. The increase in figures at the end of the 1990s and early 2000s was also explained by the deaths of 58 Chinese immigrants all found dead in a lorry container at Dover, and all counted as individual victims of homicide (Brookman, 2005:32).

To counter the effect of these deep-seated impressions clouding professional judgement, the approach to the assessment and prediction of potential dangerousness has become increasingly 'scientific' and linked with risk. This process attempts to remove subjectivity from the process as far as possible, although this is probably impossible to achieve in its entirety. Chapter 5 will explore the developing methods of risk assessment but, prior to that, an overview of definitions of dangerousness will be conducted.

Understanding and conceptualizing dangerousness

Risk and dangerousness are words used interchangeably by many people. It is increasingly the case, however, that criminal justice professionals will speak of risk, and the public and media of danger. Some years ago, the author approached a probation service seeking permission to conduct research into the supervision of dangerous offenders. In refusing permission, the research officer for the service indicated that the probation service was no longer considering dangerousness, only risk! Risk is, of course, the likelihood or probability that an event will happen, whereas dangerousness relates to the potential severity of that event, although even in this context the word is increasingly replaced by serious harm. It is, therefore, absolutely vital that assessments of risk do not begin to squeeze out the considerations of 'risk of what?' The actual nature of potentially dangerous behaviour must not be lost in a push towards claims for actuarial accuracy in assessment processes. As Horsefield (2003) indicates, '(risk) . . . obscures the individuality and hides the social origins of the behaviour which leads to people being defined as dangerous.' This is an extremely important point and reminds us of the uniqueness of most situations in which this type of behaviour occurs. It is not necessarily the behaviour itself that is unique, but the situation and context in which it occurs. Understanding this will offer many clues in assessing the likelihood of recurrence. Dangerousness is therefore, in a nutshell, the likelihood or probability of serious harmful behaviour occurring in the future. It is therefore a 'future event', predominantly but not exclusively sited in someone who has committed similar behaviour previously (although see the emerging work by Soothill (2003) on efforts to statistically predict future serious offending in those without a prior history of such behaviour). It is extremely important because society has to make decisions about people who have (mostly) indicated by their previous behaviour that they could be very harmful again. It will do this at various stages but invariably as a part of criminal proceedings, which will be concerned with sentencing, containment, release, and post-release restrictions. It is therefore closely linked with justice, fairness, and rights; issues discussed in Chapter 10.

Despite the power of the images of dangerous offenders described above, this perception has not always been predominant. In the nineteenth century for example, the so-called 'dangerous classes' were viewed in quite a different light (Pratt, 1987: 11–18). In an era when for many people threats to property were regarded as more serious than threats to the person, punishments for property crime often exceeded that for physical violence, especially if the victim of violent attacks came from the undeserving classes. It was as if their position in life and lifestyle contributed to their victim status and in a sense they deserved what happened to them. A similar line continues to run through official responses to sexual assault and domestic violence today. Well into the twentieth century there was an association of recidivist behaviour with dangerousness, with exemplary sentences available for incorrigible offenders who failed to learn from their mistakes and punishment. This recidivism was not of an exclusively violent or sexual nature. It was not until the end of the twentieth century that dangerousness became intrinsically linked with certain forms of violent and sexual behaviour and images of the people who might commit such behaviour.

Are there more dangerous people at large?

The abolition of the death penalty was undoubtedly instrumental in establishing contemporary perceptions of dangerousness. A concern quite quickly developed over what might happen when people who might otherwise have been executed were released into the community. This concern, of course, tended to overlook the rarity of capital punishment, its regular commutation and the successful release of large numbers of very serious offenders back into the community (Coker and Martin, 1985). The fact that many killers were already at large in the community without causing mayhem was secondary it appears to the loss of the ultimate deterrent. Symbolism was again proving a powerful perception builder. Specific cases were instrumental in provoking policy debate and legislative developments, just as they would again, but much more powerfully, in 1990s America and, to a greater or lesser extent, across much of the world.

A seminal case was that of the poisoner Graham Young. This teenager was responsible for the murder of his stepmother and serious illness of his father by poisoning—a process that fascinated him. At the age of 15, Young was committed to a special hospital (Broadmoor) for a period of 15 years. Discharged after eight years as fit for a return to the community, he had during his hospitalization nurtured and developed his knowledge of poisons, undoubtedly becoming one of the leading specialists in the country. His discharge arrangements entailed him working in a factory that manufactured camera lenses, offering a ready supply of poisonous chemicals. Young poisoned several workers at the factory, fastidiously recording the effect of his chosen poison (thallium) on his victims. He was eventually charged with two counts of murder and two of attempted murder. In court Young pleaded not guilty, confident that his knowledge of poisons was second to none. Unfortunately for him there was one expert with equal if not superior knowledge and Young was convicted and sentenced to life imprisonment, the state thus avoiding the chance of his early release as a result of a 'cured' diagnosis (for a full discussion of the case see Holden, 1974 and Bowden, 1996a).

The significance of the case lay not only in the actual decision to release him from hospital, but also the nature of his post-release arrangements. Young's release from hospital was what might be termed a *false negative,* where a prediction of no or low dangerousness ended with dreadful outcomes. His post-release supervision was minimal, omitting the home visits that might have yielded clues to the macabre interests he enjoyed. Young's case raises the classic issues of dangerousness and emphasize the difficulties for all involved in its assessment and management. He had been found guilty of very dangerous acts but was later assessed as safe for release. Those of an unforgiving nature might well argue that he should have at least spent the recommended minimum term of 15 years in hospital, and no doubt for many people, he should never have been released. However, treading that path would see the long term prison and secure hospital populations rapidly spiral out of control. It would also negate the view held by many professionals that offenders can change and that some behaviour, even the most heinous, may never be repeated. Distinguishing between those who will and will not repeat their behaviour is unfortunately not an exact science and mistakes will be made. One can imagine how those involved in Young's release decision would have felt when news of his latest victims broke. One can also imagine the reaction from the press and public to that original decision. Being blamed for events largely outside of one's control is an unpleasant experience and unfortunately blame culture is rife in the modern world. It is, therefore, easy to understand why practitioners might err on the side of caution but events such as the Bryan case noted above demonstrate that errors of judgement can continue to have disastrous consequences.

The government responded to the furore created by the Young case by establishing the Butler Committee, which reported in 1975. In considering the discharge and after-care of the mentally abnormal offender, the committee naturally had to consider the issue of dangerousness; indeed they had to consider and attempt to define what it was. The Butler definition has stood the test of time, and is now the basis of that employed by multi-agency public protection panels (MAPPPs). The Butler Committee held that dangerousness was 'a propensity to cause serious physical or lasting psychological harm'. The definition itself is relatively simple and extremely useful, but its problems arise from the use of the word 'propensity'—how can we assess it and how certain can we be that we are right? A further very important consideration would be the definition and understanding of 'serious'—how serious does behaviour have to be to trigger a substantial loss of civil or human rights? These central issues will be discussed in Chapter 10.

Provoked in similar fashion by concern with one notorious offender (Jimmy Boyle), the Scottish Council on Crime (1977) defined dangerousness as being, 'the probability that he will inflict serious and irremediable personal injury in the future'. We can then begin to identify the three essential components of dangerousness; it is a future event, it is likely or probable, and will have serious consequences or impact for one or more victims. Because the consideration of dangerousness invariably occurs within a criminal context, it is highly probable that there would already have been anxiety-provoking behaviour to act as a baseline. The crucial issue therefore becomes that of assessing the likelihood of that behaviour being repeated, or the circumstances and context in which it occurred being recreated. Dangerousness is not about what has been done in the past, that cannot be undone, but about trying to reduce the possibility that it will recur in the future. Dangerous people, therefore, become those who might repeat their already serious behaviour. The problem for a criminal justice system that needs to manage these offenders is, of course, to distinguish between those it thinks will and will not—and to avoid releasing early those who will, and avoiding the continued detention of those who will not. The confusion between past and future behaviour in part explains why risk of harm may be the preferred terminology for professionals—risk is very much future oriented.

Dangerous thoughts and dangerous behaviour

It, therefore, becomes essential to understand the motivations for offending, and the context in which the original serious behaviour occurred. In understanding these factors, practitioners might be better placed to predict the recurrence of behaviour. For example, the acid bath murderer noted above was alleged to have murdered his wife because he was extremely jealous. Scott (1977) regards jealousy as a 'notoriously dangerous passion' in that it is untreatable. Those offenders, for example, who murder partners as a result of jealousy may well enter new relationships upon their release. They may then, of course, become very jealous once again of their partner's real or imagined lifestyle. In such circumstances the whole murderous scenario could be recreated and re-enacted. The accepted wisdom that views 'domestic' murders as less serious or dangerous than those perpetrated by strangers, may well be generalizing on motivation and underestimating risk of danger.

Of course, if we do extend the baseline of potential dangerousness to include newer types of offending such as hate crime and Internet sex crime, then the numbers of those to be potentially included in considerations becomes almost unmanageable. It is this sheer scale of a growing baseline, however, that requires differentiation to be made between offenders. Writing in 1988, Prins considered there to be a dangerous offender population of approximately 300. Earlier, in 1980, Brody and Tarling had argued that '... those whose aggressiveness is so repetitive or obsessive as to leave little room for doubt are rare'. As will be shown below, as the baselines for potential danger, or perhaps more contemporarily, of high risk grows, so there needs to be mechanisms to restrict the scale of the problem, in numeric terms if nothing else. Therefore MAPP arrangements have refined their risk criteria at the upper end to include 'very high risk' and a group of offenders meriting the greatest restrictions known as the 'critical few'. Home Office figures put this group at 2,152 in 2003–4 (MAPPA report). The pool for potential danger is, however, far greater, for example, there were nearly 39,500 offenders on MAPPA with over 24,500 of these registered sex offenders. We also know that there are far larger numbers in the community not registered as their offending predates the Sex Offenders Act 1997, or a part of the severely under-reported pool of sexual and domestic crimes. Even if we accept that the most dangerous (or highest risk) group is only 2,152 (level 3) it is still far in excess of Prins' (1988) figure of 300. Does this suggest that there are more of these very dangerous offenders in circulation, or that the system of counting is becoming more inclusive, or that practitioners afraid of making the wrong judgement are overcautious in their evaluation? Alternatively, does the language of risk conflate a problem that is better represented if dangerousness is considered as the baseline behaviour? By definition, dangerousness should remain exceptional and, if this term remained the focus of attention, it might restrict the numbers involved.

Unfortunately for the reasonable management of dangerousness, its perception appears directly related to the public's fear of crime—as fear increases so potential danger is seen in more and more people and more and more places. As Bottoms (1977) noted, considerations of dangerousness have shifted from the behaviour to the individual, whereas it is crucial to place the behaviour in its context (as well as locating it with the individual in a given context). He also noted the change this engendered in probation practice (Bottoms, 1979). As Scott (1977) indicates, a potentially dangerous situation results from the combination of offender, circumstances, and victim. Any manipulation to this equation may well considerably reduce the risk of a potentially dangerous outcome. The problems involved in assessing potential danger are discussed in Chapter 5, but for now the point can be made that it is evident that dangerousness resides in a critical combination of people and circumstances, and its repetition in the possibility of replication and recreation of events similar to that occurring previously. In all aspects this implies a complicated and difficult process that requires a detailed knowledge of the offender and the circumstances of their original dangerous behaviour (aspects of which may not have resulted in a criminal conviction). This negates any form of simplified assessment process but must, of course, allow for the potential for subjectivity in cases where crimes may be extreme or bizarre and therefore conjure up some very disturbing images in the mind. As Scott (1977:129) indicated, 'the legal category, even murder, arson and rape, is not very useful in determining dangerousness'. If we are to keep dangerousness within the exclusive category that its seriousness merits, we will need to be sure that we are attaching the label to the right people. Undoubtedly there are dangerous people in society, people who, given the opportunity and right circumstances, will kill or seriously assault others, either known to them or strangers. But we are essentially saying that we are fairly confident that they will do so in the future rather than that they have 'simply' committed a particular crime in the past. On this basis, not all of those convicted of murder will be dangerous, but simplified, offence-focused assessment processes, would at least have them in the 'potential' category. Following this route slavishly would open the floodgates to huge numbers of offenders, thus negating the opportunity to adequately assess those who need it.

In many respects, the 'pool' of potentially dangerous offenders is enormous. It does not consist solely of people who have shown dangerous tendencies previously, or have been convicted of serious offences or indeed certain types of offences. Dangerous behaviour, if it is taken as very serious behaviour that has a lasting harmful effect, can arise in anyone. The crucial issue is, once it has happened, whether it will be repeated in the future. Naturally, we all make everyday assumptions about people, and these are that in general, other people do not have harmful intentions towards us. However, it is important to consider that people who do not normally act out, or act aggressively, can do so in certain contexts.

In stressful life situations, people will behave in ways that may be entirely different to their everyday conduct. For example, in family law cases involving disputed living arrangements for children, tensions can run extremely high. Many parents may see themselves in a situation where they have lost everything and their only recourse is to extreme measures. Women in particular may be at serious risk of harm from their ex-partners, although the focus tends to be on the potential risk to the children concerned. The very public and at times highly dangerous activities of the pressure group Fathers for Justice, and more extreme offshoots, demonstrate how high emotions can go in what might once have been viewed as a relatively quiet area of practice for family court professionals. A report prepared for Women's Aid (Saunders, 2005a), indicated that 29 children had been killed in 13 families between 1994 and 2004 during contact or residence arrangements agreed and ordered by the family courts. Ten of these children died in one year, 2002–3. In three cases, unsupervised contact or residence had been granted to very violent fathers, *against professional advice*. In 11 of the 13 families, domestic violence was seen to be an important issue. In five cases it was clear that the father had killed the child to take revenge upon the mother.

Animal rights and environmental protest are other examples of activities that are increasingly showing potential for serious violence and, perhaps on the other side of the fence, the emotions generated by the ban on fox hunting hint at the potential for future violence. None of these potential sites of violent behaviour are routinely associated with the possibility of dangerousness, yet that may be the clear outcome. Dangerousness has to be concerned with future serious violent or sexual behaviour. It needs to be considered wherever it might arise and should not be stereotyped along traditional lines.

It is not at all usual to associate these or similar activities with potential dangerousness, but perhaps the time has come to think outside of the box. If we accept that jealousy has the potential to spark serious offending, we thereby accept that very strong human emotions can create potentially dangerous situations. We should therefore look to other situations where emotions and passions can run strongly as a possible reservoir of dangerousness. Scott (1977) argues persuasively that dangerousness is situational—thus we need to not only consider a range of situations in which it might occur, but also how we might manage the risks involved. The suggestion is that those involved in working with the potentially dangerous need to look in a variety of places and think laterally. However, there is a real risk that as the agencies of public protection become increasingly concentrated into specialist units, skill and expertise will not be as widespread within the organization as the response to potential risks requires. Danger may not be everywhere, but may arise anywhere.

Making sense of images of horror

Some of the examples noted in this chapter have resulted in terrible deaths for victims, in other cases violent and or repeated sexual assault may be the result of an offender's dangerous behaviour. These images cloud perceptions to a certain extent and certainly drive public agendas. Yet even relatively minor sexual assaults of children, persistently carried out over a number of years by a person in a position of trust, must be regarded as dangerous. The potential effect on the victim is huge and long lasting. Such behaviour must be regarded as seriously as the one-off spectacular and media-friendly cases, but, as noted further on in this text, it may be regarded as outside of mainstream dangerousness, thus furthering the prospects for its continuation.

Thus, in trying to understand and deal with dangerousness should society focus upon the extremes of behaviour, or be more concerned with the potential for repetition? If we consider the persistent sexual abuser just noted, the actual behaviour might be at the lower end of seriousness but its persistence is the worrying issue, especially if efforts have been made to reduce its recurrence and have failed. Scott (1977) cites the example of a man smoking a lighted cigarette on an oil tanker. If he is asked to put it out and does so, the suggestion is that he made an innocent mistake. If, however, he refuses to do so it is possible to infer that he has harmful intentions. Dangerousness here therefore is determined by a desire on the part of the offender to persist, even if efforts are made to prevent him. Often offenders will seek to complete unfinished business, or to push on with their mission until they have been successful. In such circumstances they would remain at high risk of reoffending until their set task is finished. For example, consider the case of a man convicted of 11 rapes and sentenced to 11 life sentences. He believed that he had lost his business as a result of 17 years of police persecution. In seeking revenge he had chosen to rape 17 women. When asked why he had not chosen to act directly against the police on 17 occasions he reasoned that they would suffer maximum embarrassment by their inability to catch him. Here was a man who had not only committed 11 very serious sexual assaults (victims aged 16–72), but who had another 6 to reach his target, he was therefore on an unfinished mission. Does his behaviour make him more potentially dangerous than another man who may commit 11 opportunist rapes? It could be argued, however, that 11 opportunities is pushing the argument too far and a degree of deliberation is likely to be evident. Nonetheless, the fact that there is, according to the offender, a good reason to continue with his actions, despite his punishment, must push him into a category at very high risk of further serious offending.

Contrast this with a man convicted and sentenced to life imprisonment for strangling his wife and burying her body in a wood, because, he claimed, of her infidelity. Traditionally regarded as a domestic matter, this prisoner served a short tariff of just over five years. Whilst in prison he had befriended another woman and, upon release, remarried. Within two years he had strangled his second wife and put her body into the boot of his car with the intention of burying her in a wood. Fortunately for her she was not dead and managed to escape from the car. What had happened in this case was that the offender had exactly replicated the circumstances of his first murder. A man who was very jealous indeed had got himself back into a situation where he would again feel great jealousy and would as a result act dangerously. How closely had the circumstances of his first murder been examined? Was he what might be termed pathologically jealous? How complicit had the various authorities been in deciding that his first murder was 'just a domestic' and therefore not only not very serious but also unlikely to be repeated? Our perceptions of danger may be framed and clouded by the spectacular, and obviously such behaviour must concern all. Yet it is vital that seemingly mundane offending is also closely examined for its potential to be repeated or replicated.

Understanding potential dangerousness is therefore more than considering the instant offence, it is also examining in as much detail as possible the circumstances, context, and motivation for the crime. This might be regarded as understanding the 'quality' of the information available. A simple way of getting into this level of analysis might be, it appears, assessing the amount of violence used for a given crime. If the violence is excessive to the purpose it may be regarded as an indicator of dangerousness. Yet as Scott (1977) points out, in many cases murder victims are young and fit (usually male) and will inevitably put up resistance. Multiple stab wounds for example may be the result of resistance and difficulty in finishing the act, as well as a desire to finish it as quickly as possible. He argues that the younger the offender the more likely is the use of excessive violence.

The prison service has previously issued guidance to staff that suggests a number of offending behaviour features might increase the risks of future dangerous behaviour. These might include an analysis of any bizarre or sadistic features to the crime. Are there any areas where cruelty can be regarded as calculated (and perhaps giving pleasure), or that crimes have been fastidiously planned and organized? Have weapons deliberately been taken to the scene of the crime to increase fear, to ensure compliance, or to kill? Have victims been specifically targeted or groomed? Does the offender gain sexual pleasure or feelings of pleasure from their crimes? Are these feelings more powerful than those engendered by detection and punishment? Has the offender reconfigured his behaviour to justify his crimes, to argue that the victim deserved it or even enjoyed it really? Are there any signs of regret or remorse? (Although it is of course notoriously difficult to judge the sincerity of these feelings.) Are there known trigger factors that can be identified and can these be manipulated or managed in such a way as to reduce the prospect of future serious harm? Those assessing danger, therefore, need to have access to as much quality information as possible, information that offers real clues to the behaviour of *individual* offenders.

Constructing danger

By framing dangerousness in the way it is presented in the media, successive governments have succeeded in skewing perceptions of real risks. Offenders who commit the most extreme (and by definition the most unusual) crimes effectively set the agenda on which public agencies have to operate. Notions of the 'other', of evil, and of monsters in our midst cloud the reality of everyday dangers that pose far greater risks to the most vulnerable members of society. Extreme behaviour leads to the deployment of extreme measures by governments and creates the impression that something is being done. Yet, in many ways, this complicity with a distorted picture adds to the climate of fear and in turn leads to an endorsement of ever more severe measures with an increased expectation of safety. There is a balance to be struck between oversimplifying perceptions of dangerous behaviour and fuelling anxiety by saying that it can occur in everyday situations at any time. This is the case, however, but in the overwhelming number of everyday life encounters danger or serious harm will not result. The point is that we should not close our eyes or ears to that potential because our perceptions have been framed around very severe, unusual, and often spectacular behaviour. Governments need to be working at developing trust rather than building fear, suspicion, and hostility. Public anxiety shows no sign of abating and the political nature of dangerousness does little to help, a situation very well summarized by Hollway and Jefferson (1997:261), 'In other words, because we have no means of being sure where risk and safety lie, nothing can be trusted and anxiety, therefore, potentially finds a location in any area of daily life.'

Summary

Whether it is potential dangerousness or risk of serious harm, the issue of public protection has come to dominate the criminal justice agenda. It has emerged as a priority for not only key agencies such as police, probation, and prisons, but has also seeped out into a number of other public services. It also remains a topic that fascinates the media and, as such, is one that politicians cannot ignore. It is embedded into the public consciousness as much as it is agency policy and practice. As such it is unlikely in the present climate that the pool, in which dangerousness is fished, will run dry. Agencies are now finding that a good deal of their time and other resources are directed towards the assessment and management of high risk cases. The bureaucracy itself appears to be generating more cases to be considered, a greater number of risk levels and an almost impossible ambition to make the world a safer place. Public protection staff have to try and grasp the nettle of dangerousness and attempt to lessen its impact. It is, however, an elusive concept and is very difficult to pin down.

2

Driving the Agenda 1 — Sex Offenders and Sexual Crime

Introduction

Following on from the point made in the previous chapter that perceptions of dangerousness are frequently media driven, it is also probably true to argue that these perceptions are framed by images of sex offenders. The sex offender has emerged as the complete modern folk devil and evokes fear and loathing in equal measure. Sex offenders are danger personified; with little attempt to differentiate the risk that each might pose. They have become an amorphous threat whose ranks are continually swelled by the creation of new offences, longer sentences, and longer post-release supervision. As a result, public protection staff are forced to deal with greater numbers, which may ultimately negatively impact upon their ability to protect the public. Sexual offending therefore drives and shapes the dangerousness agenda, both distorting the true picture of sexual abuse and limiting the ability of staff to focus upon other areas where potentially dangerous behaviour may be a real possibility.

Monsters in our midst—distorting sex offending

This chapter will, by focusing on three categories of serious sexual offences, discuss how this comparatively small area of offending has become so influential in driving the criminal justice agenda. For example, sexual offending constitutes 0.9% of all police-recorded crime and offences such as rape approximately one quarter of that 0.9% (Dodd et al, 2004)—accepting, of course, the massive under-reporting of these crimes. There has been a sense, at least perhaps in the public's mind, that serious sex offending is a relatively recent phenomenon. As with many crimes, however, it may be our perception and awareness that has changed rather than any significant alteration or acceleration in deviant sexual behaviour. Soothill (2003) reminds us of a concern with prostitution in the 1950s, homosexuality in the 1960s, rape in the 1970s, child abuse in the 1980s, and in the 1990s growing concern with predatory paedophiles, switching the focus from family to strangers. There may be a variety of reasons why these offences, and others, come into and out of prominence, but it will not always be a sudden increase in offending behaviour. As Matravers (2003:2) very neatly expresses it, '... current policy responses to sex offenders both reflect and shape a view of these offenders that is a product of our own particular culture and time. As such, these responses reveal concerns and anxieties that preoccupy us. As such, they are open to change, no matter how immutable they may seem to us.' Although she sees these responses as narrow and dominated by incarceration and tracking, because it is time and space determined, she does see the potential for alternative methods to come back into prominence.

Sex offenders have been seen as qualitatively different from other offenders. They are 'not like us', they do things that are not normal and are not forgivable, although even this seemingly entrenched position can shift depending upon circumstances and victim status. As Garland (2001) describes, they are seen as being outside of the more managerialist and rational approach to offenders that has evolved in recent times. He describes this as a 'criminology of the self', where criminals are seen as an everyday problem that needs to be managed. The problem will not go away but can be kept under control. In this world, any person could become an offender. Parallel to this world is the 'criminology of the other', a world populated by evil people who do abnormal things that 'normal' people would never do. These people need more than punishment and have little if any hope of rehabilitation. Exclusion and 'penal marking' are their lot in life. It is in this climate that professionals working with sex offenders have to operate. Although they would know that the greatest risks are in the home and in other relationship settings, they are in many ways forced along the stranger–predator route. Sex offending for many is therefore framed by stereotypes and fears.

As a result, real risks remain at best underestimated and at worst ignored. This chapter will discuss three types of serious sexual offending: rape, sexual abuse of children (mainly stranger), and sexual murder. It is not suggested that these are the only serious sexual crimes; they are certainly not the most numerous. Yet they do shape people's perceptions because they generate fear. The first category will be rape where readers will be asked to consider what they consider to be the most serious or dangerous of a number of scenarios, and to consider how they form their own judgements and assessment of risk.

Coming to terms with unpleasant feelings

Working with potential dangerousness involves close contact with people who have committed awful crimes, many of which touch on the sensitivities of even the most hard-bitten of criminal justice professionals. It is these horrendous acts that set the scene for public perceptions of dangerousness and, most notably, for sex offending. Dangerousness has, therefore, become synonymous with serious sex offending. Yet, as most people involved know, these types of crime are in a very small minority and most sexual offending is at a much less serious level, although should not be underestimated because of that. Indeed, a history of minor sexual offending may lead to more serious offending in the future (Prins, 1989:107). What we do know, however, is that the public's perception and media presentation of sexual offending does not represent the reality, but unfortunately it is this distorted picture that drives policy and practice. It is not only the policy response to this type of offending that is constructed by spectacular media reporting, but the feelings and concerns of most people. Sexual offending strikes a chord with many people and feelings of fear, anxiety, horror, and disgust are far more likely to be heard than empathy or forgiveness. Although practitioners are trained to deal with their feelings in regard to sexual offenders it is unlikely that gut instincts can ever entirely be eliminated. As the public protection circle widens, so more people will become involved in the assessment and risk management of sex offenders. As this happens the type of professional training that these newcomers to the field have had may equip them less well to deal with some of the behaviour they will encounter. Understanding where they come from on a personal, as well as a professional level, will therefore be essential.

To illustrate the difficulty of this process, a number of scenarios around one offence category—rape—will be described. Only a small amount of background information is given because readers are encouraged to think about the case from their own perspective and from what they have read so far in this text. Rape is an extremely unpleasant, physically and emotionally damaging, and potentially life-threatening offence, if it does not result in actual death. It is a crime traditionally located in the public's mind with a stranger, predator rapist although, as we know, it is much more common within marriage and other relationships. According to research, the traditional stereotype of the stranger rapist is now true in only 8% of rape cases (Myhill and Allen, 2002). The 2001 British Crime Survey estimated that 54% of rapists were current or former partners, with a further 29% known to victims. It is this stereotypical but rare type of stranger rape that is likely to receive the heaviest sentence in court although convictions remain alarmingly low for this type of offence.

A report in The Guardian (17 October 2005) suggested that only 5.6% of women who report rape see their assailant convicted. Cases reaching the prosecution phase saw conviction rates drop from 28% in 1988 to 21% in 2001. It was suggested in The Observer (23 October 2005) that there were as many as

50,000 rapes in the UK in 2003, but only 11,867 were reported to the police. The same report noted concerns by the Attorney General, Mike O'Brien that even serial rapists were avoiding prosecution. He indicated that senior judges did not help when they made comments about the errors in bringing rape allegations to court without a realistic prospect of conviction. O'Brien hoped that comments such as this would not further deter CPS staff from taking cases to court, or further undermine the faith of victims in the criminal justice process.

Offenders themselves are wise to the type of sentence they might receive and to the difficulties in proving rape allegations. As a result, many offenders form 'relationships' with their potential victims, knowing that if any type of acquaintance can be proved between offender and victim, the easier it becomes to present a defence based upon a consensual agreement. The Home Office classifies rapes as stranger, acquaintance, and intimate. Acquaintanceship may be argued on the basis of knowing the person for 24 hours or less. Acquaintance rape in many ways lessens the chances for a successful conviction and it increasingly appears as if more offenders know this. Stanko (1998, in Nash, 1999a:152) argues that many date or acquaintance rapists are actually serial rapists, who know the ground and territory sufficiently well enough to cover their tracks by forming relationships with their victims. Many people, especially women, argue that all rapes should be treated in the same way. Whether domestic or stranger, acquaintance or date, all involve non-consensual sexual intercourse and should receive the maximum punishment in law (a discretionary life sentence). This, however, is not the case, and it is clear that a hierarchy of circumstances and perceived seriousness applies in fixing sentence. Before moving on to consider these issues, readers are invited to think about their own perceptions of the following rape scenarios which are very loosely based upon real cases.

Four examples of rape case scenarios

Consider the following instances of rape and try to determine your response to the following questions. Which case do you consider to be the most serious? Which case do you believe should receive the heaviest sentence? Is this the same case as you identified in question one? Which case do you consider poses the greatest risk of future offending? In all questions try also to think why you have answered in the way you have and what it is about the offence, or the offender, or both that has influenced your decision. Obviously in a real life scenario there would be evidence of previous convictions, response to any previous supervision, employment records, health records, and records from any prison sentences. Offenders would have been routinely assessed at various stages and may or may not have also been subject to a psychiatric assessment. However, if we accept that professionals cannot totally distance themselves from their subjective feelings about crimes, then thinking about these crimes in something of an information vacuum might offer some insight into how practitioners can view potential dangerousness and what informs those judgements.

....

Case 1 — the 'failed' rapist

The first case is of a man who was about to be released from custody after serving eight years for two attempted rapes. This man, regarded by probation officers as sexually inadequate, had a previous criminal history of theft offences and two counts of indecent exposure. He, as a virgin, on two occasions attempted to have his first sexual experience with a prostitute. In his first attempted rape offence he attempted to have sexual intercourse in a car but prematurely ejaculated and became frustrated and aggressive towards the woman. He reacted to her wishing to leave by forcing her to remain in his car and attempted sexual intercourse again, this time with a threat of force. He again ejaculated prematurely and his victim was able to escape. A few weeks later he repeated this scenario with another prostitute but this time abducted the woman by threatening her with a knife. In this attack he was also unable to complete the act of intercourse and his victim also escaped but was several miles from her home. In prison this offender attended a variety of courses including anger management and sex offender treatment. He was described as plausible by prison staff and as someone who knew how to 'play the game'. He had occasionally been aggressive to female staff but would quickly apologize. Several female staff said that they felt uncomfortable in his presence. He had been a regular church attendee in prison and had arranged post-release accommodation in a church army hostel. At a multi-agency conference called to consider his release arrangements the question was asked why he had selected the particular city that he had chosen to resettle in. There appeared to be no obvious connection but the police officer present reminded the conference that the area had a large population of prostitutes.

- What features of this case could lead this man to be considered potentially dangerous, or, how high would you consider his risk of serious harm to be?
- Is there anything in his offending history that is relevant, what is it and why do you consider it to be important?
- Is there anything about his past behaviour that might have increased the risk he poses in the future?
- What is relevant from his prison performance?
- What are your feelings about his proposed living arrangements?

Obviously you cannot undertake a full risk assessment in this case (or those that follow), but think about what it is about any of these cases that causes you most concern, and indeed, if you can, begin to place them in order of potential risk and seriousness.

....

Case 2—the 'angry' rapist

Our second case concerns a man who raped two women and received an eight-year sentence. His victims were both black women and he was a black man. The rapes occurred following his meeting both victims at nightclubs. They might be termed 'acquaintance' but both followed immediately on from the meeting the same night. He had one previous conviction for violence towards a man (an assault outside of a club). He enjoyed drinking but he did not appear to have an alcohol problem. He had served every day of his original sentence having lost all of his remission for assaults on prison officers. He spent almost his entire sentence in solitary confinement in a maximum security prison and had numerous periods on a 'lay down' (a 28-day period in which the offender is moved to another prison) to give his own establishment a break.

He was an extremely angry individual with most of his ire directed at two sets of people. He was very angry towards 'authority', on the basis that he believed he had been unfairly sentenced because he was black. He believed that had he been white with the same black victims his sentence would have been lighter. He was also angry towards almost all women (with perhaps the exception of his mother) and especially women in authority. He was a very large and aggressive man, verbally and physically intimidating. He had not attended any behavioural programmes whilst in prison and would return to his hometown to live with his mother. He was not to be under any form of supervision.

- Are there any specific features of this case that pose a serious risk of harm to the public?
- Who is most likely to be at risk from this man and why?
- What are the trigger factors that might be important and that people coming into contact with him need to be aware of?
- What differentiates this case from number one and which do you think, from this sketchy information, poses the greater risk and is the more serious? Why is this?

....

Case 3—the 'revenge' rapist

The third case is a man serving 11 life sentences for 11 rapes. He had no previous sexual or violent offending but had numerous petty convictions relating to his business as a motor trader. He had raped 11 different women aged between 16 and 72. All had been attacked in their own homes and he had persuaded them to allow him entry by posing as an estate agent, targeting properties with 'for sale' boards outside. He was a prisoner who had survived perfectly well in open conditions despite his crimes. He had achieved this by convincing his fellow prisoners that his attacks had been on the partners of police officers. He told prison staff that the motivation for his crimes was to cause maximum embarrassment to the local police who, he claimed, had been harassing him for years and had caused him to lose his profitable business. When it was put to him that there were other ways in which he could have achieved the same outcome, he could not provide an explanation.

He had been building up to commit 17 rapes, one for each year of police harassment as he saw it. His behaviour in prison was generally very good and he had been made a trustee. He had participated in a variety of group programmes but few felt he had 'moved on'. He was extremely plausible and was often seen in deep discussion with prison officers, exchanging photographs, talking about how much they earned and gleaning other personal information about them and their families. He appeared to be very capable of ingratiating himself with a variety of people. He had been a single man aged 35 when convicted and his rape spree had continued for over two years.

- Are there any particular features of this case that would cause you concern?
- What about his motive for offending?
- Who would be at risk in the future?
- How great do you consider the risk to be if this man were to be released?
- Is there anything about this case that makes it a greater or lesser risk than the previous two?
- Do you consider this man to be on a 'mission' and do you think he plans to complete it?

....

Case 4—the 'date' rapist

The fourth case concerns a first offender. He is a 19-year-old student who was convicted of raping a female student after they had been out together for the first time. She had invited him back to her digs but had passed out drunk. She was raped whilst she slept. In his defence the offender had claimed that the couple were building up to sexual intercourse—consensual in his view—before the victim passed out. He was sentenced to be detained for three years in a young offenders' establishment.

- This type of rape is often termed 'acquaintance'—where does it sit in your list of rape seriousness?
- Does the absence of previous convictions make any difference to the assessment of risk?
- Some people—including judges (see below)—have been sympathetic to the view that men cannot turn off their emotions and urges like a tap. What is your position on this?
- If the victim is asleep does this aggravate the seriousness of the crime in your view?

Four different rapes have been presented here. Every rape is, of course, an awful event, but practitioners will have to allocate resources to monitor offenders in the community and the assessed level of risk posed by the offender will to a great extent determine the degree of intervention. A range of factors will determine the assessment of risk. These would include previous criminal history, personal history, performance in prison or under community supervision, and of course the offender's attitude to their offending. However, a number of 'softer' factors might impact upon these judgements as well as the hard data that make up people's lives. Many people believe, for example, that 'risk' can be seen as greater when it applies to vulnerable individuals. For example, the innocence of children usually puts them at the top of the list to be protected and people that offend against them at the top of the 'must be detected and incarcerated' list. The status of the victim is also important and we might normally expect this to run through from children, through women, and then men. However, within this list there remain discrepancies and these might include married women over single parents, white over ethnic minority, middle class over unemployed. For men a similar 'grading' system might operate over straight or gay, young or old, 'respectable' or 'unrespectable'. It may be very unpleasant to think of crime victims in these terms but the presentation of victims in the media endorses this feeling. We obtain our perceptions of crime not only from how offenders are presented to us but also their victims. It is the latter that will often determine our perceptions of crime seriousness.

In 1993, the John Howard Society in Canada picked up on this point as they commented on proposed dangerous offender legislation that would, they felt, be victim-related in terms of seriousness and assumed serious harm for all child victims but not for adult victims. They said,

> we believe that this designation of different classes of victims establishes a precedent that certain victims are more deserving of special status and protection or that there is more value placed on the hurt caused to them. This creates the possibility of further classification of victims and value judgements about assessing serious harm and deserving victims. The sentence originally handed down should have reflected the level of harm done; it should be revisited at the time of release (1994:4, in Nash, 1999a:144–5).

If you return to the four rapes above, what was it about each of them that caused most concern to you? To what extent did the 'status' of the victims influence your views? If you had to allocate the four cases in order of priority of risk which would be at the top and why?

Rape assumptions

It is evident that offences not meeting the stranger–predator stereotype are not only regarded as less serious by the public and the media, but are generally punished less severely by sentencers (that is when cases actually come to court and when there is a finding of guilt—both scenarios less common than they should be). Lees (2000), in a detailed study of cases of marital rape and marital murder heard before the Court of Appeal from 1991 to 1998, found marital rape is still not treated as seriously as stranger rape, even though it is often linked with life-threatening violence. As noted in the section on domestic violence in the next chapter, Lees found that divorced and separated women were up to seven times more likely than married women to have had violence threatened. She also noted that one in three divorced women and one in seven cohabiting women had been coerced into sex (Lees, 2000:60). In citing Painter (1991) she observed that marital rape was seven times as common as rape by a stranger. However, even though marital rape may be dismissed as 'just another domestic incident', Lees warns that many men who rape their wives also rape strangers, citing Fred West and John Duffy as infamous examples. Considering the link between men who assault women and violence raised by Soothill, Francis, Sanderson, and Ackerley (2000) and discussed below, it is interesting to note Lees' comments (2000:62) that in acquaintance rape there are more choked and strangled victims (23%) than in stranger rape (15%). In England strangulation is one of the most common methods of killing by men of women they know. Lees summarizes the overall position of marital rape very well when she says, 'reported wife rape and wife murder are likely to occur when the marriage is breaking down or after separation and divorce. We also know that injuries are just as serious in cases where women are attacked by their husbands, cohabitees or ex-husbands, as where they are attacked by strangers' (Lees, 2000:67).

There is significant evidence of the severity of marital rape and violence, with the Home Office (2005) reporting, 'Research suggests that women forced to have sex by their partners experience the most severe forms of domestic violence, and that sexual coercion and violence within a marriage is likely to occur more than once with increasing frequency and intensity.' Even in the light of this, and the potential links with assault on other people outside of the relationship, the courts appear determined to erect a barrier between domestic and stranger attacks. Two judicial comments, from many that could be used, summarize the position faced by marital rape victims pursuing their case through the courts. In 1990 a man who twice raped his ex-wife was given a two-year suspended sentence with the Judge observing, 'This is a rare sort of rape. It is not like someone being jumped on in the street. This is within the family and *does not impinge on the public*' (emphasis added). A second case saw a husband sentenced to three years for the rape of his wife with the Judge commenting, 'If you had done this to a stranger the starting point would have been eight years' (both in Lees, 2000:64).

Perceptions and decisions regarding serious sexual assault on women is often framed by negative views of women from males, such as notions of 'deserving it', or really 'wanting it', thus excluding the perpetrator from blame. These notions have also found their way into judicial statements and continue to reflect a male-centric and commodified view of women that absolves men of culpability and places blame on victims. The following comments are all taken from a review of judicial competence and 'engagement with reality' conducted by Billen (1992) for The Observer (13 December 1992). For example, consider the comments of Judge Wild from a trial at Cambridge Crown Court in December 1982. In acquitting a 35-year-old man of rape, he reminded the jury of the expression, 'Stop it; I like it.' He continued, 'If she does not want it, she has only to keep her legs shut and he would not get it without force.' In many ways this runs right alongside the issue of consent and suggests that an absence of bruises or other injuries would imply consent—somewhat in contradiction of much personal safety advice. In similar vein, Judge Dean spoke at an Old Bailey rape trial in 1990, 'As the gentlemen on the jury will understand, when a woman says no she doesn't always mean it. Men can't turn their emotions on and off like a tap like some women can.' Judge Richards, at Ipswich Crown Court in 1982, fined a man £2,000 for raping a woman he had picked up as a hitchhiker. She was 17 at the time and, according to the judge, 'Guilty of a great deal of contributory negligence.' Of course, one of the most infamous incidents concerned the sentencing in what became known as the Ealing Vicarage rapes. Three offenders had broken into the vicarage and carried out the attacks in front of the victim's father. They received sentences of three and five years, and perhaps to the surprise of many observers, passed longer sentences for the burglary than the rape. Of the three offenders two committed a rape but the one who did not received the longest sentence. With this in mind it may not therefore be surprising to read the comments of Mr Justice Leonard saying that, 'I cannot pass a sentence on you that properly reflects the horror of people, as you may be imprisoned for a disproportionately long time.' His sentencing decision was in part determined by what he regarded as a 'remarkable recovery' on the part of the victim and his view that her trauma was 'not so very great'. The furore that followed these comments led to a video interview with the victim being shown to judges by the police in subsequent training sessions (for the continuing significance of this case see Hinsliff, 2003).

Rape typologies

Perhaps a more accurate method of determining sentence for rapists is not only to consider the details and seriousness of the attack but also the chances of the attack occurring again in the future. If the case scores on both counts there would appear to be a sound argument for a protective sentence. Establishing typologies or profiles of rapists may be a useful tool to assist in the assessment process. As indicated for paedophile offenders below, such tools do not provide a panacea but do offer additional weapons in the armoury. Holmes and Holmes (1996) provide a useful list of rape typologies in relation to stranger or predator rape, but it should not be forgotten that most rapes and indeed violent rapes, occur within relationships. They describe the stranger rapist as predominantly under 30 years of age and categorized them as follows:

- *The power assurance rapist.* This person is described as the least violent and aggressive, with many coming from single parent families. Although described as having some concern for their victims, their aim is to rape to elevate their own status. They tend to operate locally, on foot, and at night. They tend to believe that the victim enjoys the act and may well return. The authors believe that many of these rapists have a 7–15 day attack-cycle, a figure that if anywhere near accurate, would be extremely alarming.

- *The anger retaliation rapist.* This person is supposedly driven by a desire to hurt women borne out of a sense of injustice perpetrated by them. Common background characteristics include coming from divorced homes (80%); physical abuse as a child (56%); raised by single women (80%); and adopted (20%). Attitudes to women are said to be negative and hostile whilst they regard themselves as masculine and athletic. Their intention is to harm with behaviour ranging from verbal abuse to physical assault sometimes culminating in murder. They may enjoy sexual degradation of their victims and could well ejaculate in the woman's face. They are often mobile and may engage in blitz attacks with a 6–12 month offending cycle.

- *The power assertive rapist.* This person is described as believing in male superiority and of having a right to rape. The attacker's behaviour is characterized by aggression to secure compliance—it is important to the offender that the victim does exactly as she is told. Background features again include single parent homes (70%); foster care (33%); domestic problems; and unhappy marriages. They are characterized by loud and boisterous behaviour. They occasionally carry out multiple attacks and may suffer sexual performance problems. More often than not they will have a steady partner. Their aggression and violence escalates as their offending continues and they then may resort to weapons. Offending may occur over a 20–25 day cycle.

- *The sadistic rapist.* Holmes and Holmes (1996) regard this typology as the most sexually aggressive and dangerous. These people may well suffer from a personality disorder and may be compulsive, making meticulous plans for their attack. They are typically married and regarded as good family men. They develop an awareness of policing techniques and take care in victim selection and attack. Their assault may well include paraphernalia to terrorize their victims and be characterized by excessive degradation and profanity. They may address their victim by another name that may well be that of a lover or even their mother. They are very ritualistic in their methods and may need certain things to happen in a particular sequence to bring them to sexual arousal.

Many of these characteristics have been confirmed in a review of the evidence by the eminent authority Donald West (1996:51–8). For example, he found that a super-macho stance, along the lines of 'she was asking for it', are attitudes linked with increased risk. Aggressive sexual predators who harbour irrational grudges against women and use forced sex to satisfy sex and anger impulses are believed by West to be particularly dangerous. He argues that aggressive sexual fantasies and a fascination for sadistic pornography may also be very relevant but are difficult to evaluate, but should not be overestimated perhaps if it has not so far been acted out. More recognizable danger signals include social isolation, persistent sexual dysfunction, and a build-up of hostility towards women. Anti-social personality traits such as impulsive aggression, alongside general criminality and indifference to harm done are found in many rapists (West, 1996:57). As with many other experts, West is anxious to play down the more simplistic links drawn between mental illness and serious offending or dangerousness. However, he does note that schizophrenics with active psychotic delusions about sex are dangerous. The Madonna–whore complex is related to a belief that sexual temptresses are evil and extremely violent behaviour may ensue between such people and the person they have had sex with, once their sexual desires are satiated.

Are clues helpful in everyday practice?

Are these profiles of any practical use? Clearly each attack is unique and it would be a mistake to try to read too many common features into these very serious and distinctive type of cases. However, there may be two practical applications for such information. The first might be in deciding upon an appropriate sentence. These characteristics might offer clues concerning motives that would indicate risk of replication and repetition. The second might be to assist in rehabilitation plans for these offenders. Profiles might give useful clues to an offender's behaviour and offer possible areas for therapeutic intervention, or for the style and intensity of post-custodial supervision that is required. In essence all information is useful in assessing future dangerousness and the more complete and accurate it is the more helpful it will be. Finally, another mechanism may also be helpful, the analysis of previous convictions. Soothill et al (2002) in a detailed study for the Home Office, found increased risks of rape and other serious sexual assaults on adult women by men with certain previous convictions. The increased risks were of the order of 19 times for those with a previous offence of unlawful sexual intercourse (USI) with a girl under 13; for USI with a girl under 16 it was three times; and 26 times for those with a history of attempted rape. Another offence that triggered considerably increased risks of further serious sexual assault and murder was kidnapping—an offence that according to the authors merits more research. Of course, we can also be fairly confident that, as indicated by self-report studies, the actual incidence of serious sexual offending among those who have perpetrated the crime may be much greater than criminal records indicate. West (1996:55) cites an American study of incarcerated rapists indicating eight times as many rapes as shown on their previous history. Even allowing for bravado, this does, somewhat ominously, suggest that serious sexual offenders are far more likely to repeat their offending than many other less aggressive sex offenders. Utilizing all available information to try and reduce future serious assaults is a key task for criminal justice staff.

Serious sex offending against children

Despite the seriousness of all rape cases, if the John Howard Society's comments are to be believed, then offences against children will generally be regarded as more serious than any other sexual crime. If rape offences test our emotions, offences against children do so even more. If there is a hierarchy of rape victims, children are more likely to be seen as one group demanding protection and the maximum sentence for their perpetrators. Yet we know that even this is not true, with familial abusers receiving lighter penalties than strangers, despite the evidence that the long term trauma is worse in cases where a significant family or friend figure breaches a position of trust. This social construction of sex offending against children focuses on the notion of predator danger at the expense of domestic abuse. It inevitably means that sexual abuse in the home is downgraded in its seriousness compared with that posed by stranger danger, a replication of the way in which rape cases have been traditionally handled by the criminal justice process.

It is this focus on a stereotype that negates attempts to differentiate between offenders in terms of the risks they pose. Generalizations tend to over- or under-estimate risk and prevent a finer assessment of each individual case. If planning for the management of risk in the community is to be effective and efficient then this more discriminating approach needs to be taken. The widespread use of the term 'paedophile' demonstrates this approach to child sex offenders. It is a word deeply embedded in the public's consciousness and seemingly important in determining the policy response of governments. It has come to epitomize sexual offending against children and, in so doing, reinforces the stereotype of predator or 'groomer' in a narrow and unhelpful fashion. Its perceived meaning and public understanding partly explains why so many seemingly respectable people are able to persist in their abusive behaviour over a number of years. What emerges strongly is that those involved in the assessment and management of serious sex offenders need to avoid this narrow approach and to be aware of research that perhaps offers clues to the repetition or indeed first commission of serious sexual offending. The remainder of this section will explore some of the work that may assist in this process.

Patterns of behaviour

Soothill et al (2000) examined the criminal profiles of the four most common groups of male sex offenders over a 32-year period, finding a more complex pattern of risk than might be expected in the generality of sex offending. For example, in terms of future sexual offending, the most risky group (ascribed predator status by the authors) were men convicted of sexual assault on a male. These offenders had a reconviction rate for 'other' sexual offences of over 41%, almost double that of the remaining sex offenders in the research (indecent assault on a female, indecency between males, and unlawful sexual intercourse (USI) with a girl under 16). This group of offenders therefore would appear to pose the greater risk of future sex offending, whilst those committing USI had much higher rates of future violent offences, burglary, and theft (Soothill et al, 2000:61). There was a clear and significant relationship between sexual offences against women and future violent crime, another confirmation of the circumstances involved in much domestic abuse.

Grubin (1998) neatly summarized the state of play in terms of the pattern of sexual offending against children, perhaps the area surrounded by the greatest number of myths. He noted that 60–70% of child molesters target girls only, 20–33% boys only, and 10% either sex. Significantly, in 80% of assaults on children, the perpetrator knew the victim (although granted this can be a wide definition and has in part been addressed by new offences in the Sexual Offences Act 2003). Grubin observed that in 25–40% of cases there was a recurrent and intense sexual attraction to children that was sufficient to attract a label of paedophilia. Soothill et al (2000) indicate that these people are likely to be mostly those who offend against males, although a more generic approach to their victims cannot be ruled out. Although this figure is too high for any concerned parent, it does perhaps put into a different light the more populist view that all who offend against children are paedophiles. Grubin noted that the vast majority of sex offenders act alone, although there has to remain significant concern over the activities of groups or 'rings' because they have the ability to generate a large number of victims, especially if these rings are of the 'virtual' variety.

Nonetheless, the notion of stranger danger remains deeply embedded in the public's consciousness. It is evident that extremely serious offending by people, many of whom hold intractable views, does pose a threat to a small number of victims. The problem is identifying these offenders and best managing the risk they pose to potential victims. The term 'paedophile' has assumed a generic meaning of essentially 'those who offend against children'. This is not helpful to those charged with assessing risk, passing sentence, and attempting to both change and manage offending behaviour. Definitions are numerous and do not always agree, although most would accept an erotic and enduring attraction to pre-pubertal children. In most cases this would exclude one-off incidents and those offending against children over the age of 13, although age bands will bear little relationship to physical maturity. It is likely that 'true' paedophiles prefer sexually immature children and for some clinicians, these should be victims from outside of the family unit (Silverman and Wilson, 2002:31). The preference for immature children will be recognized by practitioners who see in some family abuse cases the perpetrator moving down the age band within the family, targeting the next child entering the preferred age/maturity band and abandoning the one who has matured.

It is important to be able to distinguish between those who offend against children. This is necessary so that risks can be gauged as accurately as possible and that resources, both therapeutic and punitive, are directed towards those for whom they are most appropriate. Therefore separating the one-off from the persistent is important, and it is this feature that appears in a definition used by the American Psychiatric Association, 'The Acts or fantasy of engaging in sexual activity with prepubertal children as a *repeatedly preferred* or exclusive method of achieving sexual excitement' (Holmes and Holmes, 1996:135—added emphasis). The authors describe different types of child molesters with a view to assisting risk assessment, namely situational and preferential. The former refers to offenders who may not have a true or enduring interest in children but who experiment and could well abuse any vulnerable person. Within this grouping, Holmes and Holmes (1996:175) identify four sub-categories, as follows:

- *The repressed paedophile*: children are used as a temporary measure, usually as a result of the offender's self-image. This person has normal adult relationships and the child (victim) may be experienced or used as a pseudo-adult. Girls are the most likely victims and the offender usually has a stable, employed and married background, but suffers from low self-esteem. This person may well respond to therapeutic intervention.

- *The morally indiscriminate paedophile*: this person is described as an abuser of all available persons.

- *The sexually indiscriminate paedophile*: a sexual experimenter, a 'trysexual' with a wide variety of victims.

- *The naive and inadequate paedophile*: a person probably suffering from a mental disorder who is unable to determine right from wrong in terms of sex with children. This person is probably a loner, is not usually violent, and does not feel threatened (but for a contrasting view see Prins, 1986:175— below).

The second type of child molester identified by Holmes and Holmes was the preferential, and thought by them to be the more dangerous. In these cases children are preferred for pleasure—that is preferred over adults. Within this group, two further sub-groups were noted:

- *The sadistic molester*: associates sexual gratification with fatal violence. Features of their offending behaviour may include abduction with force, pain, and death. This person has no 'love' for children—a cognitive distortion frequently used by paedophiles to justify their actions.

- *The seductive molester*: courts or lures children·with gifts and affection. These offenders are fixated on an earlier age and stage of development. They have a persistent and compulsive interest and generally prefer male victims. They are likely to be single and immature (Holmes and Holmes, 1996:135–40).

Prins (1986:174) points out that differential assessment is extremely important in all cases of serious sexual offending and, more generally in all serious cases. For example, he cites Crawford (1982) as suggesting that it is essential to distinguish between those who use force as a means of gaining cooperation in the sexual act and those for whom the infliction of pain or terror is an end in itself (Prins, 1986:173). He suggests that this will help distinguish between those who claim an overpowering love of children and those for whom the issue appears to be hate. As indicated in the work of Soothill et al (2000) above, it is equally important to distinguish between homosexual and heterosexual child sex offenders. Bluglass (1982, in Prins, 1985:174) suggests that the former category is more likely to have had previous sexual involvement with children, to prefer them as sexual partners, and to show patterns of deviant arousal. Heterosexual offenders, however, were more likely to be situationally motivated and may well prefer adult women but seek children out at times of stress or other problems. With this need for as much information as possible, the following is a summary of typologies that both reflect and enhance those described above, all taken from Prins (1986:174–5).

He differentiates between young and adult child sex abusers. In the former category he describes two groups, the first being 'ambi-sexual'. These are described as inadequate adolescents who frequently bribe young children to engage in deviant (and of course illegal) sexual practices. He points out that many of these offenders have been placed in a position of trust by parents, for example, as child minders. The second group are described as more dangerous, engaging in serious sexually assaultive behaviour and themselves often revealing a pattern of childhood sexual abuse (but remember some of the conflicting research in this field in Chapter 3).

With adult child sex offenders, Prins notes five categories. Readers should perhaps think how these offenders may be helped, if at all, to recover from their deviant activities (some of which are suggested by Prins, 1986:176–8). Differentiation may be useful for treatment or therapy purposes but might also serve as an additional indicator of the levels of harm that might be posed by future activity. Such information may well impact upon release and post-release management decisions. Prins' five categories are:

- *The middle-aged heterosexual paedophile*. This person is characterized as lonely and isolated, seeking the (non-threatening) company of small girls. Such people may be socially incompetent and unable to form age-appropriate relationships.

- *The senile or pre-senile paedophile.* These men are characterized by their sexual predilections not dulling with age although their physical ability may be. (Think about the occasions on which an elderly paedophile has been sentenced and the judge has commented that by the time he is released he will be unable to offend in the same way again—Prins somewhat negates this notion!) He is concerned that as their physical ability wanes they may become angry and frustrated, less in control and thus potentially more dangerous.

- *Paedophiles of low or subnormal intelligence.* These offenders, according to Prins may offend because they simply do not know the consequences of their behaviour or even know that it is wrong. They may lack social skills which, when rebuffed, provoke a violent reaction. Others may not appreciate their own strength and, because some will be 'playing' with people they regard as their peer, will cause considerable harm.

- *Those whose offending is part of a wider failure to achieve social conformity.* These offenders may well demonstrate a history of alcohol abuse and non-sexual offending.

- *The exclusively homosexual offender—the pederast.* This person may set himself up as a protector of children and does not regard his activities as wrong or illegal. He may well exert a powerful and coercive influence over his victims and, according to Prins, may be quite impervious to treatment.

No one is suggesting that typologies such as these provide a magic template to assess future risk and punishment/treatment requirements. They do, however, enable those with the appropriate information to begin to break down generalized assumptions and attempt to provide a more individualized assessment for each offender. Of course, the ability to do this relies absolutely on having the required information and, in particular, this means the full details from the police investigation. However, many agencies will pick up vital clues about an offender's past behaviour and future intentions, notable among them prison and probation staff. It is essential that this information be systematically recorded, as noted by Scott (1977:129), 'it is patience, thoroughness and persistence in this process rather than any diagnostic or interviewing brilliance, that produces results. In this sense the telephone, the written request for past records, and the checking of information against other informants, are the important diagnostic devices.' If computer records, information databases and e-mail were added to this list it would serve very appropriately for modern practitioners.

As with rape offences, we do know that sexual offending against children is massively under-reported and under-recorded. Self-report studies, again as with rape, indicate a much higher prevalence of offending, although, with children, the extent of the gap is extremely worrying. In citing Abel et al (1987) in an American study, West (1996:54) noted that non-familial child molesters self-reported an average of 23 sex acts with girls and 282 with boys, mostly with different victims. Familial offenders reported lower rates, although the balance between male and female victims was reversed, with an average of 81 incidents with girls and 62 with boys. Again, allowing for the offender's own needs to inflate the extent of their activities, there is a suggestion here that once offenders start a serious sexual offending history, there are very strong prospects for it not only continuing but also extending.

As with domestic abuse, child protection is increasingly seen as a multi-agency issue, rather than one that has traditionally resided with social services departments. Interim guidance on the identification of those who present a risk to children has been issued by the national probation service (Probation Circular 32/2005). This suggests a change in the term *Schedule 1 Offender*, in use since the Children and Young Persons Act 1933, and used to describe anyone who has committed an offence in Sch. 1 of the Act against a child. The Circular indicates that the existing provisions define offenders by their history rather than by the risk they present for the future and is not linked to other offender assessment systems such as OASys. It is suggested that the term 'Schedule 1' be replaced with 'Risk to Children', thus feeding into the full probation assessment process. The duty to protect children is now much more central to the work of the probation service and the Children Act 2004 places a duty on the service to make arrangements with local authorities to promote the wellbeing of children. This example further illustrates the growing breadth of public protection arrangements and areas of responsibility. Single agency responsibility for offenders who pose risk of serious harm is increasingly being consigned to the bin of history.

Sexual murder

Sexual murders appear to be comparatively rare, although this may be because the motive was not always obvious to police investigators. For example, would murder committed as result of sexual jealousy be regarded as a sexual murder or a rage or anger murder? West (1996:51) suggests that in the 40% of female homicides committed by a sexual partner, sexual jealousy is a common motive and is, as indicated by Scott (1977) a notoriously dangerous passion. In stranger sex murders, perpetrators were often fuelled by anger that was itself fed by the victim's resistance. Insults to their self-esteem or concerns with their own sexual adequacy further increased the chances of a fatal outcome to their attacks.

The extremely rare phenomenon of the serial killer would fit with aspects of the sex murderer, although not all would necessarily be for this reason. An examination of serial killer typologies initially developed by Holmes and Holmes (1998) and subsequently empirically tested by Canter and Wentink (2004), offer echoes of the characteristics noted above for rapists and certain serious child molesters. Holmes and Holmes typologies are as follows:

- *The visionary killer*. This person murders because they have had visions or heard voices, from demons, angels, or God, telling him to kill particular individuals or groups of people.
- *The mission killer*. This person takes it upon himself to rid the world of people he has judged to be unworthy.
- *The hedonistic killer*. This category is divided into two sub-groups:
  a) *The lust killer*. This person kills for sexual gratification and sex is the focal point of the murder, possibly after the victim is dead. Various acts such as cannibalism, necrophilia and dismemberment may be present.
  b) *The thrill killer*. This person kills for the pleasure and excitement of killing. Once the victim is dead the murderer loses interest so the whole process may be drawn out to maximize the pleasure.
- *The power or control killer*. This person murders for the pleasure and gratification drawn from having control over a victim. Again, there would be a great need to extend the process of murder.

Canter and Wentink (2004) were keen to discover what could be extracted from the crime scene rather than drawing inferences from other variables. Following this methodology, the three types of serial murder most relevant to this section are lust and thrill and power/control murders. All three murders share the following crime scene variables; multiple crime scenes, torture, victim alive during sex acts, and vaginal rape. Thrill and power murders may be characterized by different types of strangulation whereas lust murder may show more features of mutilation. All are likely to make efforts to conceal the body and lust and power murderers may take parts of the body away with them.

Obviously clues such as these are of most use to profilers and investigators. However, other criminal justice personnel will have to work, albeit rarely, with these individuals. Information taken from the crime scene may reveal patterns of behaviour that might assist in release plans if such people were to be returned to the community. More importantly perhaps, people who talk about interests in the areas noted here, or showing attitudes matching these, should certainly provoke some alarm in their supervisors. Although not all people who share these attitudes graduate to murder or serious sexual assault, this, possibly with other clues, may certainly help to identify future warning signs with some individuals.

Summary

This chapter has briefly discussed three forms of very serious sexual offending. All three types of activity remain comparatively rare, although they are likely to be much more prevalent than their place in official statistics suggests. However, their importance lies in their power to shape perceptions and agendas. Fear of crime has increasingly featured on government agendas and as such has provoked legislative responses aimed at calming that fear and giving the impression that something is being done. It is offences such as these that most interest the mass media and therefore shape public perception of sexual offending. They confirm everyone's worst nightmare whilst the great well of risk that dwells in the domestic sphere goes largely unreported and unremarked. Serious sexual offending does indeed drive the legislative agenda at the beginning of the twenty-first century—certainly more than other offence categories. Attitudes to certain sexual behaviour do change over time and as a result changes do take place to the criminal law. However, attitudes to these very serious matters do not change and because they are constructed as *the sexual problem,* remain the driver of policy responses despite their rarity.

3

Driving the Agenda 2— Behaviour Causing Concern

Introduction

The previous chapter indicated how sexual offending has framed and driven the dangerousness agenda. As a result, other 'traditional' and increasingly more recent or modern forms of offending are, if not excluded, certainly marginalized in dangerousness discussions. This chapter will remake the case for so-called domestic violence and sexual assault to enter the dangerousness sphere on equal footing with public danger—not least because it is more prevalent and may well produce many more victims of very serious crime. It will also consider serious offending by children alongside Internet offending and hate crime. All these forms of crime have the potential to produce seriously harmed victims yet often remain tangential to the mainstream dangerousness agenda. The following is intended to generate discussion around this issue, and argue that a bureaucratic and formulaic response to specific types of offending may lead to potentially seriously damaging behaviour being overlooked.

New sites of concern

At the time of writing, the latest social menace had recently been identified in the press and elevated to a starring media presence. This was the phenomenon known as 'hoodies'. These were (predominantly) young people who wore a sports top with an integrated hood. The 'problem' was that the hood was worn over the head (and often over a baseball cap) and as such was deemed to be threatening to the public. It symbolized the threat of the young and, in crime prevention terms, made the identification of any potential criminal more difficult. At a stroke a whole generation of young people, for some of whom the hood was part of their school uniform, were branded as a threat to social order and became subject to bans from shopping centres. It was in effect a significant display of social exclusion supported by many people who swallowed the media message that young people dressed in this way presented a threat to 'normality'. Although not reaching the status of a group triggering public protection concerns, the hoodies are a good example of how society can quickly pick up and run with an idea that strikes a chord—that chord usually being one of fear and anxiety. It also shows how easily mass labelling can take hold and reflects the ease with which whole groups of offenders can be considered to pose the same threats with little attempt to distinguish between them.

This is an inherent and core problem in how society reacts to potential danger and is the cause of a seemingly unending expansion in the public protection infrastructure. However, it should not be forgotten that for some young people the hood will be serving a very specific purpose, namely to disguise their features from surveillance mechanisms such as CCTV. They are for some the modern equivalent of a balaclava hat or even a mask, the problem is then to distinguish between the innocent and potentially criminal hoodies.

This chapter is concerned with behaviour that causes public concern but is perhaps a little outside of the mainstream public protection agenda, or indeed is included with perhaps a less than rounded rationale for doing so. In Chapter 1 it was suggested that potential dangerousness is too easily pigeonholed, by offence or by offender, usually based on a range of violent and sexual offences (a list that is growing considerably—see Chapter 6). This approach both narrows the perspective by focusing on particular crimes to the exclusion of others, and of course considerably enlarges it as those offending within certain offence categories are all regarded as posing the same or similar levels of risk. This chapter could therefore equally be titled 'behaviour that should cause concern', in that every encouragement should be given to explore the potential for danger in a variety of settings and emanating from a diverse range of offending behaviour.

'Out of the blue danger'—or were there signs all along?

Perhaps one of the most pressing problems for criminal justice agencies is to attempt to assess and predict danger in people or circumstances where there has not been a previous (obvious, ie conviction) indication of such behaviour. Many of those who have committed some of the more spectacular crimes in recent history, such as the mass killings at Hungerford and Dunblane, do not have previous convictions for serious violence. Research by Soothill, Francis,

Ackerley, and Fligelstone (2002) indicates that 32% of first time murderers and 36% of serious sex offenders had no previous convictions. As such there was no reason to predict that they would offend in the future and in any case, unless known to the authorities for other purposes, there would be no reason to assess them. However, many people do come to the attention of police, probation, prison, and mental health services, for a variety of reasons, but are not necessarily known for their violent or sexual histories. Nevertheless, there may be sufficient clues in their behaviour, or their specific context, to anticipate the possibility of what are often described as 'out of the blue' crimes. It is, of course, absolutely impossible to eliminate all risk of serious harm, but many people do come into contact with a variety of state (and voluntary) workers and many of these will not be in the public protection sector. That does not mean, however, that the person they are working with does not pose a risk of danger or that these staff should not be vigilant towards signs of potential harm. The remainder of this chapter will now explore possible sites of dangerous behaviour that may frequently be overlooked, especially perhaps by the sensation-hungry media, which does much to shape our understanding and perception of dangerousness.

Violence against women—is 'behind closed doors' public enough?

Studies across the world confirm the extent and severity of violence against women, perpetrated by men. Yet, the vast majority of this violence is prefaced by the words 'domestic' or 'private' and as such, assumes a mantle of being somehow less serious than if a stranger had perpetrated it. This is simply not the case. This downgrading of domestic abuse, physical, sexual, and emotional, masks a range of behaviours that can culminate in murder, rape, or suicide on the part of the victims. This is a huge and complex topic warranting its own literature and that may act as an excuse for public protection staff to overlook this significant social problem. This section can only touch the surface of this area, yet it is believed that those working in the public protection field should consider it as a legitimate site for public protection interventions—the public sphere needs to enter the private realm at times of serious risk of harm. It may be 'private' violence but both victim and perpetrator are members of the 'public' and domestic abuse, in a supposedly safe setting, should rightly be considered as a site of significant potential dangerousness (Saraga, 1996). If nothing else, staff in a variety of agencies need to be able to listen to and understand what women may be telling them—and more importantly acting upon this information where it is possible to do so. Developments reported at the end of this section offer prospects of a more rounded professional consideration of this issue, if matters such as professional and personal cultures can be overcome.

Watts and Zimmerman (2002:1232–7) list what can only be described as a catalogue of horror committed against women worldwide. The behaviours include female genital mutilation; dowry deaths; acid throwing; stoning; honour killings; rape; and sexual brutalization. They cite evidence from more than 50 population-based surveys as indicating that between 10 and 50% of all women who have ever had male partners have been physically assaulted at some time in their lives. This is essentially a list of crimes and is, as such, rightful territory for public protection staff.

Domestic abuse

It is extremely difficult to gain a real picture of the extent of domestic violence, not least due to the fact that so much is either unreported by victims or unrecorded by police officers. However, Mullender (1996:32) cites several surveys conducted in London that indicate significant levels of violence against women. In one such study she refers to a north London survey (Mooney, 1994) that found 30% of women reporting they had been subject to violence that was more than being grabbed, pushed, or shaken. She also referred to a study in Islington that revealed 25% of women reporting physical abuse, almost all (92%) severe.

Mullender indicates that much domestic physical abuse starts with a slap and is often dismissed as low level—although she makes the point that 'even' this is unacceptable. However, what has emerged from the research is that over time this low level violence escalates and becomes increasingly dangerous and life threatening. In the Islington survey, one quarter of the incidents involved weapons and objects such as bottles, glasses, scissors, sticks, and clubs.

Mooney (2000:13) breaks down violence and injuries as follows:

- Grabbed, pushed, or shaken   32%
- Punched or slapped   25%
- Kicked   14%
- Head-butted   6%
- Attempted strangulation   9%
- Hit with object/weapon   8%

Injuries were recorded as:

- Injured   22%
- Bruising/black eye   26%
- Scratches   12%
- Cuts   11%
- Broken bones   6%

Mooney (2000:38) also reported a series of vignettes presented to men, detailing a number of stereotypical conflict situations, asking them if they could see themselves hitting their partner in any of the situations. Of the sample, 37% said that they could never see themselves hitting a woman in any situation. Approximately 50% of the men indicated that they could see themselves harming women in up to two of the vignettes and 17% felt they would be violent in every scenario. The most frequently cited situation likely to lead to violence was sexual infidelity, with 33% of the men saying they would use violence in this scenario. Approximately 19% of the respondents indicated that they had already used violence in similar situations to those posed by the vignettes.

It is not difficult to see the potential for extremely dangerous violence in such cases. It should also be noted that, as with potential dangerousness legislation and policy, it could be the prospect of harm as much as its actual incidence that can cause distress and alarm. The UN Declaration on the Elimination of Violence Against Women defines it as gender-based violence that results in, *or is likely to result in*, physical, sexual, or psychological harm to women. Just as public protection might look for trigger factors in those they supervise, so should all staff be aware for the potential escalation of domestic abuse into the highest levels of violence and sexual assault. For example, Browne (1987) cited in Mullender (1996:21) identifies factors that might increase the risk of very serious harm in people who have shown domestic violence to their partners. These warning signs indicate a potential for men to kill their partners and include the following: threats to kill (how often are these taken seriously?); bringing a weapon into the house after making such threats; locking the women in the house; inflicting multiple injuries in each attack; and killing the woman's pet. Escalation of violence may also be influenced, to some extent, by the availability of weapons, thus in North America guns may be used to threaten or actually harm women more than other parts of the world (the increased use of guns in the UK could well have other 'collateral' effects than many might think). One fifth of all homicides are men killing their partners or ex-partners (Mullender, 1996:21), whilst one third of these were actually separated at the time of their death.

The Guardian newspaper carried a graphic account of a case perfectly illustrating this situation on 7 June 2005. The author, Fran Abrams, reported on the death of Julia Pemberton, 14 months after she had separated from her husband and after he had met and moved in with a new partner. However, threats to her had continued throughout this period and on several occasions her husband had vowed to kill her. The victim had told police and family court judges of the threats. She did at one point have a six-month injunction that was temporarily extended. However, lacking faith in the willingness of the police to enforce it she was eventually persuaded to downgrade the injunction to an 'undertaking'. This, Abrams reported, would not lead to an automatic arrest following any breach. To cut a very tragic story short, Alan Pemberton visited the family home ostensibly to take his 17-year-old son for a driving lesson. Following an argument it appears as if the son was murdered on the doorstep and then Alan Pemberton broke into the house and shot his wife who was hiding in a cupboard. The whole incident was recorded by the police from the victim's mobile phone call requesting 999 help. It appears that, despite a catalogue of reported incidents over the 14-month period, the police did not know Julia's address.

The case is to be the first to be made subject to a homicide review under the Domestic Violence, Crime and Victims Act 2004.

Separation from an abusive partner therefore does not necessarily bring safety or even respite, and many men will use legal measures to contact their children to track down their partner. Separation of partners with children is an enormously stressful period for all concerned. Recently, militant fathers groups have shown how far they will go to secure what they term as a fair deal for fathers in disputes concerning residency of and contact with their children. Fathers 4 Justice (disbanded in January 2006 but survived by the more militant Real Fathers 4 Justice), for example, have thrown purple powder over the Prime Minister in the House of Commons; chained themselves to a balcony at Buckingham Palace; handcuffed themselves to the Children's minister; and spent a weekend demonstrating outside the home of the most senior family judge. Perhaps in a more threatening way they have caused criminal damage to public property and intimidated and threatened children and family court advisory and support service (CAFCASS) staff and sent suspect packages through the post. In many ways this might be regarded as a form of urban terrorism but again the 'civil' nature of the issues appears to downgrade the seriousness. Because the scenario is often clouded by concerns over rights *to* children, rather than rights *of* children, its criminal and serious harm potential is overlooked. This area of civil work could be regarded as a significant site for criminal dangerousness.

A variety of reasons might be given to explain why men behave as they do, but too often these explanations (invariably offered by males) blame the victim in various ways. In summary the more common rationales would include the following; it is only a few bad men (the rotten apple thesis)—however, male on female violence appears to be far too common for that explanation to hold water. Another suggestion is that violence represents loss of control (but this doesn't explain why women become the chosen target (see the example of the rapist in Chapter 2) and why men are able to control themselves much better outside of the home). Ptacek (1988) found 17 out of 18 abusers claimed to have lost control but only five did so outside (in Mullender, 1996:39). Another common explanation is that women 'invite' violence by, for example, continuous nagging. In citing Kennedy (1992), Mullender (1996:46) recounts the case of a man given a suspended sentence for the manslaughter of his wife with the judge claiming that living with the defendant's wife 'would have tried the patience of a saint'. In many sexual attacks women are also said to 'have asked for it' because they wore provocative clothing—a misogynous comment supported by many judicial statements.

Too often then, violence against women (and children) has been sidelined into the private sphere by criminal justice agencies and, at least until recently, been outside of public protection arrangements. Happily, this is increasingly less the case although, even in recent times, agency practice has been found wanting. A report in The Guardian (29 July 2004) suggested that the probation service 'fails domestic violence victims'. In a report from the Chief Inspector of Probation, only 21% of sampled cases were rated as good in terms of both identifying cases and managing the risks, with none rated as excellent. Only 34% of cases sampled gave sufficient consideration to the safety of the victim. When children were in the household, risk to them was assessed in only 59% of cases and only 29% of cases were reassessed after a further concerning incident occurred. Assessments of risk were regarded as sub-standard and there was a lack of collaboration with probation records and other sources. The same newspaper report also referred to the police service recording less than half of all domestic cases reported to them, with an incident reported every minute and, alarmingly, two women being killed by their partner every week.

The probation service is now making use of the Spousal Assault Risk Assessment Guide (SARA), a tool developed in Canada over a number of years. The tool utilizes a range of 20 risk factors and, although not producing a score, does aid risk judgement. Furthermore, the emerging National Probation Service *Domestic Abuse Policy and Strategy* (NPS, 2005) explicitly links domestic use with MAPPA. The strategy makes clear that tackling domestic violence is an important component of the probation service's Priority 2 (of the NPS Business Plan), which is 'Protecting the Public from Harm'. This is an important step towards mainstreaming domestic violence and abuse, a behaviour with such a high rate of incidence and tragic outcome. The strategy is encouraging in its description of domestic abuse as a widespread social *and criminal* problem. The document indicates that one in four women are likely to have been victims of domestic abuse (it also cites the British Crime Survey, 2002, as indicating that about one fifth of incidents were against men). It is also clear that the national probation caseload contains large numbers of both victims and perpetrators. Data from the Offender Assessment System (OASys) from November 2004 revealed the following:

- up to 14% of assessed male offenders are current domestic abusers;
- 28% of all violent offences are committed by men who are current domestic abusers;
- up to 38% of all female offenders are victims of domestic abuse (NPS, 2005: para. 1.8).

In terms of dangerousness being incidences of future serious crimes, the document offers compelling evidence in the argument for the centrality of this form of violence. It notes that 0.2% of the NPS caseload are offenders under probation supervision who have committed a serious further offence and 35% of these offences was a domestic abuse offence. A matter of chilling concern according to the report is that there may be as many as 35 incidents before the abuse is reported to the police. If the matter does not receive the attention it deserves it is understandable that the victim may not report it again. Although a number of domestic abuse perpetrators may not meet the level 2 and 3 thresholds (see Chapter 8 and Annex 4), it is regarded as essential that they are managed through local multi-agency arrangements, not least to facilitate referral to MAPPA if and when this becomes necessary.

This strategic approach to domestic abuse has to be a good sign. By making it a part of the public protection priorities of criminal justice agencies it is bringing the problem out from behind closed doors. There are far too many victims to ignore and to regard it as somehow a different sort of crime from 'public' offending is short sighted and blinkered. These recent developments are to be applauded but, as the Guardian report noted above observes, there may yet remain work on attitudes and culture to be done.

A similar shift in attitudes would be welcome in 'domestic' rape cases. The Home Office (2005:20) rape attrition study found that 19% of rapes are committed by current or ex-partners (with another 33% of assailants regarded as acquaintances). It further suggested (pages 33–4) that marital rape was extremely brutal and sadistic and is characterized by repeat victimization. As the study notes (2005a:33), 'Rape is a more frequent and mundane crime than conventionally believed, with current and ex-partners featuring strongly, and for a substantial proportion of women rape involves repeat victimisation.' The report highlights the perceived difference between the 'real rape' template and other assaults, the former being characterized by resistance and physical harm. It indicated that even victims tended to view rape alongside the 'real rape' template. A telling point is made in the report concerning the overlap between domestic violence and rape, and the implications for other offences to be committed. It said:

> Overlaps between rape and domestic violence have received limited attention in either research or policy development ... This overlap however clearly deserves greater exploration, not least with respect to protection issues victims may need addressing in order to sustain a prosecution, and the finding that women who kill abusive partners are much more likely to have been subjected to repeated sexual violence ... (Home Office, 2005:34)

Alcohol abuse and sexual assault

In late 2005 the British government radically overhauled the licensing laws to considerable concern over the potential increase in alcohol fuelled violence, sexual assault, and general anti-social behaviour. This section will in particular focus on the links identified in the research literature between alcohol and sexual violence. It will examine how women might be at increased risk from drunken men and their own vulnerability whilst under the influence of alcohol. The majority of what follows in this section is taken from Feeney (2004), Home Office Findings 215.

We have already discussed a number of studies exploring the extent of physical and sexual assault against women. Studies have also attempted to place the role of alcohol abuse in these attacks. Feeney (2004:2) cites a British study (Grubin and Gunn, 1990) indicating that in a study of 142 men imprisoned for rape, 58% had been drinking in the six hours prior to the rape. A further 12%

had used a combination of alcohol and drugs. A remarkably similar figure for those drinking at the time of a rape (57%) had been revealed in a much larger American survey (Bureau of Justice Statistics, 1983). Caution was expressed, however, in the sense that in some self-report alcohol abuse admissions, this may have been exaggerated in an attempt to minimize their culpability. This situation is known as 'drinking in the event' and it should be noted that this could also apply to the victim, thus reducing their ability to protect themselves. Feeney cites six American studies showing that 6–36% of victims had been drinking prior to their assault. In another review of seven US college surveys, between 35 and 81% of victims had been drinking 'in the event'.

At various points throughout this book the message is repeated that most incidents of behaviour with seriously harmful outcomes occur within the home, and this includes sexual assault. However, it appears that where alcohol is a prime agent in the assault, this does not hold true. Feeney (2004:3) cites several studies indicating that alcohol-related sexual abuse is more likely to occur between people who do not know each other well. Alcohol was consumed most often in cases of casual dates (and more contemporarily acquaintance rapes), rather than spousal or family assaults. A number of other factors emerge from the links between alcohol abuse and sexual assault. These are increases in the likelihood and severity of victim injury and victim humiliation, although other studies may offer a contrary view to this. One is that if the offender has been drinking there may be a lower chance of rape completion on the basis of more effective victim resistance—this again may also be debatable. Victim vulnerability through alcohol abuse can be seen in the views of those who regard women as more promiscuous and available if drunk, and, of course, that men are somehow less culpable if the victim was drunk. Alcohol may therefore lower men's sexual inhibitions and lead to more aggressive sexual behaviour whilst at the same time increasing the vulnerability of victims in a number of ways. A significant increase in alcohol-related, sexually motivated assaults may therefore be a direct outcome of the more liberal licensing laws.

Children who sexually abuse other children

Although 'children who kill' may make the more lurid headlines, it is sexual abuse by children on other children that is much the more common activity. It has been estimated that approximately a third of all sexual offences are committed by children (Grubin, 1998). This is a figure replicated around the world and in some instances the figures may be higher. It appears as if modern society is increasingly prepared to demonize its children, although seeing children and young people as a threat to established social order is not new and has a long historical pedigree (Pearson, 1983). However, in recent times, and perhaps particularly following the killing of toddler James Bulger in Liverpool in 1991 by two boys aged 10 and 11, some (but maybe not all) societies appear to be more prepared to write off their troublesome youth and increasingly forget that they are children. Actions are regarded through adult eyes and ascribed with adult motivations when, on many occasions, this is clearly not appropriate. This perhaps in part explains the way in which young people demonstrating inappropriate sexual behaviour have been labelled, although the real issue may be more complex.

Numerous research studies have indicated a link between children who have been victims of sexual abuse and their subsequent sexually abusive behaviour towards their peers. In many ways this creates a simple, understandable explanation for behaviour that adults find unacceptable and often inexplicable in young people. It has been described as a cycle of abuse, meaning that their abusive behaviour has been learned, or is a reaction to their own abuse, or is their way of dealing with that abuse. In reviewing a range of studies, Calder (2005) found figures of between 40–80% of children and young people who sexually abuse reporting that they had themselves been abused as children. However, Johnson and Doonan (2005:34), in citing Silovsky (2002), report a study where 65% had no history of being sexually abused, but 47% had been victims of physical abuse and 58% had witnessed domestic violence. Exposure to domestic violence again featured prominently in a list of factors associated with a propensity to sexually abuse during adolescence (Hunter and Figueredo, 2000, in Carpentier, Proulx, and Lussier, 2005:59). A Department of Health (2003:16) report suggests that at least 750,000 children witness domestic violence and that nearly three quarters of children on the 'at risk' register live in domestic violence households (in Saunders, 2005b). Other influential factors included early victimization; a high rate of abusive incidents; a long period between the first event and its report; a lack of support following disclosure as well as exposure to domestic violence. Saunders (2005b) also cites a case featured on a national radio programme as illustrating the difficulties faced by women caught up in the domestic violence and domestic sexual abuse scenario. The problems for the mother involved were summarized as follows:

- The lack of an independent witness (of course, also regarded as a major problem in many rape allegations)
- Failure to report domestic violence to a statutory agency before leaving the abuser
- Children's reluctance to disclose before it is safe to do so
- The mother was being abused but she thought he would never hurt the children
- Dire threats from the perpetrator
- No guarantee of protection from the courts
- The terror of knowing that their abuser will be listening to everything they say.

The author concludes that it was this type of scenario unfolding that inevitably led to courts making orders for contact, without detailed risk assessments or a recognition of these domestic dynamics, resulting at times in serious harm or death to children. It could also be argued that, if a percentage of those who are abused become abusers themselves, then courts could be complicit in returning children to situations which places them at risk of being abused and also possibly becoming abusers.

Wilcox, Richards, and O'Keefe (2004:339) also review the literature to reveal a range of somewhat contradictory findings. They cite Johnson's (1988) finding 49% of a sample of 47 pre-adolescent males in treatment for sexual aggression as having been sexually abused themselves and in a similar study of girls the same author (1989) found all girls in his sample had experienced sexual abuse as a child, however, the sample was of only 13. Wilcox et al (2004:340) also note the findings of Ryan et al (1996) where 40% of adolescent male sexual offenders reported their own sexual abuse as children. However, in individuals who sexually abuse adults the incidence of their own child sexual abuse is much lower, with other forms of abuse such as emotional, physical, and neglect being more prominent and most noticeably, wide-ranging experiences of domestic violence. If the link between being sexually abused as a child and future sexual offending behaviour were as clear as many might argue, it would create a substantial well of future risk. It has been estimated (Laurance, 2000 in Wilcox et al, 2004:342) that 1 in 100 children are sexually abused by their father, and 2 in 100 by their siblings. If most of these victims became sexual abusers themselves we might anticipate 3% of the adult population being sex offenders. This figure would not appear to equate with the degree of sexual offending reported to the police, although the evidence of under-reporting does remain strong.

The message here is that there is not conclusive evidence to claim that child victims of sexual abuse will themselves become juvenile sexual abusers and indeed adult abusers. Undoubtedly a number of juvenile sexual abusers have themselves been victims, but it is equally likely that exposure to physical abuse and neglect may be equally influential factors. Exposure to domestic abuse (sexual or violent) also appears in a number of studies to be an important precursor to disturbed behaviour among adolescents. There are worrying indications that, if males are abused and later offend, they may use more violence than is necessary in carrying out their abusive attacks as juveniles and adults.

Surrounding this concern with deviant juvenile sexual behaviour is the notion of 'what is deviant?' and 'what is natural curiosity?' Johnson and Doonan (2005:37) cite several cases where there appeared to be sexual curiosity among children, discovered by or reported to adults. Their feeling is that many adult professionals assume the behaviour to be 'wrong' and therefore seek a perpetrator and victim. The former is likely to the older, stronger or brighter, or the male. The authors argue that some professionals may persuade children that other children have abused them. This they believe may encourage children to explain their apparently worrying sexual behaviour in a way that becomes acceptable to the officials working with them. What it does do of course is further cement the alleged link between abused and abusers. This undoubtedly has the very negative labelling effect of those victims of sexual abuse, rather than being regarded as deserving victims, being viewed as potential offenders. This is unlikely to assist their recovery from traumatic events, especially if their sexual abuser has been a parent or other person in a position of trust (Wilcox et al, 2004:338). Intergenerational transmission remains a powerful belief among many, although Kaufman and Zigler (1987 in Johnson and Doonan, 2005:36) argue that the figure is approximately 30%, plus or minus 5%. They also argue that this figure included child victims of all forms of abuse and therefore conclude that two thirds of victims will provide adequate care for their children. They conclude, 'the time has come for the intergenerational myth to be put aside and ask researchers to cease asking, 'do abused children become abusive parents . . .' and ask instead, 'under what conditions is the transmission of abuse most likely to occur?'

It is probably right to be concerned about the impact that childhood sexual abuse will have on the child's future behaviour, indeed that concern should include all abuse suffered by children. It is, however, extremely important not to see each victim as a perpetrator in waiting and to ensure that all are given every opportunity to recover, especially those suffering from other factors noted in this section that might increase the chances of their becoming juvenile and adult perpetrators.

Internet crime

Images of potential dangerousness have recently become over-associated with predatory sex offenders or men who have already shown extreme violence to others. As such, assessment and prediction have focused upon their potential to recreate their offending in given situations, and indeed the imminence of that behaviour. Yet not only is this stereotype inaccurate in terms of individuals, but it also diverts attention from new, emerging, and fast-increasing forms of criminal sexual behaviour. An example of this might be the growth of sexual crime associated with the development of the Internet. The worldwide growth in the use of home computers and the Internet has not only opened up massive new opportunities for sex offenders to network with other offenders, but also to access and store huge numbers of illegal pornographic images, much more easily than with printed material. More recently, the development of Internet-linked mobile telephones has further expanded the possibilities for creating and sharing abusive opportunities.

The National Criminal Intelligence Service (NCIS) has claimed that, 'the arrival of the internet has changed the nature and extent of networking' (NCIS, 2003). They further claim that Internet-based child abuse images have replaced the printed document as the main source of child pornography. Paedophile Internet networks they suggest, are very hierarchical with new members having to provide evidence of their illegal activity to gain status and trust. In a major case of Internet pornography, new members to a group known as the Wonderland Club had to provide 10,000 new images of child pornography each as an entry fee. The club was 'protected by powerful gatekeeping and encryption devices and had a rule book providing tips on how to avoid detection by police' (The Guardian, 14 February 2001). Those members who put others at risk of detection may find viruses sent to their computers to take them out of the group. The police investigation of this paedophile ring, known as Operation Cathedral, eventually resulted in the conviction of seven men for distributing more than 750,000 images. These men were eventually sentenced to custodial terms of between 12 and 30 months, being spared the then maximum of 3 years as a result of guilty pleas. Despite police descriptions of the terrible suffering endured by the child victims of this form of sexual abuse, it appears as if it remains sufficiently 'virtual', or distant, to be considered less of a problem or indeed danger, than the images of the real sexual predator.

Jewkes and Andrews (2005:42) note the comments of a detective inspector saying that child pornography images were like sunken wrecks, they were there but unseen. He said that the Internet had brought these images to the surface. That said, the authors argue that Internet abuse appears to be less of a priority for police services. There may be several reasons for this. These might include a lack of resources, a lack of specialist staff, the sheer scale of the problem, and the absence of this work from key performance indicators—although if considered in the same light as 'real' rather than 'virtual' abuse, it most certainly would be a priority. Another very important issue to consider is the reaction of the public to Internet abuse. Undoubtedly the notion of paedophiles potentially entrapping their children via chat rooms does cause public consternation and new laws appear to be an attempt to tackle this issue (see below). However, the mass of images, the vast majority of which represents a truly awful crime, are seen as too remote and often emanating from distant countries, to generate the panics witnessed elsewhere in the world of paedophile offending.

Another issue, referred to by both Jewkes and Andrews (2005:52) and Silverman and Wilson (2002:86), is the question of how many users or observers of Internet pornography become abusers—what has been described as the difference between 'lookers and doers' (see discussion below). In many ways this question should not even be asked. Those purchasing and watching this material are supporting the commission of a crime—if there were no market there would be no crime. Indeed, as real time videos appear over the Internet, the lookers are actually watching a crime taking place live before their eyes. It may be that the lookers are easier to detect than the producers of this material, especially as organized crime has taken over from the 'dirty' brigade (Silverman and Wilson, 2002:91).

Internet-based sex offenders find it easy to gain the trust of potential victims, appearing sensitive to their problems or by presenting as being much younger than they are. Similarly chat room and Internet-based dating services offer opportunities for abuse to develop. Paedophiles are able to use commercially available encryption packages to protect transmission and store illegal material. This is, of course, a global problem just as the medium itself is global. For example, in Japan during the first six months of 2002, police reported one murder and 23 rapes connected with Internet dating. Overall 800 Internet-related sex crimes were reported in those six months, 70% of which involved teenage girls. Japan has 55 million users of Internet-equipped mobile phones (BBC news world edition, 22 August 2002).

An indication of how the use of technology can worsen the situation is illustrated by the increasingly inexpensive and portable nature of web cameras (webcams) to show real time sexual abuse to a number of viewers, potentially all across the world. The Internet Watch Foundation (IWF), which monitors web content, received 20,000 reports of potentially illegal content in 2003. The major sources by country are the USA (55% of all sites) and Russia (at 23%). Sites originating from the UK are down to 1%, perhaps reflecting the more proactive stance taken on Internet offending and the success of activities such as Operation Ore (IWF, 2003). Operation Ore aimed to track down Internet child abuse users by tracing their credit card information. The police indicated that a significant proportion of the 7,000 UK users of a particular group of websites were previously unknown to them, suggesting that this problem is widespread among previously non-criminal groups (NCIS, 2003). Jewkes and Andrews (2005), however, report on the continuing difficulties for the police service in tackling Internet child abuse, partly for some of the reasons mentioned above, but also because of difficulties with legal definitions both in the UK and elsewhere, alongside the usual problems of the cultural differences in what constitutes acceptable and unacceptable behaviour. Added to this the authors argue that for some senior police officers, cyber crime is still not real police work. It is possible that this attitude permeates the criminal justice system.

Naturally, the growth of Internet-based sexual abuse concerns parents and law enforcement agencies. It means that children can become victims in the safety of their own homes, with parents having little idea of the dangers their children may be facing. As a result, organizations such as the National Prevention of Cruelty to Children (NSPCC) offer advice to parents on how to protect their children online whilst also entering the debate on policing sex crimes online. For example, the NSPCC called for a new police unit to be set up to enable online sex offending to be reported and in particular called for an online '999' service to enable live, webcam abuse to be reported as it happens (NSPCC, 30 November 2004). The police service has responded to the growing threat of Internet abuse, and the National Crime Squad established the Paedophile On Line Investigation Team (POLIT) in January 2003. This team aims to support, coordinate, and assist national and international investigations of Internet-related child abuse. It has also helped to develop *ChildBase*—a sophisticated database to assist with not only the identification of victims of abuse but their abusers as well. Polit also chairs the Virtual Global Taskforce (VGT), which basically aims to 'police' the Internet. With the active participation of Internet providers such as AOL, BT, and Microsoft as well as mobile phone companies such as Vodaphone, working together with, for example, the FBI, Royal Canadian Mounted Police, and Interpol, it is hoped to demonstrate that cyberspace can be policed. Essentially the tactic involves establishing a website purporting to show images of child abuse and takes viewers through a series of pages frequently prompting them to withdraw. If they choose to continue they are advised that they have entered a law enforcement website and that their details have been captured (Virtual Global Taskforce, 13 December 2003).

It is likely that police and probation officers will increasingly encounter Internet sex offenders under post-custodial supervision. In many ways the approach to their offending behaviour should be little different to that than if it took place in the 'real world'. The offender's motivation to engage in this activity may be no different and the attempts to manage their behaviour in the community may be similar, but more difficult. Although no system of monitoring or surveillance guarantees safety, at least with a 'real person' in 'real life' situations, certain controls and exclusions may severely limit the risk. In the virtual world this is far more difficult. The availability of cheap mobile telephones, Internet cafes, and home computers, make it extremely difficult to control Internet abusers. We shall consider later how recent changes to the criminal law have attempted to tackle this emerging problem. Yet for practitioners concerned with monitoring offenders in the community it may be a case of very careful questioning and listening to what they say about their life style. Giveaway information that suggests that they are 'technology aware' may also be indicative and opportunities to steer the conversation towards computers and the Internet, even for those without such previous convictions, may be useful.

The National Probation Service has issued guidance on this issue primarily for pre-sentence report authors (Probation Circular 14/2003), an indication that this may be becoming a more observable problem. Echoing points made in Chapter 5 over the use of actuarial methods for low base-rate offenders, the Circular questions their applicability to a group with little reconviction data, stressing instead the need for an assessment of dynamic risk factors. The circular also poses questions over the link between Internet pornography and hands-on offending, but does suggest that those with a predisposition to commit other sexual offences will also view pornography. Work carried out by the University of Cork is cited as indicating five classes of Internet child pornography:

1. Downloading child pornography
2. Trading child pornography
3. Distribution and production of child pornography
4. Engagement with Internet seduction of children
5. Contact offences

These classes are not mutually exclusive or indeed incremental in that one leads automatically to another. However, one may facilitate the commission of another and as such, offenders operating within these groups need to be assessed for their capability of committing linked sexual offences against children. The Circular puts this scenario very well when it says, 'As the viewer becomes familiar and bored to the pornography, they seek out more "intense" contact. The combination of disinhibition, increased risk taking, entrenched cognitive distortions and the need to seek more intense experiences suggests the possibility of escalating behaviour into seeking opportunities for "real-life experiences" and "hands-on abuse".' A small survey conducted by the West Midlands Probation Area found, in a self-report study, that 86% of sex offenders reported using pornography as a precursor to offending. Thus, although not absolute, there may well be a link in some cases between viewing pornography and seeking out real life victims to abuse.

Finally the Circular cites the work of Carnes, Delmonico, and Griffin (2001) suggesting that online activity becomes particularly problematic in three scenarios, when it is *compulsive* (entrenched habits and routines), when it *continues despite consequences* (eg effect on relationships) and when it is *obsessive* (a preoccupation to the exclusion of other parts of life). They suggest a line of investigation that might reveal information indicating an increased risk for further sex offending. Their list is:

- Preoccupation with sex on the Internet. This is more than just thinking about online sex. It is finding that the offender regularly thinks about how they can arrange their time to spend more time online.
- Frequently engaging in sex on the Internet more often and for longer than intended.
- Repeated unsuccessful attempts to control, cut back or stop engaging in sex on the Internet.
- Restlessness or irritability when attempting to limit or stop.
- Using sex on the Internet as a way of escaping from problems or relieving feelings such as helplessness, guilt, anxiety, or depression.
- Seeking more intense or higher risk sexual experiences.
- Lying to family members, therapists, or others to conceal involvement with sex on the Internet.
- Committing illegal acts online.
- Jeopardizing or losing a significant relationship, job, or educational or career opportunity because of online sexual behaviour.
- Incurring significant financial consequences as a result of engaging in online sexual behaviour.

Understanding where an offenders 'is at' in their criminal careers is important in determining future risks. Carnes et al (2001) suggest that a continuum of experience might provide a useful template. They argue that this would range from a *Discovery Group*, who have no previous problem with online or other sexual behaviour, through to a *Pre-disposed Group*, who have had their first out-of-control online sexual behaviour after years of fantasies, and culminating in the *Lifelong Sexually Compulsive Group*, those whose out-of-control online behaviour is part of a wider pattern of severe sexually problematic behaviour. In assessing online pornography offenders, and having gathered some of the information noted above, the authors conclude by summarizing well-known dynamic risk factors, which could help determine the nature of risk presented by the offender. These include: sexual pre-occupation, sexual entitlement beliefs, distorted attitudes concerning children and sex, emotional congruence with children rather than with adults, sexual arousal to children, poor self-esteem, external locus of control, victim stancing (passive or active), impulsivity, poor problem recognition, and problem solving skills. Many of these behavioural and personality factors will be familiar to those who work with sex offenders and their inclusion in the assessment of online sex offenders will considerably enhance the overall picture.

Internet sex offenders may therefore appear to be down the list of seriousness in the minds of many people, mostly because the victims appear to be at least one step removed from reality. However, the evidence from this section suggests that it should be treated as seriously as real time abuse, especially if some of the aggravating factors in terms of escalation are present.

Hate crime

Elsewhere in this book the point is made that criminal justice practitioners need to listen to and hear what offenders are saying to them. The reason for this seemingly obvious statement is that many people actually do what they say they will do, or threaten to do. It is all too easy to turn a deaf ear to some of the things that people say—they may be too uncomfortable to hear, or demand too much of the listener. It may therefore be easy for the listener to convince him or herself that what the offender is saying is merely bravado and that they will not follow through on their threats. Yet some do, with disastrous consequences. As ever, the perennial problem is sorting out those who will from those who will not. Throughout this book a range of indicators is given to readers, not with an intention to reach some magical point when a dangerousness threshold has been crossed, but to assist in building a holistic picture, one that increases the likelihood of a prediction being right. A consideration of the phenomenon now known as hate crime comes into this category. It offers another insight into the lives and thinking of some of the offenders dealt with by criminal justice staff. Although a 'contested issue' (Hall, 2005a), hate may well offer valuable pointers to future violent behaviour, so a brief summary of the issues will now follow.

For criminal justice staff, especially perhaps probation officers, it will not be an uncommon experience to hear offenders under their supervision espousing racist, homophobic, or sexist vitriol. Such language would of course be unacceptable, undoubtedly challenged, and, at the very least, banned from the office. Policies of zero tolerance may be politically correct but could, of course, pass up on an opportunity to work with people who may become potentially dangerous. An issue lying behind the hate 'façade' therefore is that of any connection between thought and deed. If the offender speaks about violence towards a group of people, how likely is he to carry it through? Are there other clues in the offender's character, background, or present circumstances that might increase the risk of violence? The likelihood of crimes related to hatred appears to be increasing. Just as reports of serious crimes increase fear, so certain incidents, perhaps on the world stage, increase hate. There is a danger that, as with domestic violence, hate will be shunted into a siding, in this case marked 'political'. Political and domestic are then viewed as outside of mainstream criminal justice and therefore do not receive the priorities they may well merit. It may also be an unpleasant fact that victims of so-called 'hate crime' may be regarded by some as less deserving because of who they are, and the offences perpetrated against them by default as less serious. However, even those whose actions may be driven by strong political beliefs exist, generally, in the normal social world. They could therefore be under probation supervision like anyone else, and may at times give clues as to their intentions. It is these signs that demand attention.

Hall's (2005a) contention is that the notion of hate crime is oversimplified by a series of definitions, constructions, and legal responses. He cites Sullivan (1999) in asserting that there are many strands to hate, or more accurately prejudice, and that some may be perfectly acceptable. For example, he refers to Sullivan's view that it would be perfectly normal for the Jews to have hated the Nazis during the Holocaust. It may also be understandable for one person to hate another if they felt themselves to be grievously wronged by that person. We therefore get into complex territory around degrees of hatred and prejudice, around tolerance and intolerance, and freedom of expression. It may be much clearer if there are obvious examples where high prejudice or hate is a prime motivator in offending behaviour (Hall, 2005a:15–16). Any move away from this fairly clear association muddies the water a great deal. For example, should we be very concerned with a person who constantly refers to black people in very derogatory terms, but has no history of violence or other offending against them? Their choice of language may be unacceptable to us but will it, on its own, lead to violence? This book is concerned with identifying future dangerous behaviour, and people with extremely prejudiced and hate-filled views can enter that category, but by no means will all. One piece of behaviour does not automatically lead to another, but it may be a building block in determining future risks.

Establishing a typology of a typical hate offender is, however, very difficult. McDevitt, Levin, and Bennett (2002 in Hall, 2005a:83–5) suggest, from their examination of 169 cases in police files, that four categories of offender emerge. The first and largest at 69% of all, was the thrill offender, usually a youth, who offended for excitement and out of boredom. Victims were selected for their 'difference' and this in itself does suggest a degree of planning and forethought, qualities that may up the stakes in considering future serious offending. Set against this might be the relative youth of the offenders and the expectation that many will grow out of it. The second largest category, at 25%, were those termed 'defensive' offenders, those who struck against those perceived as outsiders or intruders in the offender's territory. Retaliation was the third highest category at 8%, with the retaliation often following a perceived hate offence. Incidences are likely to increase at given stress points when high profile offences linked with hate have been reported. It would be reasonable to expect such offences to be on the increase following recent events in the USA and the UK, although politically this would be a worldwide problem. Finally, at less than 1%, is the 'mission' offender, those whose hate and bigotry is such that the objects of their hatred have to be eliminated.

On their own, these typologies will not necessarily help the criminal justice practitioner in their dealings with offenders. However, they may, along with other factors, hint at the chances for escalation, repetition, and possible deterrence. For example, many of these offenders characteristically offend with others. Are they likely therefore to lead or be led? Will they be susceptible to peer pressure to behave violently? If operating in groups, will the violence escalate? Is the person linked with extreme hate groups, or even legitimate political parties? Is their body tattooed with racist slogans? Are they threatening to commit violence against particular people simply because of their colour, sexual orientation, or gender?

The Guardian newspaper (17 October 2005) carried a report of a vicious murder on Clapham Common, London of a 24-year-old man. He was gay and it is alleged that the two men who beat him to death had been shouting out anti-gay slogans during the attack. Police were concerned about a repetition of the attack because they believed the level of violence was such that this was unlikely to have been a first incident. An adviser to the Metropolitan Police on gay issues suggested that there were five to six homophobic murders in London each year and he suggested that only one in ten attacks were reported to the police. Racist and homophobic prejudice is widespread and, at certain times, may increase significantly. In particular, probation officers may hear this form of abusive language quite often, but so also will police officers and other public sector workers. How and when can this information be used? Awareness of abusive and prejudiced language may not prevent assaults, but it may well serve a useful purpose in estimating future dangerousness. It could become part of a range of aggravating features used to justify longer than desert sentences, it may be used to prevent early release or to include conditions in a release plan. It may simply be an important part of the bigger picture and the message has to be that this information should not be overlooked but used where relevant to offender attitudes and offending behaviour. This should especially be the case where offence-aggravating features are revealed. As Court (2003, in Hall, 2005b: 211) indicates, '... until the probation service and youth offending teams develop the skills and confidence to explore racial hostility, in particular where the victim rather than the court alone have identified it, assessments of harm to the public can only be partial at best, and at worst, dangerously misleading.'

Cruelty to animals

Finally this chapter will consider those with a history of animal cruelty. This may be another of these issues that is easily overlooked because it is not seen as mainstream offending—and this in a nation of pet lovers! However, despite huge public sympathy for the plight of animals at various times, this well of feeling does not seemingly stretch far enough to make any links between those who are cruel to animals and those who are cruel to people. Lockwood (undated) has listed a number of features that he has found common to animal abusers that he believes can be read across to other dangerous acts. In his list of 25 factors he believes that the presence of five is a cause for serious concern and ten shows a high potential for serious violence. For example, he considers (animal) victim vulnerability to be important, where small and harmless animals increase the offender's sense of power and control. Lockwood suggests such people may pose particular risks to children. He proceeds to cite the number of victims, the number of instances in a limited time frame, the severity of injury, the repetition of injury and multiple forms of injury all as poor signs for other offending behaviour. He cites the intimacy of or witnessing the suffering of the animal as a poor predictor, as would be taking photographs to enjoy revisiting the harm later. Writing this book close to 5 November it was sad to note a perfect example of this behaviour. Three young men were alleged to have tied fireworks to a dog and essentially blew the animal apart, filming the whole act on their mobile phones (The Guardian, 31 October 2005).

Other factors closely linked with potential people violence Lockwood argues, is the burning of a live animal, tying animals in a bag or ritualistic abuse of animals. It may be the case that many readers may regard this information as a little 'off the wall'. However, it should not take a giant leap of the imagination to believe that people who can be very cruel to animals could take that cruelty into human interactions. The author, for example, knew a man who had been detained in a special hospital for stabbing his girlfriend in the chest. He had many previous incidents of animal cruelty in his history. He was known to have regularly pulled the legs from live spiders and had also stabbed a parrot dead for making too much noise. His human and animal crimes may not be linked in any way, but they surely add to the picture of a man prepared to use forms of violence in a variety of settings.

Painting the whole picture

The purpose of the examples used in this chapter has not been to imply that an occurrence of certain behavioural factors naturally leads to the development of potentially dangerous behaviour. More, it is suggested that if these behaviours or attitudes are revealed, they need to be used to create a wider, deeper understanding of the offender in question. They can offer clues that might enhance the fairly bald picture drawn by concentrating on certain offence types. This process could be described as trying to predict the future by making sense of the past, depicted by Hawkins (1983) as 'patterning and characterisation'. It is about questioning information about the offender's life, and their motivations for what they do. This is a much more 'clinical' process than an actuarial one and requires an almost forensic approach to information interrogation.

Clues might be found in an offender's choice of occupation for example. Sullivan and Beech (2002) suggest that some perpetrators choose their occupations because they offer a ready supply of potential victims. Others such as Prins (1988:600) suggest that the chosen occupations of some offenders, butchers for example, allow those with a fascination for blood, knives, and cutting to practise their interests and obsessions everyday. This in no way suggests that all butchers or abattoir workers, or mortuary attendants, do those jobs because it feeds obsessions and offending behaviour. It may just offer further, additional clues to the lives and offending lifestyle of some people. As Prins argues, 'the painstaking assembling of facts and the checking of information from a variety of sources are essential'. The type of information summarized in this chapter is but a part of that process (1988:600).

Summary

The behaviours noted in this chapter do not necessarily constitute new problems, but they are reflective of concerns that are increasingly reported upon by the media. Dangerousness is not simply about the spectacular sex and violence cases that can fill page upon page of the tabloid press, or gain widespread television coverage. These cases are of course often extreme, but remain relatively rare. However, killing and serious sexual abuse are more common but often occur in contexts that are less media-friendly. As such a distorted impression of dangerousness is given. This chapter has selected a few areas where serious harm can result but has been dealt with less prominently by the media, hence less attention has been paid to it by politicians and thus it has been a lower priority for criminal justice agencies. The examples given here, however, do suggest that there are signs of change. Previously sidelined issues are moving centre-stage and as a result, agencies have developed policies to tackle these issues. By expanding the range of behaviour that may be included in the public protection agenda, there may be greater protection for previously unseen victims. It will, however, place increasing strain on limited resources, but perhaps this can be helped by working with those presenting real and imminent risk, a clear case for targeted risk assessment, rather than the inclusive and diffuse range of risks currently targeted by government legislation.

4

Dangerous Severe Personality Disorder and Psychopathy

Introduction

This chapter will consider government plans to manage what is portrayed as a new, emerging threat to the public, in the form of people said to be suffering from dangerous severe personality disorder (DSPD). It will also consider the considerable objections raised to these proposals, particularly from the psychiatric profession. It will also briefly outline the characteristics of a psychopathic personality in the light of work within the prison service to develop treatment programmes for this group. There are widespread assumptions made by the public linking mental illness with all types of dangerous behaviour. In many respects these new measures brought in by the Labour government do little to confound these associations.

Penal trends

The legislation outlined in Chapters 5 and 6 share similar themes in their approach to potentially dangerous and very serious offenders. Since the early 1990s, legislative attention has switched between an offence focus and a behaviour focus, with occasionally a combination of the two. Successive governments have pushed through tougher, more punitive legislation, not only in response to perceived public demand, but also in an attempt to ensure that courts follow through on parliamentary intentions. Automatic mandatory minimum penalties have been one attempt to ensure that courts pass longer sentences in specific cases. However, basing these provisions on the commission of a given range of offences, rather than the seriousness or severity of those offences, led to many judges rejecting these measures. Other measures have focused upon the release of offenders from custodial sentences, particularly those that the prison service considers still to be dangerous at the point of release. Policies have therefore concentrated on extending the length of post-release supervision, increasing opportunities for recall, and enhancing the quality and nature of supervision through the work of multi-agency public protection panels discussed in the next chapter.

For those offenders considered to be potentially dangerous, various ways have been devised to deal with them. Measures include sentences that are longer than desert (a departure from proportionality), or for an indeterminate period until they are considered safe for release, or until their risk is considered to be at an acceptable and manageable level. Certain offenders are considered to present such a risk, or their crimes to be so heinous, that they will never be released, as they qualify for the 'whole life' tariff. As we have seen in earlier chapters, and note below, many of the approaches to dangerousness developed in recent years have significantly altered the way in which criminal justice agencies have had to operate. Police officers, for example, have had to become much more adept at risk assessment whilst probation officers have seen their role shift towards a more controlling and intrusive style of supervision, or perhaps surveillance. The extension of the public protection 'family' to a range of agencies such as housing, education, and even leisure services has made an impact upon many people who would not have considered themselves as 'law and order officials'. However, perhaps nowhere has the debate about the changing role of professionals and public protection been as fierce and contested as in mental health, and in this chapter we will explore why this situation has developed.

The contested area of mental illness and dangerousness

We have already indicated the myths that abound over the connection between mental illness and dangerousness. Despite the best efforts of mental health practitioners and researchers to demonstrate the absence of that connection, it remains embedded in the public consciousness. Stark, Paterson, and Devlin (2004:636) reviewed a range of studies that indicated a public association between mental illness and violence ranging from 33–49%. They further cite Crisp et al (2001), whose study of public attitudes to schizophrenia indicated that 70% of survey respondents perceive this group as dangerous. The reporting of mental illness stories again has high associations with violence, according to the 1996 Health Education Authority Survey (Stark et al, 2004:637).

Undoubtedly, certain cases such as that of Timothy Bryan (see Chapter 1) fuel public anxiety, not only reaffirming their belief in the link, but also confirming their lack of faith in the ability of mental health practitioners to adequately protect the public. As with the notoriety afforded to certain paedophile offenders, discharged mental health patients who go on to reoffend earn particular censure, as do those who decide they are safe for release. Unlike fixed-sentence prisoners who had to be released by law even if still considered dangerous, experts exercising their professional judgement declared mental health patients fit for release. As with released life sentence prisoners, it was the cases of discharged patients that went wrong that attracted publicity, rather than the hundreds of successful resettlement cases. It was to be the public reaction to certain notorious cases that would lead the government to embark upon another of its efforts to close the stable door, although this time for many patients the door may never now open, yet alone give them an opportunity to bolt.

We will not spend much time reviewing existing mental health legislation and will instead, focus on where these new mental health provisions overlap with those for potentially dangerous offenders, and in particular, a newly invented group of offenders and even non-offenders, said to be suffering from dangerous severe personality disorder (DSPD). However, it is worth noting that much of the debate surrounding the new measures outlined below, reflect similar discussions about criminal legislation. That is the view held by many that existing legislation, when used appropriately was adequate to do the job without the need for newer, and more draconian provisions. The new provisions in mental health also mirror those in criminal legislation that appear to single out and isolate certain groups of offenders for special treatment, with the common themes of restricted or non-release and indeterminate detention reflected in both health and criminal provision.

As a generality, there is no absolute evidence to suggest that mentally disordered offenders reoffend in any significantly higher rates than mentally ordered offenders (Peay, 2002:749), but studies reviewed by Hare (2003) discussed below, do paint a gloomier picture, at least where psychopathy is considered. Homicides committed by patients released from psychiatric care, or known to psychiatric services, are not as common as many people believe but when they do occur they attract spectacular publicity. In the 1990s, two cases in particular, the murders of Jonathan Zito and Lynne and Megan Russell, caused a public outcry over the discharge of people from psychiatric institutions. The Zito Trust, formed by Jonathan's widow, estimated that between 1992 and 1997, people known to the psychiatric services committed 104 homicides. This figure should of course be viewed in the light of an annual average of approximately 600 homicides per annum in the UK during this period (Brookman, 2005:31), these 'psychiatric' murders therefore only constituting approximately 3%. The Zito Trust also estimated that 70% of patients discharged from hospital would stop taking their prescribed medication within two years (Crow, 2001:159). However, somewhat in contrast to the perceived danger to others posed by these patients, it has been suggested (Royal College of Psychiatrists, 1996 in Crow, 2001:160), that they are a far greater danger to themselves, with 240 recorded suicides in England and Wales between June 1993 and December 1994.

Partly as a result of cases such as those just mentioned, regarded as high profile failures of the system of community care, a review of mental health provision for certain mentally disordered offenders has been instigated. In 1998, the Labour government, only a year into its term of office, set up a panel of experts to undertake a root and branch review (Department of Health, 1999) of the Mental Health Act 1983, with the first consultation document appearing in November 1999. Probation officers, social workers, and mental health staff will of course be familiar with the sections of the 1983 Act that dealt with treatment in the community and in hospital. Section 12 provides for a probation order to have a condition of psychiatric treatment included following conviction. Section 37 provides for a hospital (or guardianship) order without necessarily having a conviction, but two doctors, one of whom must make a bed available within 28 days, must agree the diagnosis. For those practitioners used to working with dangerous and disordered offenders, s. 41 is likely to be the most familiar. This allowed for a restriction order to be imposed in cases where a hospital order had been made by a Crown Court. In practice this meant that an offender could not be transferred or discharged without the authority of the Secretary for State or a Mental Health Review Tribunal. It is estimated that approximately 120 restricted patients are released each year back into the community on conditional discharges (Crow, 2001:150). A section inserted into the Act (s. 45a), by the Crime (Sentences) Act 1997, provides for a hospital and limitation order or a hybrid order. This allows the court to sentence an offender to custody if he is suffering from a treatable psychopathic disorder whilst at the same time ordering his immediate admission to hospital for treatment. This section emphasized the increasingly blurred distinction between health care and custody and, as we shall see below, begins to see health care used in an increasingly coercive and punitive fashion.

Speaking in Parliament in 1999, then Home Secretary Jack Straw stated: '... there is, however, a group of dangerous and disordered individuals from whom the public are not properly protected ... there should be new legislative powers for indeterminate, but renewable detention of dangerous personality disordered individuals. These powers will apply whether or not someone was before the courts for an offence' (Straw, 1999 in Feeney, 2003). Just as in so many criminal justice proposals, the DSPD measures were to become another example of loophole plugging, or in this case, gap closing. The then Health Minister, Alan Milburn, put the government's case succinctly:

> At present, neither the law nor services are geared to cope with the risks posed by dangerous people with severe personality disorder. Many cannot be compulsorily detained in hospital because under current law they can be defined as untreatable. Many are sent to prison after committing a serious crime and

are a danger to the public upon release. As a consequence there has been a gap in the protection mental health laws should afford the public—a gap we will now close. In place of the flawed concept of treatability new criteria will separate those who need treatment primarily in their own best interests from those who need treatment because of the risk they pose to others.

This speech reflects another government statement that 'gaps will be closed', offering the public a notion that safety can be achieved. Treatment is also blamed for previous mistakes, being a 'flawed concept'. As a concept it will be redrafted to become a public protection intervention.

Once in, will you get out?

It was to be the proposals to deal with the DSPD group that would spark such a hostile reaction from the psychiatric profession as well as human rights activists. The new form of detention, lacking the treatability clause of the 1983 Act, would lead many psychiatrists to oppose the proposals. Indeed, in a very early comment on the proposals, the leading psychiatrist Professor Gunn was moved to say in response to the DSPD group, 'I don't know who these people are' (Yamey, 1999:1322). Gunn moved on to explain that, in his view, dangerousness was something ascribed to people permanently, like eye colour. He thought it more sensible to talk about risk, which could be managed, predicted, treated, and measured. In the draft mental health bill the government have proposed that care plans will be put together to deliver treatment. The plans must be designed to give therapeutic benefit to the patient *or* to manage behaviour associated with mental disorder that might lead to serious harm to other people.

Concerns have been expressed that the definition of mental disorder has been defined too broadly and that many more people may get caught up in compulsory powers. As noted by Leung (2002:179), the White Paper broadened the definition of mental disorder to include any disability or disorder of mind or brain, whether permanent or temporary, which results in an impairment or disturbance of mental functioning. Leung's concern was that matters normally described as 'social problems' might be caught up in the new DSPD measures. In determining that treatment does not have to be beneficial the door is open to the indefinite detention of people suffering from what might be regarded as untreatable personality disorders. Brindle (2001) preferred to see a wider use of guardianship orders as a good example of a non-stigmatizing tool, but saw great problems with this idea. He argued that '... since 1998, the initial goal of compulsory community treatment has become yoked, grotesquely, with a second idea of preventive detention ...'; a situation he ascribed to the dominant influence of the Home Office. Brindle concluded, 'to get anywhere further forward, and retain any hope of broad-based support for reform, the two things have to be decoupled. Health ministers must tell their Home Office colleagues to do their own dirty work.' Coid and Maden (2003) reported that the Royal College of Psychiatrists has stated that the only rationale for psychiatric intervention is for the benefit of a patient's health and that public protection should be secondary. Batty (2002) quotes Peter Tyrer, a professor of community psychiatry at Imperial College London, as saying, 'we know people are dangerous. We know people have personality disorders. What we do not know yet is the link between the two is so strong that we can make a diagnosis of DSPD.'

The issue for many people is the problematic nature of assessment and prediction of dangerousness, as discussed in Chapter 5. Farnham and James (2001) confirm the scepticism of many commentators over the effectiveness of assessment when they say, '... Would be clairvoyants engaged in this form of assessment exercise will make use of "tools" in the form of actuarially-based checklists, which give spurious scientific value to estimates that perform less well than chance.' As with many other experienced practitioners they argue that forecasting dangerousness is similar to weather forecasting in that short term predictions can be reasonably accurate but there is much less certainty in the long term. In a systematic review of prediction studies, Buchanan and Leese (2001) came to the conclusion that six people with DSPD would have to be detained for a year to prevent one person from acting violently that year. They calculated that for every ten people with DSPD who would be violent, five would be identified and detained and five would be missed, and for every ten who would not be violent, seven would be identified and released and three would be detained. Their view was that 'there was no value at which prediction can be said to be of acceptable accuracy.' The acceptability of the rate of error was they believed a moral issue, determined not only by the level of mistakes but also by the conditions under which people would be detained. In a 'risk society' (Beck, 1992) the former is likely to be more important than the latter. The expectation that psychiatrists can predict violent and sexual behaviour is called into question by Feeney (2003), and that even if it were possible to treat personality disorder, that this would reduce the level of dangerousness. It is interesting, however, to digress on this issue briefly. Despite the acknowledged difficulties in assessing dangerousness, in a re-analysis of 58 data sets, Mossman (1994) found that actuarial instruments significantly outperformed clinical judgement (although this performed better than the chance levels many experts indicate). Krauss and Ho Lee (2003) found that in mock juror trials, however, real 'human' experts were much preferred to actuarial tools, even when the failings of clinical judgement were explained to them. Public faith in psychiatric opinion may therefore be higher than that of the government or the media.

Reconfiguring the concept of health care

Farnham and James (2001) argue strongly that the new proposals change the nature of the Hippocratic injunction to do no harm to patients and replace it with a duty to prevent the patient harming others. They see the situation changing from one where doctors treat the sick to one where they become agents of social control (although this would not be a new idea to readers of Foucault, for example). However, to read of psychiatrists quoting Garland's *Culture of Control* (2001), perhaps illustrates how they are viewing their changed role. Birmingham (2002) reminds us that four conditions should be met before compulsory powers can be used. These are that there must be a mental disorder; it must be of a nature or degree warranting medical treatment; treatment must be necessary for the health and safety of the patient or the protection of others; and that appropriate treatment must be available for the disorder. Alongside these are general principles that patients should be involved in decisions made about them, that those decisions are made fairly and openly, and any treatment given imposes the minimum level of intrusion. The increasing dominance of the public protection agenda, however, suggests that these principles may be misapplied in certain situations.

In the view of MIND (2005), the breadth of the criteria for compulsion will make it very difficult to satisfy the conditions for their release. The government have estimated numbers of potential DSPD offenders to be between 2,000 and 2,500, although many critics argue that the broadly defined criteria will see many more included, as well as the accumulation effects caused by the difficulties of earning a discharge. Szmukler (2001) argues that although the measures are meant to be aimed at a small group of offenders, 'it is not obvious what prevents their wider application'. He continued, 'the crux of the matter is whether the ascription of mental disorder is being applied to a group of apparently risky individuals as a means of securing their preventive detention under a veneer of ersatz healthcare.' There is a clear backlash against what many health professionals see as a major ethical issue. The Clinical Psychiatry Network say that, 'the attempt to extend medical authority into preventive detention without treatment (detaining persons with DSPD) who had not yet committed a dangerous offence would breach both medical ethics and Human Rights legislation.' In their view the proposals showed disturbing parallels with past examples of political abuse of psychiatric power, citing the example of the Soviet Union as demonstrating how psychiatry can be used to routinely seek out those who do not conform. Leung (2002:180) believes that doctors will be unable to fulfil their traditional role as healers as the conditions of DSPD are untreatable. Instead, they were being asked to become 'public protectors' and, he anticipated, compulsorily treat and monitor people whose health problems may have been in remission.

The opposition to these new measures has been widespread and prolonged. In many ways they recreate the united practitioner and academic opposition to the measures considered in the first 'dangerousness debate'. Moncrieff (2003:8) noted that the mental health bill had 'succeeded in uniting almost every pressure group, charity, and professional grouping against it' (the only exception being the Zito Trust, which has supported it). Peay (2002:780) indicated that, 'the initiative (DSPD) does not bode well. It has shocked our North American cousins who have observed that even there such proposals had not been countenanced.' Despite a significant majority of psychiatrists opposing the measures (estimates of 66–75%), it appears as if the government will pursue its agenda. Psychiatrists will then be left to debate their role in the process, just as probation and police officers have had to do within the criminal justice public protection framework. The government have argued that the DSPD measures are entirely compatible with human rights legislation. White (2002:95) suggests that, at least in terms of public reaction, they may have got it right. He cites the Public Health (Control of Diseases) Act 1984, reinforced by s. 5(1)(e) of the Human Rights Act 1998, that allows several public authorities to preventatively detain non-criminals who have major communicable diseases such as cholera, smallpox, and plague. He argues that the public are unlikely to object to these measures in the interest of public protection and may think the same about the dangers presented by personality-disordered offenders. In a thoughtful piece, Leung (2002) cites several European Court judgments that would appear to support the government's view that its legislation will be human rights compatible. For example, proposed measures designed primarily for the protection of others will focus mainly on managing behaviours arising from disorders and may not involve any benefits for the patient. Leung notes that in *Ashingdane v UK* (1985) it was held that article 5(1)(e) of the European Convention on Human Rights (ECHR) does not require treatment to be given during detention. In terms of compulsory treatment in the community, Leung again cites a European judgment, *W v Sweden*, indicating that forced medication on discharge from hospital was not characterized as a deprivation of liberty, thus he felt that compulsory community treatment would be regarded as legal. However, he did express concern over how broadly drawn the definition of mental disorder had been and that future issues that might come before the European Court could be much more difficult to rule on than those until now. In other words, human rights compatibility may only be temporary and the government could be mistaken in believing that it would not face successful challenges to its DSPD proposals.

Populist policy-making

Despite its undoubted 'good intentions', it is difficult not to conclude that the DSPD proposals are another example of populist policy-making. As Moncrieff notes, having professionalized the process of dealing with the 'mad' in 1959, the government appeared to be taking back power unto itself, in the belief that psychiatrists are not locking up enough people (in criminal terms read judges for psychiatrists). The proposals certainly represent another clear example of policy flying in the face of expert opinion, although again it is equally clear that human tragedy lies behind these initiatives. Undoubtedly though, and importantly for the government, they would engender widespread public support. The public may also, however, be some way apart from that expert opinion. The intent may therefore be understandable but the suspect legal and medical underpinning of the measures must lead to serious human rights concerns, particularly as there appears to be such scope for significant net widening of the potential DSPD population. Recently elected Labour governments have made a great deal of their determination to push through evidence-led policy, but, as Peay rather devastatingly summarizes, this does not appear to be so with its DSPD measures:

> This is not to be an evidence-based programme. And how, anyway could it be? If there is no agreed definition, no clear diagnosis, no agreed treatment, no means of assessing when the predicted risk may have been reduced, and no obvious link between the alleged underlying condition and the behaviour, how could outcome measures be agreed upon and then evaluated? The potential for the demonization of this group and discrimination against them thereafter is self-evident (Peay, 2002:780–1).

Notwithstanding widespread opposition in principle, and indeed a high percentage of psychiatrists (30%, Critical Psychiatry Network, 1999) saying that they will not implement the proposals, the government is pressing ahead. It says that it can operate within the existing Mental Health Act 1983 and does not need new legislation. It has already established over 300 high security places in Whitemoor and Frankland prisons as well as in Rampton and Broadmoor hospitals. The government argue that its target group are people who have not accessed mental health services in the past (as personality disorder was not considered to be treatable—but see Asen, 2005) but who are dangerous as a result of their personality disorder. The DSPD programme is based on three factors; risk of serious harm, personality disorder, and the existence of a functional link between the two. It is said that a candidate for the high secure units can be admitted for treatment if assessment confirms that:

- he is more likely than not to commit an offence that might be expected to lead to serious physical or psychological harm from which the victim would find it difficult or impossible to recover; and
- he has a severe disorder of personality; and
- there is a link between the disorder and the risk of offending (Home Office, 2005—note PC 40)

It is envisaged by the Home Office that suitable people would include those assessed as high or very high risk according to OASys and have previously been assessed as having a severe personality disorder (this measures by a high score on the PCL-R and/or a diagnosis of two or more personality disorders). According to Annex A of Probation Circular 40/2005, personality disorder occurs in approximately 10–13% of the general population. However, among those presenting to primary or secondary care services that figure can rise to 50% and, in the prison population, to between 60–80%.

With such a large number of individuals potentially at risk of getting caught up in these measures it may be useful to reprise the different types of disorder as defined by the Diagnostic & Statistical Manual of Mental Disorders (DSM—IV). The disorders are presented as clusters as follows:

Cluster A—'odd' or 'eccentric'

- Paranoid—interpretation of people's actions as deliberately demeaning or threatening
- Schizoid—indifference to social relationships and restricted range of emotional experience and expression
- Schizotypal—deficit in interpersonal relatedness with peculiarities of ideation, odd beliefs and thinking, unusual appearance, and behaviour

Cluster B—'dramatic'

- Histrionic—excessive emotionality and attention seeking, suggestibility, and superficiality
- Narcissistic—pervasive grandiosity, lack of empathy, arrogance, and requirement for excessive admiration
- Anti-social—pervasive pattern of disregard for and violation of the rights of others occurring since the age of 15
- Borderline—pervasive instability of mood, interpersonal relationships, and self-image associated with marked impulsivity, fear of abandonment, identity disturbance, and recurrent suicidal behaviour

Cluster C—'anxious' or 'inhibited'

- Obsessive-Compulsive—preoccupation with orderliness, perfectionism, and inflexibility that leads to inefficiency
- Avoidant—pervasive social discomfort, fear of negative evaluation and timidity, with feelings of inadequacy in social situations
- Dependant—persistent and submissive behaviour

Many criminal justice professionals will recognize these behaviours in offenders they have dealt with—and several of those offenders will have more than one of them. To be regarded as present, the disorder needs to be chronic or persistent (continuing for a long time or frequently recurring). The pool of people who may therefore be potentially included in the DSPD provisions is a not unreasonable sample of the offender population at large. The DSPD programme may therefore become something that probation and police officers might become familiar with.

The DSPD team have also been working closely with the Prison Service's Offending Behaviour Programmes Unit (OBPU) to develop a programme to reduce violence in violent offenders who score over 25 on the Psychopathy Checklist—Revised. The programme will use cognitive behaviour therapy and skills training to target the dynamic risk factors associated with an individual's violent behaviour. In an early evaluation of violent behaviour within the new units (Taylor, 2003), a significant decrease in expected violent incidents was recorded, although the report acknowledged that a number of factors external to the unit could have been influential in the reduction of violent incidents.

Psychopathic disorder

Criminal justice practitioners and criminology students alike will be familiar with the term 'psychopath'. Just as there is a public association between mental illness and violence, so there is a similar association between psychopathy and dangerousness. In particular, those individuals displaying very aggressive behaviour and violence will be too often termed a 'psycho'—it has become the label of choice for those whom the public should avoid. However, as ever there is much confusion about the term, even in one noted case, its endearing application to a former 'hard man' England footballer and now successful premier league manager. The murder in Feltham young offenders institution of Zalud Mubarek, in his cell by his 'cell mate' Robert Stewart (because he 'felt like it') saw the term 'psychopathic personality' raised in court and is another example of confirming the association of psychopathy and dangerousness in the public mind. It should be noted however that Stewart was an avowed racist who had already stated his intention to cause harm to Mubarek—leading to an admission by the Director of the prison service that his organization suffered from institutional racism. If the clues noted in earlier chapters had been acted upon (hatred of visible minorities, doing what he said he would) then this young man's life might have been saved by the simple measure of not putting him in the same cell as an avowed racist. Thus to conclude this brief diversion into mental health issues a short section on psychopathic disorder will follow. The Mental Health Act 1959 first recognized psychopathic disorder and defined it as 'A persistent disorder or disability of mind (whether or not including significant impairment of intelligence), which results in abnormally aggressive or seriously irresponsible conduct.' Kirkman (2002) attempts to draw out the distinctions between incarcerated and non-incarcerated psychopaths with a view to isolating the emotional behaviours that may give rise to severe anti-social behaviour. But first he believed it important to identify the key features of psychopathic disorder and cited Cleckley (1964) as a leading figure having distinguished 16 key features:

- Superficial charm and good intelligence
- Absence of delusion and other signs of irrational thinking
- Absence of nervousness or psychoneurotic manifestations
- Unreliability
- Untruthfulness and insincerity
- Lack of remorse or shame
- Inadequately motivated anti-social behaviour

- Poor judgement and failure to learn from experience
- Pathological egocentricity and incapacity to love
- General poverty in major affective reactions
- Specific lack of insight
- Unresponsiveness in general interpersonal relationships
- Fantastic and uninviting behaviour with drink and sometimes without
- Suicide rarely carried out
- Sex life impersonal and poorly integrated
- Failure to follow any life plan

Cleckley, in the *Mask of Sanity*, distinguished further between primary and secondary psychopaths. The former were regarded as charming, socially skilled, often intelligent, and showing few signs of anxiety. The latter group were regarded as impulsive and lacking in moral sensibility, socially inept, and withdrawn. Many members of the public might recognize some of these characteristics in their own behaviour, or in people they know. It has been estimated that 1% of the general population are psychopathic to a degree whilst in the criminal population the figure is much higher at 15–25% (in the new DSPD units that figure has been recorded at 60%, Taylor, 2003). However, for a diagnosis Cleckley (1964) believed that the majority of these characteristics should be present in an individual. However, the question remains, is even a majority of these characteristics enough to suggest that a person will be violent or dangerous?

Helibrun (1990) suggests that psychopathy linked with low intelligence may be a factor, indicating that several studies demonstrated that psychopathy and intelligence status were sound predictors of future violence. He indicated that when intelligence is lacking in a poorly socialized individual, the possibility of dangerous acts (such as violent crimes) occurring might escalate as temporary cognitive restraints on grossly anti-social behaviour (eg alternative plans, anticipated consequences) fail to materialize (1990:142). He concluded that men who combine high antisociability and low intelligence tend to be those who commit the most dangerous crimes. Heilbrun concluded that as a society we are considerably better informed about the anti-social behaviour seen in psychopaths than we are about the emotional difficulties that are the risk factors for the development of the anti-social behaviour. He believes that non-incarcerated samples can yield rich information untainted by incarceration or institutionalization. In others words, studies of those with the characteristics of psychopathy but not the criminal behaviour may lead us to better understand attributes specific to psychopathy and to criminality. Such a distinction would of course inform much of the DSPD debates outlined as above. Peay (2002:779) makes a similar point, suggesting that the Hare checklist identifies two dimensions of psychopathy. The first related to interpersonal and affective disorders (selfishness and callousness, for example) and the second to socially deviant behaviours (irresponsibility and anti-social behaviour, for example). Violence would invariably be drawn from the second dimension.

An issue of concern is perhaps that the behaviour displayed by psychopathic offenders is often so extreme that it is generalized across all types of mental disturbance. But, even in allowing for this, is there a significant link between psychopathy and not only reoffending but also serious offending? A range of studies reviewed by Hare (2003) does suggest that those scoring highly on the Psychopathy Checklist—Revised (PCL–R) do have a higher recidivism rate. A brief summary of the items in the checklist (each scored 0, 1, or 2 with a maximum of 40 points) reveal a range of behavioural factors that many people might recognize to a greater or lesser extent in people they know.

Factor 1: Interpersonal/affective	Factor 2: Social deviance
1. Glibness/superficial charm	3. Need for stimulation/proneness to boredom
2. Grandiose sense of self worth	9. Parasitic lifestyle
4. Pathological lying	10. Poor behavioural controls
5. Conning/manipulative	12. Early behavioural problems
6. Lack of remorse or guilt	13. Lack of realistic, long term goals
7. Shallow affect	14. Impulsivity
8. Callous/lack of empathy	15. Irresponsibility
16. Failure to accept responsibility for own actions	18. Juvenile delinquency
	19. Revocation of conditional release
*Additional items	
11. Promiscuous sexual behaviour	
17. Many short term marital relationships	
20. Criminal versatility	

In the United States a score of 30 is considered high, but in England it is 25 or 26. A number of studies linking recidivism with psychopathy will be discussed briefly below. Psychopathy is also linked more specifically with certain types of offending, notably violence but also to a lesser degree, with sexual offending. As Hare (2003:35) indicates, it should not be surprising that connections between psychopathy and violence are made. He says that many of the characteristics that inhibit anti-social and violent behaviour, such as empathy, close emotional bonds and a fear of punishment, are absent or seriously deficient in psychopaths. He cites an FBI investigation in 1992 showing that almost half of law enforcement officers killed in the line of duty were killed by strangers who closely matched the personality profile of the psychopath.

Citing a 1998 study by Hart, Kropp, and Hare, Hare (2003:37) notes that failures from custody (reoffending or parole violation) over a three-year period was linked with high psychopathy scores (80%), medium scores (62%), and low scores (37%). Citing a French study over a shorter time frame of one year, the figures were high 60%, 30% medium, and 10% low. Links with sexual offending also emerge, but these appear to vary according to the type of offence. For example, high PCL-R scores (30 or over) appeared in extra-familial molesters 6.3%, incest offenders 10.8%, mixed molesters 6.3%, rapists 35.9%, and mixed rapists and molesters 64% (recall Scott's 1977 comments on the poor prognosis for exposers who combine with other offences).

It appears therefore as if high PCL-R scores are associated with more aggressive and predatory sexual offending. When the high PCL-R score is combined with deviant sexual arousal patterns, the combination becomes 'deadly' according to Hare (2003:42). There is an increased risk of pre-index sex offences, more kidnapping and forcible confinement, more general non-sexual offences, and more violence. High PCL-R scores may therefore be closely linked with violent and aggressive sexual recidivism. Lower scores appear to witness a reduced risk with concentrations being smaller in less aggressive offences.

Summary

For those working with potential dangerousness, or, if they prefer, high risk offenders, a little knowledge about mental disorder may itself be a dangerous thing. However, in situations where a variety of information about offenders is revealed and too often filed away, it may be that certain factors about a person can be useful as potential indicators of dangerous behaviour. It is extremely unlikely that practitioners can have too much information to hand and everything can be used to build a picture of individuals. Heilbrun's suggestion that we attempt to be clear about which dimension the disorder may be drawn from is particularly helpful to non-mental health specialists who will frequently come across these individuals within criminal justice circles. At the same time, it would be right to proceed with caution. As noted earlier, there are many common associations about mental illness and violence that are patently incorrect. Yet the association remains a powerful one, right through to court hearings. Peay (2002:783) cites Solomka's (1996) study of the first 35 Court of Appeal decisions under s. 2(2)(b) of the Criminal Justice Act 1991 'dangerousness' provisions. Of the 35, 22 involved psychiatric evidence. It was noted that even the appearance of a mental disorder to a lay audience was enough to lead to a request for a psychiatric report. Significantly, even if the report did not lead to a therapeutic recommendation, it often indicated worrying features, which persuaded courts to pass longer than proportionate sentences.

A range of people have been given social demon status in recent years both by governments and the media. In the mid-1990s, these included groups seen as more of a threat to the 'establishment' than to life and limb. Among these would-be travellers, ravers, animal rights protesters, and squatters. Each was subjected to new laws to effectively criminalize what had been perfectly lawful activity. The target then shifted towards drug offenders and to those recidivists who were not apparently learning their lesson. Throughout the decade the focus never shifted from sex offenders, however, with predatory paedophiles in particular singled out for a constant ratcheting up of punitive interventions. Violent offenders have not quite reached the level of notoriety in recent years although, where violence has been linked with mental illness, it most certainly has. It is to this final group that the government has now turned its attention.

Two major issues will continue to cause debate for some while. The first is that the new DSPD proposals appear to open the door for prolonged compulsory detention for those who have not committed a crime, but pose a risk of doing so. Their disorder does not have to be amenable to treatment, as with current legislation, and can simply be to 'manage their behaviour'. As the Mental Health Alliance indicate, the lack of certainty over the criteria to be deemed a DSPD patient (or prisoner) may make it very difficult to meet any conditions set for release. The second issue in these proposals appears to be the reluctance of the mental health profession to support them. There appears to be a sizeable majority who are not supportive of the DSPD concept and a sizeable minority who indicate that they will refuse to implement the new measures. The recent history of criminal justice legislation is one of rapid policy-making with a strong populist element, an ever-increasing level of punitiveness, and a series of reforms, rejections, and new proposals. It will be interesting to see if the new DSPD measures end up going the same way.

5

A Look into the Future —Predicting the Risk of Serious Harm

Introduction

Assessing and predicting dangerous behaviour has long been the preserve of psychiatrists and psychologists. Yet with the growth in the dangerousness problem since the early 1990s, a number of other professionals regularly and routinely assess and predict the risks posed by an ever-increasing number of offenders. As a result a number of risk assessment tools have been devised, several in shortened format, for a wide variety of practitioners from different disciplines and with different types of experience and training. In many respects all of these people are attempting to predict the unpredictable, as the less common the behaviour the more difficult it becomes to apply standardized prediction methods. This chapter will explore a number of prediction methods and argue that sound knowledge of the offender and awareness of key trigger behaviours remains central to effective assessment.

Repetition, risk, and realism

Violent and sexual offending are, thankfully, uncommon behaviours. These offences at any level constitute approximately 20% of all recorded crime, but those offenders operating at the extreme end of the seriousness spectrum are a much smaller percentage of this group (approximately 96,000 out of nearly 6 million police recorded crimes, Home Office, 2004). Yet serious, unusual, and vicious crimes hog the headlines, offering an impression of a much more widespread problem. The problem is one of product inflation—public concern and anxiety fuelled by the media leading to more common offences being escalated up the seriousness ladder. Those working with potential dangerousness have two tricky tasks to undertake. The first is to determine the nature and quality of behaviour that merits the label and the second is to determine if that behaviour will be repeated. Criminal justice professionals need to avoid falling into the trap of regarding all occurrences of a given behaviour as potentially dangerous. If they do not differentiate between offenders and their behaviour, the public protection system will inevitably collapse in very short time. At the same time acknowledgement has to be made of the fact that serious assaultive offending behaviour can arise in those without a previous history or in those committing completely different types of crime. In other words, there is a need to operate outside of the stereotypes. Those who have committed heinous crimes may not repeat their behaviour, whilst much less serious offenders could be showing all the signs of serious escalation and repetition. But if no one is looking for these signs, or they are looking in the wrong place, they will go unnoticed.

It could be argued that any person convicted of certain types of criminal behaviour, for example violence, sexual crime, arson, kidnap, and similar matters could be considered by default as dangerous. The commission of these particular crimes also by default, sets them up to be considered as potentially dangerous in the future. Their offending behaviour to date is likely to have involved victim suffering, to greater or lesser degree. That suffering may be physical, psychological, or both. Death may have been an outcome. The seriousness of their offending will, rightly, determine the severity of their punishment—a fundamental principle of sentencing as encapsulated by the Criminal Justice Act 1991. Yet that same Act enabled a departure from this principle if an offender was regarded as presenting a further risk to the public—this deviation focusing upon the offender rather than the offence. The message here was that certain offenders displayed particular traits that increased the risk of their repeating or escalating their offending in the future. This is the essence of potential dangerousness and the response to it is generally additional punishment for a possible future crime. The problem then becomes cutting through the morass of offence-based categories to determine those who may well continue to pose a serious threat in the future—this assessment influencing length and type of sentence, their release decision, and their post-release supervision and management arrangements. The assessment of potential dangerousness is therefore a crucial process, for the offender and the wider public because potentially huge harms or a huge loss of rights rest upon it.

Assessing dangerousness is not an easy task and is undoubtedly one fraught with potential pitfalls. Getting it wrong may prove calamitous, with either an offender being unnecessarily detained or a new serious crime that might have been avoided. The word 'dangerous' is itself in common usage and is frequently used to describe people and situations inappropriately. It is therefore at risk of losing the 'exceptional' focus that it should entail. It is important that this exceptional element is maintained for the simple reason that the measures available to the state and used against these offenders are themselves exceptional. The role of criminal justice professionals is to rise above generalized understandings to apply knowledge and experience in order to separate the wheat from the chaff. Yet, in arguing that this professional knowledge is better than the view that anyone can recognize potential dangerousness an onerous responsibility unfolds. By claiming expertise, professionals are arguing that they can do the job better, more accurately and less emotively and it is here that one reaches the nitty-gritty of assessment and prediction. By claiming expert knowledge, professionals need to deliver accuracy in their assessments with these having a sound theoretical and increasingly scientific basis. Odds of about evens, or slightly better than chance, are unlikely to prove acceptable to the public or politicians. Claims to scientific rationality will therefore need to be made and tools and mechanisms developed to increase the effectiveness of assessment. However, the question will remain whether scientific, actuarially based assessment and predictive tools, based upon aggregated data, can be brought to bear upon rare and extreme behaviour.

As already noted, dangerousness is about a possible future act. It is an event that might happen but of which no one can be certain. The only certainty is when something does not happen, but again, no one could know if it would have happened regardless of any intervention. The degree of that intervention, and the numbers regarded as dangerous or not, will likely be influenced significantly by factors outside of the individual. These factors will include the sense of security felt by the public and politicians as they decide upon acceptable levels of risk. The more secure people feel the greater the risk they may be prepared to face, and conversely insecurity will decrease levels of tolerance. In Canada the changing nature of risk acceptability was noted by the John Howard Society (1995, in Nash, 1999a:161), 'What is judged to be an acceptable risk is bound to change over time. In the current political climate, it is reasonable to assume that public pressure to detain potentially dangerous individuals will result in more offenders being judged as high risks.' This point is supported by Douglas (1990, in Horlick-Jones, 2003:158) when she says; 'Note that the reality of the dangers is not at issue. The dangers are only too horribly real ... this argument is not about the reality of dangers, but about how they are politicized. This point cannot be emphasized too much.' Commentators therefore note the absence of neutrality from the risk process, because of its centrality to political dynamics. Horlick-Jones (2003:167) makes this point well when he argues that, 'Risk may be viewed as both a language and asset of techniques, however, it is not neutral in its framing of the world, or its associated accounts and practices.'

Public protection workers do not therefore operate in a vacuum. They operate in a context in part defined by their own feelings about particular crimes, and the political and media climate driven along by spectacular incidents. These staff are charged with the task of making the future safer and, as techniques and methodologies are said to improve, so public expectations of greater accuracy will increase. As Rose (1999, in Horlick-Jones, 2003:154) offers, '... risk is a particular style of thinking that has brought the future into the present and made it calculable', a scenario described by Kemshall as attempting to 'colonise the future' (1998:294). Her words are a fitting finale to this introductory section and put into context the difficulties faced by staff involved in this process on a daily basis, who may increasingly less often be able to step back and really think about what they are doing. She described '... an inexorable widening of the risk net as those held accountable for risk attempt to reduce its inherent uncertainty through the use of precautionary techniques and invasive systems of information collection ... In our attempt to colonise the future through risk ... we may make that future very bleak indeed.'

Risky views and risky methods

Trying to accurately assess the risk posed by potentially dangerous offenders has taxed practitioners, academics, and increasingly commercial organizations, for a long period of time. Assessing risk has in the main been carried out within two camps, the clinical and the actuarial. The former, essentially carried out by clinicians but also probation and social workers for example, relies upon expert knowledge and professional judgement. It is characterized by the gathering of information and a number of interviews, and, to be effective, needs to be painstaking in its research and analysis (Scott, 1977). Of course, commendable as this approach might be, it is by definition very time consuming. The problem here is that the massive growth in the public protection business has ensured a huge increase in the number of cases to be considered. Time will inevitably be at a premium; although the MAPPA guidance (Home Office, 2004:6) argues that time is essential to consider all the available relevant information. This chapter will therefore review some of the arrangements available to 'predict the unpredictable'.

For many people, the prediction of risk and harm is an ongoing, never-ending part of their daily working lives. Probation officers, for example, in both regularly meeting with offenders and constantly gathering new information, have to update their assessments and maybe change their predictions. Is the risk greater, is it more imminent, or has it diminished? Because of the potentially severe consequences of both over- and underestimating risk, its assessment must be regular and thorough. All the time, practitioners are keeping in mind two vital points, how great might the risk of harm be and how likely is it to happen in the near future? Not all risk decisions involve long term assessments of offender's future harm, there may be a more pressing need for instant assessments and decisions when staff face possible harm to themselves. In such scenarios, basic common sense and an ability to be in tune with one's human senses is vital—if the hairs on your back are up, or if the offender's facial features change, or his colour alters, it may well be the time to be considering the exit route (which hopefully would have been established *before* the interview took place).

For many criminal justice staff the risk of physical harm in specific situations needs to be addressed. If we consider the potential situations in which police officers might find themselves, the point might be illustrated better. Let us consider a possible scenario, which could result in severe violence. A man mugs a woman in a public street and runs off. The public shout for help and a solitary uniformed constable gives pursuit having seen that the victim is OK. The officer chases the man into a cul-de-sac. The man, who is carrying a bag, shouts out that he has a knife. The officer immediately has to assess the likelihood of this being true, whilst determining, if it is true whether the man will use the knife. Even this assessment is not simple as the victim could be the police officer or the offender. If the man then produces the weapon, a new scenario unfolds. Certain information has been firmed up and the risk has clearly increased. Will the officer attempt to disarm the man? Does the offender look as if he knows how to use the knife? Is he reckless through drink or drugs? How fit does he look? What will the officer's training be telling him and will the adrenalin of the moment override this? Will he believe he can save other members of the public from being victims? Will he think he could be stabbed himself? Should he just call for help but then what if the man attempts to get past him? There is nothing new in this scenario and it perhaps shows the types of decisions we could all face any day. Although all are unlikely to be as serious as these decisions, they all share common characteristics of multiple options with information changing rapidly, and becoming more or less important. As those options close down though, the need to take decisive action increases. All the training in the world may not overcome human reactions and instincts, and all criminal justice practitioners trying to predict future risk of serious harm will face similar issues with quantities of information, often conflicting, and a number of potential outcomes. All practitioners have to keep in mind how the changing context in which the offender operates, and the dynamic nature of his harm triggers, can increase or decrease the risk of harm in a short time span.

Often the bottom line of risk assessment is to try to make the unpredictable more predictable, to bring greater certainty into a very uncertain scenario, and this is far from an easy task. Severe violence and sexual crime is thankfully an infrequent occurrence and, as a result of that, often has distinctive situational or contextual qualities to it. Therefore seeking common features upon which to build behavioural patterns to assist prediction is not easy. It is of course this patternization across large numbers of offender groups that forms the basis of actuarial assessment, but with more common offending types. It is likely therefore that combinations of key factual information, baseline predictions, professional training and judgement aided by human instinct, will be the best that we can currently do, but this will not yield perfect results. Another everyday example involving the author can illustrate the point further.

Whilst working in a category 'A' (maximum security) prison, the author, then a senior probation officer, was called to a prisoner's cell. The prison was at the time in a state of high security and all prisoners were locked behind their (single cell) doors. The prisoner's cell door was unlocked by the prison officer who immediately returned to his wing office, some distance away. On stepping into the cell, with the prisoner lying on his bed, the author was immediately aware of another person standing behind the door. Clearly, this was a highly dangerous situation with great potential for hostage taking. A quick word with the prisoner and an immediate step back outside the cell resolved the problem. The prisoner went back into his cell and the door was locked. Upon leaving the wing the prison officer staff were asked if everyone was back 'behind their doors', a question met with a cursory 'of course'. When asked if this meant two to a cell and the location of the 'extra' man was identified, the level of activity was extreme to say the least. This was a highly risky situation, whether there was an intention to cause harm or not. The decision to get out quickly and not panic was obvious and sensible, but still required judgement and experience. These human qualities and professional skills cannot and should not be minimized, even if the push towards a more systematic and formulaic assessment of risk gains pace. If there is a moral in this tale it is that no matter how scientific the process of offender risk assessment might become, it will still involve assessing unpredictable human beings. This process will continue to require professional judgement, and will need to be recognized as requiring personal skills that are not held by everyone. It should, in other words, remain a task for the skilled and professional practitioner; risk assessment reflects a human response to a human problem.

Aside from the daily assessment and prediction of future risk, there are also particular crucial pinch points where decisions are vital. Obvious ones would include the decision whether or not to charge a person, whether or not to grant bail, the sentencing decision, and the decision to release. At each of these points there is always likely to be a number of pressures on those making the assessments. These pressures might include a shortage of time, a shortage of resources, media and political pressure, local feelings, and a concern to avoid getting it wrong. A case reported in the national press in September 2005 illustrates a number of points relating to predicting dangerousness and it is worth examining in some detail. Many of the points raised will be discussed further in this chapter. A 23-year-old man was sentenced to 14 years for the rape of a 19-year-old woman. Although perhaps at the upper end of rape sentencing, there were a number of factors in the case that should cause significant concern and could perhaps have justified an indeterminate life sentence (The Times, 16 September 2005). Newspaper reports do not of course include all the relevant case information so the following comments need to be treated with an element of caution, but the identification of 'dangerousness indicators' is a useful exercise. Offender and victim met at a nightclub in Lancashire and were seen to kiss. Significantly, the newspaper reported the 'couple' as leaving at 2:00 am ostensibly in search of a taxi. When do two people become a couple? If they are described as a couple, are we not entering the territory of acquaintance rather than stranger rape? If we accept the research noted in Chapter 2, can we consider that the offender deliberately planned to kiss in public so that he could claim an acquaintance and therefore argue that sexual activity had been consented to?

Further details of the case suggest other reasons to be very concerned about this individual. One was the level of violence perpetrated on the victim, resulting in a broken jaw necessitating the insertion of a metal plate into her mouth. At the time of the trial, she was continuing to receive psychiatric assistance to cope with the trauma of the attack. The offender used his own mobile phone to film himself committing the rape, apparently intending to show his friends later. Other violence research, for example, that perpetrated against animals, suggests a strong link between videoing the violence and the offender's reinforcement of power and sexual satisfaction from such events (Lockwood, undated). A further matter has some relevance to this case. The offender had a previous conviction for indecent exposure which, according to Scott (1977), is an indicator of significant concern when it is mixed with other crimes. Overall, we therefore have a very pessimistic picture. A very violent sexual assault, allied to a range of other potential indicators of future dangerousness, is somewhat clouded by notions of consent and acquaintanceship. The judge in the case described the offence as, '... particularly grave, horrendous and abhorrent causing the height of violent violation, fear and distress and very serious physical injury to the victim. It may well be impossible for her to come to terms with her trauma.' In assessing the character of the defendant the judge summarized, 'I consider you are extremely dangerous to women. The violence that you used was extreme to the point of being sadistic. You are a man with no conscience and remain vague, dismissive and evasive about what you actually did.' This case indicates a number of factors suggesting that the risk of future harm is considerable. It ticks a number of the boxes contained in the Sexual Offences Act 2003 that might lead to a protective sentence. These same factors were surely pertinent to the consideration of a discretionary life sentence—yet a protective sentence was not passed. There may be good reason for this but if we are to retain discretionary sentences based around notions of dangerousness, cases such as this appear to be more appropriate than many.

Those predicting dangerousness therefore have to work with all the information at their disposal. Prediction should not be about guesswork, although to a large extent it remains more of an art than a science. The information should be used to build a picture of the offender and their behaviour in order to try and estimate the chances of their doing something very serious in the future. Some of this information will be actuarial in nature, relating to base rate behaviours among a number of similar offenders. In other instances, it will include some of the information noted in the case outlined above, where both academic and practitioner research and experience will be used to inform others. The prediction of risk will therefore be a complex and dynamic process. It should be conducted by experienced practitioners but it should also be acknowledged that some of those with the least amount of experience may have to both form judgements and take decisions at times when others may not be available. It is therefore important to stress that the assessment and prediction of risk and dangerousness is an organizational and collective responsibility, and should not rest on the shoulders of individuals.

The prediction process

If one message should have come out of this chapter so far, it is that predicting risk of serious harm is a difficult job. There is not a simple solution, a formula, or template that can be applied to all cases. There are, however, good practice principles that should be followed, as closely as possible in every case. The essential point is that as much information as possible be gathered, that opinions be canvassed, and knowledge and information be updated. For too long the whole dangerousness debate has been argued upon the relative merits of actuarial and clinical methodologies whilst it has been abundantly clear that neither on its own is satisfactory—even in combination they are not foolproof! Both 'sides' have their proponents, although increasingly the combination argument is the one that wins out. Nevertheless, fundamentally opposing views are taken by each protagonist and it is unsurprising that practitioners and the public are unclear. For example, Janus and Prentky (2003:36) quote a statement from the Minnesota Supreme Court that might be unusual when policy and practice in the USA is considered in general. The judgment was as follows, 'Not only are the statistics concerning the violent behaviour of others irrelevant, but it seems to me wrong to confine any person on the basis not of that person's own prior conduct but on the basis of statistical evidence concerning the behaviour of other people.' Others of course take diametrically opposing positions to this against the alleged weakness, bias, and unreliability of clinical judgement. The same authors say that, 'In the clinical method the decision-maker combines and processes information in his or her head. In the actuarial or statistical method the human judge is eliminated and conclusions rest solely on empirically established relations between data and condition or event of interest' (Janus and Prentky, 2003:11–12). Therefore, in such a contradictory world, what information will best serve decision-makers and practitioners on a daily basis?

Before attempting an answer to this question, it may be useful to explore the context of risk assessment a little further. It is patently obvious that errors in assessment can have terrible consequences and it is equally obvious that in such instances, people will be blamed. Gray, Lang, and Noaks (2003:149) express the situation well, '... the risks of failure faced by professionals charged with responsibility for the management of risk—one of the "risks of risk" as it were—have themselves become grave; in terms of blame, public humiliation and job insecurity.' They go on to say how public responses to sex offenders, at street level, have fundamentally altered the public perception of those practitioners involved. They refer to '. . . the widely perceived shortcomings of a range of public sector workers, seen in some circles as hate figures; probation officers, social workers, physicians and so on' (2003:163). Underlying this situation is the belief that risk *can* be accurately predicted and therefore, when it goes wrong, someone has clearly failed and not done their job properly. This is not the case however. For example, Buchanan (1999:465) refers to Dr Boyd, a former Medical Director of a Canadian maximum security hospital, when he said that only 10% of his detained patients would kill again, but he did not know which 10%. This figure is below that of 'evens', which has often been cited as a reasonable baseline, but even this figure suggests one in two cases will be wrongly predicted. Glancy (2005:13) suggests that progress has been made since Monahan forecast prediction accuracy at 33% in 1981. Yet, if base rates are not much better than evens, what can be done to improve the process? Risk assessment, something that has 'largely replaced the notion of dangerousness' (Gray, Lang, and Noaks, 2003:149), implies a scientific rationality that is probably absent in reality. Risk assessment remains a very difficult task, given the low base rates for serious violent and sexual offending.

The problem for practitioners is that the research and available evidence continues to paint an uncertain picture. For example, for some while it has been something of a truism that predictions are more effective in the short, rather than medium or long term. Yet, doubts have been cast upon this assertion. The Royal College of Psychiatrists concluded in 1998 that, following a systematic review of risk factors, '. . . there was no clear consensus on items that would be clinically useful for short term predictions'. Hanson (2000:106) points out that a range of exceptional policy measures have been directed towards sex offenders and these have been predicated on an assumption practitioners have '. . . the ability to accurately distinguish between those individuals who are at risk of committing another sexual offence, and those who are not'. O'Rourke (1999:11) is perhaps even more emphatic in questioning the efficacy of prediction, 'I believe it is impossible to predict human behaviour or reduce it to a set of numbers.' Before moving on to consider some of the variables that research has indicated may be a useful aid for practitioners, one final example might emphasize the actuarial/clinical conundrum. Buchanan (1999:469) raised an example of predicting crashes for aircraft and related this to predicting human behaviour. His example neatly summarizes the issue around actuarial and clinical prediction. He said:

> If one wishes to know the probability of an aircraft crashing during a flight, one can review the statistics for aircraft of that type on that route. Alternatively, one can inspect the aircraft. The inspection may bring to light a fault of a type that causes aircraft to crash, which in turn, leads the inspector to rate the chances of a crash much higher than the statistics would allow.

In other words, baseline data receives added value from additional information, in this instance gleaned by inspection, in others from interviews. Buchanan concludes that, because people often do what they intend, if practitioners can determine intentions, they may be able to predict that which has not occurred before—something a table of numbers will not do. Stepping outside of predicting serious harm for a moment, comparisons can be made with the study of meteorology. For some while it has been accepted that predicting serious harm is easier in the short term, rather like weather forecasts. A mass of static data can be obtained, but it does not make the job of long term forecasters very much easier. The following quote taken from The Guardian (20 September 2005) illustrates the point, 'The data, as climate scientists point out, can be as precise as you like; it is the predictions based on those data that tend to be a bit more difficult. This is because the world's climate is a dynamic system, changing before your eyes.' If human behaviour is substituted for climate, the message is probably the same. In this particular climate prediction, the suggestion was that there was a two-thirds chance that the winter of 2005–6 would be colder than the average of the previous 50 years—in the world of potential dangerousness these odds appear to be rather good! Those involved in the assessment and prediction of future serious harm therefore need more than baseline data and will probably benefit from increasing their knowledge of a range of indicators that research has indicated may increase risks. A range of these ideas will now be explored.

Dynamic and static factors

Hanson (2000:107) reported the results of 61 studies, examining 69 potential predictors of sexual offence recidivism and 38 predictors of non-sexual recidivism, involving nearly 29,000 offenders. The factors related most significantly to sex offender recidivism were those related to sexual deviancy. These included deviant sexual preferences, early onset of sexual offending, a history of prior sexual offences, choosing strangers as victims, male victims, and committing diverse sexual offences. These baseline factors are 'enhanced' in terms of prediction by sexual interest in children, assessed phallometrically, alongside an antisocial personality and the total number of prior offences. Hanson and Thornton (2000, in Hanson 2000:107), argue that moderate accuracy in predicting sexual offence recidivism can be achieved by using a relatively simple list of variables. This combination of demographic and offence history variables included the offender never being married, having any stranger victims, any male victims, any unrelated victims, their age being under 25, non-contact sex offences, total number of prior sex offences, any violent offences and total number of prior offences.

However, no matter how long the list of significant factors becomes, they still have to be applied to an individual, and, as we have seen with climate prediction, this is a constantly changing dynamic. What the information will do is to assist practitioners to build a more complete picture of the offender, which will help them in the exercise of their professional judgement. Horlick-Jones (2003:158) suggests that this judgement, gained through knowledge and experience, remains important to effective prediction. He suggests that risk practitioners need to employ skill and judgement to operate effectively. He describes these as craft skills that require experience and an ability to improvise and adapt, skills learned through practice. The unspoken suggestion here, of course, is that those practitioners may not always be right—prediction is not an exact science.

The wider social climate though may still tend to invest a degree of certainty into predictions, even where they do not exist. For example, Krauss and Ho Lee (2003:115) cite research indicating that mock jurors in death and dangerousness trials are unduly influenced by expert testimony, often being swayed by the expert's presence rather than what they actually say. They say mock jurors can appear overwhelmed by complex actuarial data and prefer the human expert. Yet this expectation is not borne out by those charged with predicting harm and dangerousness. Feeney (2003) makes the point clearly, 'There is an unrealistic expectation that psychiatrists are able to predict violent and sexual crime in those they assess and that they are therefore able to protect society.'

This scenario creates something of a dilemma for those assessing and predicting risk of harm. Although clinical judgement is probably only a little more effective than an educated guess, there are many in society prepared to invest almost mystic powers in these professionals. It is therefore understandable that clinicians may begin to favour actuarial methods because failure can then be blamed on the method, rather than their clinical expertise. In 2003, a psychiatrist in America was found to be liable for failing to prevent a patient's violent crime. This individual had been treating a man with a history of psychiatric trouble, substance abuse, and obsession with hurting or killing people with a vehicle. The professional responsibility of the psychiatrist was to inform the department of motor vehicles—but he did not. The outcome was that two people were run over and one killed. The doctor became liable to $8.6m in compensation. Perhaps if the doctor had followed the advice above that people often do what they threaten to do, he would have carried out his legal responsibilities. The more unusual the behaviour, the more difficult it can be to predict. As Buchanan (1999:471) notes of actuarial and clinical methods, 'both approaches face the problem that rare events will always be more difficult to predict than everyday ones, because as the base rate of the behaviour being predicted falls, so the ratio of mistakes to correct predictions increases'. In this climate of legal liability and public vilification, what can the risk professionals do?

In many respects those charged with the onerous responsibility of protecting the public need to ensure that they have 'done all they can'. It is unreasonable to expect more. Clearly our American psychiatrist did not do everything he could because he chose not to warn the motoring authorities. This may, of course, have been a result of his professional judgement and perhaps emphasizes the need for second opinions or multi-agency discussions. This process has been dubbed 'defensible practice' by the official Home Office guidance (2004).

Horlick-Jones (2003) suggests that risk, '... seems to provide a shared language and a structured framework for negotiation, so facilitating a mutual audit-ability of actions'. Doing all you can is likely therefore to involve exercising clinical/professional adjustment and utilizing actuarial and other research data wherever possible. This is not, however, a quick process and there are no real short cuts. As the 'problem of dangerousness' increases, time will be at a premium and the temptation will be to resort towards formulaic responses, which in turn run the risk of under- or overestimating the scale of the prob-lem. Yet professionals operate in a climate of high public expectation and to a certain extent imply that they can 'manage', if not solve, the problem. Lieb (2003:212) eloquently describes this as 'joined-up worrying' and claims that 'MAPPS set very ambitious goals for their work, often with a vague descrip-tion of actions that will be used to accomplish these expansive responsibilit-ies. The list of dangerous people is ever expanding, with resources likely to be stable at best.' An additional problem is that the more research that is under-taken with dangerous, high risk offenders, the greater the number of 'indicat-ors' that are revealed. Indeed, the range of factors is such that undoubtedly a number of people reading this book may be aware of one or more of these in their own life, and if not, others may see those qualities in them. The import-ant point is that none of the factors in isolation is enough, and maybe not even more than one. All information has to be considered and applied to the offender in situ—in other words risk assessment is dynamic and needs to be ongoing.

Building the bigger picture

This next section will continue to identify a variety of predictors that have emerged from a range of studies. It is unlikely that busy professionals will have the time to follow up original sources but what might emerge are a number of key areas that can act as pointers and warning signs in respect of offenders they are involved with. They may then be in a position to chase up further research relating to specific risk triggers. Much of this information will not easily surface in baseline data but as a result of investigative interviewing and hearing what people say. Herschel Prins (1998) offers seven areas of questioning:

- Have past precipitants and stresses in the offender's background been removed? Has the worker the courage to deal with them and avoid 'not want-ing to know' certain information. He cites a phrase, 'I wish I didn't know now what I didn't know then.'
- What is the offender's current capacity for dealing with provocation? Has dis-placement, especially in attacks on women, been identified? There is a need for detailed accounts of previously provoking incidents.

- How does the person view himself? Are there unresolved conflicts with women; is there a history of revenge, serious sexual assault, or violence and degradation?
- Is there any change in the person's capacity to feel empathy?
- Take it seriously if people talk about killing with hatred in their voice. Do they take pleasure in talking about violence, pornography, torture, or the occult?
- How much attention has been paid to the offender's behaviour at the time of the offence? Did they blot it out, call for help, or eat a meal?
- Have they come to terms with what they did?

This approach requires painstaking collection of evidence (which will again demand time and space) and, importantly, understanding what to do with that evidence. Prins (1998) cites Freud when he said, 'I learned to follow the unforgotten advice of my master Charcot; to look at the same things again and again until they themselves began to speak.' This is often referred to as the forensic examination of evidence and, although this expression may not have sat easily with traditional probation practice for example, it is certainly an increasing aspect of their modern role.

Psychopathy and dangerousness

Of course, in creating pictures, just as in painting with numbers, it can be all too easy to make more than the sum of the parts. For example, Prins (1998:1360) reminds us that considerations of dangerousness are all too often 'contaminated' by considerations of political expediency, and that feelings of worry on the part of the professional can be transcribed into the language of risk. The busy professional is operating in a political and social context. They need short cuts because they do not have the time for full and thorough assessments on the massively increasing number of potentially dangerous cases. Yet, they also need to be thorough enough to be in the position of making defensible decisions that are compatible with human rights, balanced as ever with the need to protect the public. Such short cuts may link mental health conditions with dangerous behaviour, a link all too often drawn by the public that all people suffering from mental ill health are dangerous. Despite the limitations of this assumption, there are certain research indications that conditions such as psychopathy may be linked with increased risks of serious harm. A glance at the features of psychopathy as detailed in Cleckley's 1941 list (in Feeney, 2003) reveals how general they are and how easy it would be to read them into the lives of many offenders under supervision and before the courts.

Interpersonal

- Superficially charming
- Grandiose

- Egocentric
- Manipulative

Affective

- Shallow, labile, and emotive
- Lack of empathy
- Lack of guilt
- Little subjective distress

Behavioural

- Impulsive
- Irresponsible
- Prone to boredom
- Lack of long term goals
- Prone to breaking rules

These will be personality characteristics familiar to many criminal justice professionals, and indeed, to those outside of the system. The issue then is not to count a number of these traits and produce a prediction, but to consider any evidence of them against all other information and the context in which the potential offender may be operating. That, of course, takes us into the territory of risk management, in other words predicting the level of risk in a given context and seeking means of lowering that risk by manipulating the environment. Such manipulation may involve long periods of incarceration. Feeney (2003) summarizes this position well when he says,

> Dangerousness best describes the action rather than the individual, and is transient and dependent on circumstance. As a concept, it has been superseded by assessment of risk. Psychiatrists are unable to control many of the factors that influence dangerousness. Furthermore, there is little evidence that treatment of a personality disorder, if possible, would reduce the level of dangerousness.

Gunn (1996:120) supports this notion, saying that psychiatry should forget about prediction and concentrate upon management. This is of course a rational position to adopt but there is still a need to create a baseline—the management has to be of someone who has exhibited certain behaviour that has led to the initial concerns. Although dangerousness may be an increasingly unfashionable term, it does continue to convey the concerns that professionals have about certain people. Focusing too much on the management of certain categories of offenders may lead us to overlook the individual. Heilbrun (1990:141) argues that 'dangerousness is arguably the most important individual difference variable within the domain of personality research, as far as the understanding and amelioration of societal problems are concerned'. He again affirmed the link between psychopathy, low intelligence, and future violence. He argues that those who combine high anti-sociability with low intelligence are those most likely to commit the most dangerous crimes involving violence.

Yet, as mentioned earlier, it is important to stress that not all people demonstrating a 'critical number' of psychopathic traits will commit very serious violent crime. Mitchell and Blair (2000, in Kirkman, 2002:158) suggest that we need to try and disentangle the emotional difficulties that are the risk factors for the development of anti-social behaviour. They suggest that, 'by researching those who have the characteristics of the psychopath but whose behaviour does not reach the level for prosecution, we could eventually disentangle those attributes which are specific to psychopathy, and those which are related to criminality.' Nonetheless, whilst work may be ongoing to separate emotional difficulties and criminal behaviour, a mounting body of work continues to establish the links between psychopathy and violence. Such associations are not surprising when generalized descriptions of psychopaths are considered. The following example illustrates the point:

> . . . psychopathic offenders demonstrably are more egocentric, callous, manipulative, impulsive and irresponsible and less capable of experiencing empathy, guilt and remorse than other offenders. (They) lack a normal sense of ethics and morality, live by their own rules, and are prone to use cold-blooded, instrumental intimidation and violence to satisfy their wants and needs, and generally are contemptuous of social norms and the rights of others. (Gretton et al, 2001:428)

Members of the public reading such descriptions would undoubtedly be very fearful of meeting anyone matching these criteria. Such fear may also be felt by criminal justice professionals, especially perhaps those without a mental health training, and may, as noted earlier, convert their own fears into risk. Research linking psychopathy with serious sexual offence recidivism has been discussed in Chapter 4.

There does appear therefore to be evidence linking psychopathy with violent offending, although there remains a clear need to separate out the behaviours of criminal and non-criminal psychopaths to avoid over-labelling. The Psychopathy Check List—Revised (PCL–R) does, however, indicate that the condition does play a major part in sexual offending, evident in 10–15% of child sexual offenders and in 40–50% of rapists (Gretton et al, 2001:429). Gretton et al (2001) cite Harris and Hanson (1998) who suggest that offenders with a high PCL–R and behavioural file evidence of sexual deviance had committed more pre-index sexual offences, more kidnapping, forcible confinements, more non-sexual offences, and were more likely to violently recidivate (2001:430). However, a range of other, and perhaps more common factors might also help predict future serious sexual offending provided of course that the same precautions are taken against over-generalizations.

Attempting to predict serious sexual harm— a popular method

As noted in Chapter 2, fears of predatory sexual offenders have fanned the fires of the risk agenda and been prominent in its escalation. Assessing the risk posed by such people is therefore not only a difficult task in itself, but one more likely than others to be subject to intense public scrutiny. As a result a public perception has grown that all sex offenders pose a risk of serious harm and, as a result, an ever-increasing range and number of offenders are drawn into the public protection circle. For example, there are 87 specified sexual offences listed in the Criminal Justice Act 2003. Working in this context quite obviously increases the chances of over-assessing risk, 'to be on the safe side', an understandable position to adopt if working in this arena. Thus it is likely that professionals will seek to use a range of information and checklists to establish risk of serious harm and justify their decision as defensible. There is certainly a mounting body of evidence that confirms the commonality of a range of factors that frequently appear in the lives of serious sex offenders. However, caution must be taken not to brand people as potentially serious sex offenders simply because of what might have occurred in their own lives. Rather as with psychopathic behaviour, an attempt needs to be made to disentangle criminal and non-criminal characteristics.

For many people there has been a growing belief that children who have been sexually abused grow up to be abusers themselves, the so-called 'cycle of abuse'. However, even though there may be degrees of truth in this assumption (discussed below), such a position may mask the real issue. That issue is that these children are and have been victims, but it is all too easy to reconstruct them as potential offenders. Being marked as a future criminal is not the same as being helped as a past victim, but a risk-averse society may well prefer the former position, as unpalatable as this may appear. Johnson and Doonan (2005:33) report that by the mid-1980s, being abused as a child was regarded as the major etiological factor for children with sexual behaviour problems. Quoting a small study by Friedrich and Luecke (1998) they note that 75% of sexually aggressive boys and 100% of sexually aggressive girls were themselves abused as children. They also cite Johnson's (1988) study indicating that 50% of abusive children had been victims of abuse but added that virtually all of the boys had also suffered harsh physical punishment. To confuse the picture a little more, Drach et al (2001, in Johnson and Doonan, 2005:34) reported no significant relationship between being a victim of sexual abuse and the presence or absence of sexual problems in children. Suffering harsh physical abuse (47%) and witnessing domestic violence (58%) were more significant than having a history of being abused (35%), according to Silovsky and Nice (2002, in Johnson and Doonan, 2005:34). The link between future sexual disturbance and the witnessing of domestic violence reappears in the literature with some frequency, creating an association in children's minds of sex and aggression. This is further evidence of where the so-called 'private sphere' can influence public events very seriously.

Being a victim of child sexual abuse should not therefore become an absolute predictor of future sexual offending, although it has to be acknowledged that the evidence does suggest an association in a number of instances. However, as with other predictive factors, this information needs to be taken alongside anything else that is known about the child's background and experiences in an attempt to build the bigger picture. Carpentier, Proulx, and Lussier (2005) note that several studies indicate poor social skills, social isolation, poor attachment, and a tendency to experience negative emotional states as risk indicators alongside being abused as a child. Many children reported sexual activity as a prominent strategy to cope with emotional distress. Unpacking the cycle of abuse a little more, they cite a study by Hunter and Figueredo (2000) that suggests a range of additional factors that might be important. These include early victimization, a high rate of abusive incidents, a long period between the first event and its report, a lack of support following disclosure and exposure to domestic violence. All of these factors are positively associated with a propensity to sexually abuse during adolescence. Kaufman and Zigler (1987:192, in Johnson and Doonan, 2005:36) report that the best estimate of intergenerational transmission is 30%, +/− 5%. This suggests to them that approximately one third of all individuals who were physically abused, sexually abused, or extremely neglected, will subject their offspring to one of these forms of maltreatment, whilst two thirds will provide perfectly adequate care. They conclude, '... the time has come for the intergenerational myth to be put aside and for researchers to cease asking; Do abused children become abusive parents and ask instead, under what conditions is the transmission of abuse most likely to occur?'

Wilcox, Richards, and O'Keeffe (2004:338) report that sexual abuse is more damaging for children when it involves a betrayal of trust and the child is not listened to or believed. The scenario that unfolds then is not only the historical one of actually dealing with child sexual abuse, but being aware that the response to it could increase the chances of victims becoming a perpetrator themselves. Children, if resilient, may be able to better survive if they can place the blame with the perpetrator rather than themselves, although this again may be contingent upon the response they receive. There may be considerable concern if, for whatever reason, an abused child's mother has been involved, complicit, covering up, or actually involved in abusing her own children. In such circumstances the child may feel completely alone with no one to tell their story to. In such cases, the ability of the child to recover may be seriously damaged.

Aside from determining which abused child may grow into an adolescent or adult abuser, the other key question for criminal justice practitioners is, once they have offended, will they do it again? Predicting sex offender recidivism is not an easy task, as with any other type of offending. However, in the present climate, such predictions perhaps hold far greater significance due to the growth in indeterminate sentences and lifelong supervision for these offenders. Overall, the observed recidivism rate for sexual offenders is relatively low. Hanson (2000:106) reports a survey of 61 recidivism studies involving 24,000 offenders finding a new sex offence rate of 13.4% within 4–5 years, with 12% committing a non-sexual offence. However, these bald figures do little to indicate future risk of harm. Quite clearly, a situation without any recidivism would be the ideal but failing this impossibility, then a reduction in the more serious types of reoffending would be very desirable. This involves a differentiation between offenders and potential risk. For example, in the same study, Hanson notes rapists reoffending at 22% whilst child molesters do so rather less at 10%. This does not of course answer the age-old question, which 22 or 10% will reoffend?

There is also evidence to suggest that the longer the follow-up period the greater the percentage involved in reoffending and of course, all estimates are likely to be beneath the actual rate. Grubin (1999) adds to the picture from his research, indicating that 60–70% of child molesters target girls only, 20–33% boys only and 10% either sex. Confirming a great deal of other work, he suggests that 80% of offenders assault children known to them. He also finds that in only 25–40% of offenders is there a recurrent and intense sexual attraction to children that might attract the label of paedophilia. As noted on several occasions in this chapter, it is identifying this particular group that is the particular worry for criminal justice professionals. It is these offenders of course who most frequently fall into the predatory offender category.

Making sense of the future

If anything emerges from the foregoing, it is that attempting to predict future behaviour is a process fraught with difficulty. Yet, arriving at firm and accurate predictions is what the public increasingly expect and, in many ways, are led towards this expectation by governments. The language of risk assessment and management largely confirms this belief, shrouding predictions in a pseudo-scientific language that affords credibility to what is extremely uncertain. This explains why using assessment 'tools' has become increasingly popular among practitioners. It is unsurprising that people who are not trained psychiatrists are reluctant to stand by their expert professional judgement, as this is always likely to be regarded as inferior to medical expertise. Indeed, the respect given to the medical profession still means that, largely, their professional standing is sufficient validation for their expert testimony. Police and probation officers, with a quite different professional background and experience, may find this more difficult in this particularly difficult field of practice. Thus, the increasing use of tools not only offers an assurance of scientific respectability, but also an opportunity to deflect blame if the situation goes badly wrong—in other words it was the tool getting it wrong, not me!

However, if we revisit the nature of risk it may be possible to determine that there is certainly not an easy, simple, or single solution to risk assessment. These assessment tools undoubtedly have their place, but so does professional judgement. That judgement should be valued from whatever relevant area of the criminal justice system it comes from—it does not have to be medical. Assessing the risk of future serious harm is a situation where, in most respects, the greater the amount of information, and the more diverse its sources, the better. We have already noted that risk has replaced dangerousness in the everyday language of criminal justice staff. This is understandable because it does hint at the possibilities of systematic calculations being made, and management planned accordingly. Yet, it should not be forgotten that 'dangerous behaviour' is what is being predicted overall, and the elimination of the word could just begin to undermine its significance and lead to over-inclusion of lower levels of risk.

The following definition of risk (Hart, Laws, and Kropp, 2003:209), illustrates a number of points.

> A risk is a hazard that is incompletely understood and whose occurrence can be forecast only with uncertainty. The concept is multi-faceted, referring to the nature of the hazard, the likelihood that the hazard will occur, the frequency or duration of the hazard's consequences, and the imminence of the hazard; also, the concept of risk is inherently contextual, as hazards arise and exist in specific circumstances.

Unpacking this definition leads to many imponderables. It implies that risk is in many ways an amorphous concept, but is widely regarded as something that can be fixed. Prediction is uncertain, and there are serious concerns over the nature, likelihood, and imminence of any potential harm. These are precisely the questions that practitioners need answers to and yet, according to many people, are most unlikely to be met with standardized risk assessment tools. The final part of the quote is significant, specifying as it does the specificity and contextual nature of risk—it is, in other words, a very dynamic and unique concept. The words of Her Majesty's Inspector of Probation report (HMIP, 1997) are both worth recalling for their importance but also to compare them with the present probation position which has seen the increasing roll out of standardized risk assessment methods. The report noted:

> Potentially Dangerous Offenders do not necessarily have anything in common except the likelihood that they may seriously harm someone else. A key to effective supervision is therefore to approach each case individually and tailor supervision to its particular needs bearing in mind the overall objective of public protection. (in Robinson, 2002:9)

The message concerning the individuality of the potentially dangerous and the uniqueness of their behaviour is one that must remain at the top of the agenda.

Assessment tools—a brief review

Hart, Laws, and Kropp (2003) consider the relative merits of actuarial risk assessment tool and types of clinical judgement. They describe three types of professional judgement; unstructured, anamnestic, and structured. The first is said to be person centred, using unaided clinical judgement studying the unique aspects of the case in hand. It is likely to reflect a long psychiatric tradition but has many detractors, as noted below. Anamnestic risk assessment uses concepts derived from medicine and relies upon a limited degree of structure, or prompts, to identify personal and situational factors. These are then used to identify links in the chain, but do assume repetition. Finally, structured professional judgement follows guidelines aimed at improving consistency and transparency (an argument for actuarial methods), but may limit intuition and lack objectivity (Hart et al, 2003:210–12).

Many people argue for the greater reliability and more objective nature of actuarial risk assessment. Here tools are devised on a mechanical or algorithmic model, utilizing tests and structured samples of behaviour. Weaknesses have been identified in test selection, the great range of tools in existence, and the tendency to rely upon one test only. Hart et al argue that the adjusted actuarial risk assessment may be better in that it starts with the basic prediction and is later adjusted in the light of additional infractions—a dynamic instrument in other words. Where does this leave the increasing army of criminal justice staff charged with risk assessment? Evidence such as that reported by Hanson and Bussière (1998, in Hart et al, 2003:217) suggest that meta-analysis reveals unstructured professional judgement to perform little better than chance, although structured judgement performed better. They noted that the penile plethysmograph was the best single predictor of sexual violence recidivism (for a fuller discussion of this somewhat contentious claim see Laws, 2003). Numerous mechanisms have been developed, including the Rapid Risk Assessment for Sex Offence Recidivism (RRASOR), Static-99, Structured Anchored Clinical Judgement (SACJ-Min), the Violence Offences Risk Appraisal Guide (VRAG), and a similar one for sex offences (SORAG) (see discussion of scoring methods in Craig, Browne, and Stringer, 2004). The VRAG is worth examining to identify the range of factors that appear elsewhere in other assessment tools. VRAG is based upon 12 variables as follows; separation from parents before the age of 16, elementary school maladjustment, history of alcohol abuse, never married, history of non-violent offences, failure on prior conditional release, age at index offence, victim injury in instant offence, male victims in index offence, diagnosis of any personality disorder, schizophrenia, and Hare's PCL–R score.

In many respects some of these assessment tools represent a means of trying to broaden the ability of a wider range of criminal justice professionals to undertake assessment. At the same time, recognizing their non-clinical or psychological training, the tools are often abbreviated to allow for easy use by a range of busy staff. Hence Thornton's structured anchored clinical judgement is followed by 'min', suggesting an abbreviated version of the tool. He revised his assessment tool to include stages and data sets, with the earlier or lower levels still offering predictive ability. In stage 1, documented convictions were coded in five areas and these were; any current sex offence, any prior sex offence, any current non-sexual violent offence, any prior non-sexual violent offence, and four or more prior (distinct) sentencing occasions. If four or five of these factors are present the offender is automatically deemed high risk, two to three factors indicate medium risk and zero to one low risk. In the second stage this data is built upon by using sets of variable factors regarded as potentially aggravating. These include, any stranger victim, any male victims, never married, and convictions for non-sexual offences. Thus a number of largely static factors, with the addition of a few dynamic items, will determine initial risk levels. This will be helpful for criminal justice professionals but will need updating with as much qualitative, dynamic information as possible.

The chances of many of those people caught up in the criminal justice system having one or several of these factors in their lives must be high. It suggests that many have the potential for violence but in essence we know that. What we all really need to get better at is understanding when and how seriously it will happen.

Many readers will be familiar with one or more of these tools and, in many American states, different and unique tools have been developed. Hart et al (2003:220) believe that the naturally brief checklists, relying on static and background information, do not prove to be reliable predictors of risk and bemoan the lack of good, supportive manuals. They quote a survey by Grove et al (2000) comprising a comprehensive quality review of decision-making and concluded as follows:

- in 40% of direct comparisons, actuarial methods were superior;
- in 40% of direct comparisons, both methods were equal, and;
- in 20% of comparisons, clinical methods were said to be superior.

On first reading, this survey appears to point towards the supremacy of actuarial methods. However, a different reading might be taken which implies that clinical methods are equal or superior to actuarial methods in 60% of cases. Their conclusion is as follows, 'At present then, the superiority of actuarial decisions making is an article of faith rather than fact … it is entirely reasonable to conclude that the weight of scientific evidence is sufficient to reject altogether the use of or reliance on actuarial predictors.' This is a strong claim and may go a little too far in its assertion. However, it should perhaps spark a little caution as what appears to be a rush towards actuarial methods gathers momentum.

Risk of dangerous behaviour— is there a way forward?

It is clear from the foregoing that both clinical and actuarial methods of assessment and prediction have their supporters and detractors. The nature of public blame and shame has perhaps increased the momentum in favour of the more scientific approach, as have the claims for greater accuracy. Yet the lingering doubts remain about the effectiveness of applying methods based upon aggregated data to behaviour with a low baseline rate of occurrence. This chapter will conclude by summarizing the actuarial versus clinical contest.

Janus and Prentky (2003:7) suggest that, 'risk has greater utility and more flexibility than dangerousness'. They believe that it is dimensional and continuous, rather than dichotomous. This is a response to an enduring dangerousness problem in that the offender either is, or is not, dangerous. Clearly in this situation, the reluctance of professionals to make this hugely important either/or judgement is understandable. The consequences of getting it wrong are extremely serious and it is therefore likely that caution will dominate. Risk assessment therefore enables a continuum to be established, which perhaps enables finer assessments such as medium, high, and very high risk to be established. Such a fine division of risk does, of course, serve a very useful role in the deployment of resources, the greater the risk the more the resources. It implies that risk (of serious and dangerous behaviour) can be finely judged and can be manipulated as more information becomes available or the offender's situation changes. Here of course the human element returns, because that new information has to be observed, recorded, and acted upon. It therefore has to be recognized as important and therefore requires the professional to recognize that importance. Janus and Prentky (2003:9) say that 'actuarial risk assessment involves facts in the real world', yet these facts do not stand in an isolated risk guide, they still need to be gathered, used, and interpreted. Those involved in risk assessment still need to keep their professional assessment skills finely tuned—the risk lies in leaving judgement to assessment tools and forgetting the human input. Reliance upon actuarial assessment methods may lessen the experience of practitioners, they could deskill. In denying human judgement they deny human intuition. If for no other reason than their own personal safety, that judgement and intuitive feeling must be preserved if risk to staff is not to become a more serious problem.

Is there a way forward for prediction? Is it better to focus upon risk because it is something that can, according to its own methodology, be quantified? Is dangerousness a concept to be eliminated from the discourse because it has a sense of dichotomy attached to it, rather than the graduated scales of risk? These questions are not easy to answer but it is clear that the tide is flowing in favour of the scientific approach. Undoubtedly in an acutely political context defensive decision-making assumes the ascendancy and for busy and pressured professionals this is understandable. However, the bottom line must always remain that actuarial measures are of certain kinds of behaviour and that behaviour is serious and dangerous. The behaviour must not be forgotten and in understanding the chances of it recurring, its situational and personal context must be explored. This must, by definition, involve an appreciation of the offender as a person and in his social setting. It is this knowledge and its application by skilled professionals to actuarial devices that offers the best prospect of protecting the public from serious harm.

6

Legislating Against the Dangerous Offender

Introduction

This chapter is concerned with the sentencing of dangerous offenders and the seemingly unending upward spiral of punitiveness since the early 1990s. The close relationship between the political fortunes of governments either side of the Atlantic and the 'alleged' public voice of their voters ensured that already tough legislation would undergo frequent makeovers. The interludes between these upward shifts did not appear to be marked by a significant worsening of the dangerousness problem, although the media ensured that certain cases assumed a critical mass in fuelling public fear. In the UK in particular, this period has been marked by the interplay between the legislature and the judiciary, the one striving for supremacy, the other fighting for its independence. The outcome would be that legislation aimed at potentially dangerous offenders would increasingly drive and influence policy and practice for all criminal justice activity. This chapter will therefore focus on protective sentencing, whilst the measures aimed at managing and containing potential dangerousness in the community will be considered in the next chapter.

Offence or offender?—The crux of the dangerousness debate

Since the early 1990s in the UK, and a little earlier in North America, a significant trend in legislation has been a continued and determined focus on potential dangerousness. The provisions themselves have more often than not been triggered by certain categories of offence, before the individual offender's actual dangerousness has been considered. In other words, certain broad categories of crime have been targeted rather than the actual seriousness of the behaviour constituting the offence, making whole classes of offenders social pariahs (these might be viewed as general rather than individual dispositions). The reactions in the UK to the media publication of sex offender's details (see next chapter) demonstrates that certain members of the public have no intention of differentiating between offenders within the same offence category, or even within generic groups such as 'sex offenders'. They appear to be happy to accept universal labels, especially if they come emotionally packaged as monsters and predators (however, for an alternative view see Williams and Thompson (2004a and b) and discussion in Chapter 7). The populist nature of legislation since the Criminal Justice Act 1991 (CJA 1991) suggests that there is little likelihood of a more rational approach to law-making and sentencing. Whilst a sensation-hungry media fuels public fear, perceptions of danger will remain distorted and exaggerated. British governments meanwhile, of whatever political hue, would appear only too ready to listen to the public voice and develop ever-more draconian legislation. In so doing they appear more than prepared to take on those who stand in their way, such as the judiciary, by tackling professional discretion and moving towards more rigid sentencing frameworks. This chapter will explore legislative developments starting with the CJA 1991 and consider the trends that have increasingly seen certain offenders suffer a progressive loss of rights and freedoms, based more on what they might do in the future, as much as what they have actually done in the past.

The Criminal Justice Act 1991

The 1991 Act had, in many ways, treated the subject of dangerousness in a realistic manner. The Act was built upon the principle of proportionality; meaning that offence seriousness would in most cases, determine sentence severity. It could be argued that the intention behind this principle was liberal in its ambition, being to reduce the prison population by encouraging sentencers to focus on the instant offence, rather than increase the sentence based upon the offender's previous criminal history. In essence the Act sought to prevent an increase in sentence length for those with previous convictions although, in one notable exception, this was permitted. Section 28 of the Act allowed for previous convictions to be considered in current sentencing if the *circumstances* of those offences revealed a pattern of offending which aggravated the seriousness of the present behaviour. An example of the relevance of previous convictions might be a pattern of domestic burglaries (revealing a 'professional' approach), or offending based on a specific set of attitudes (such as racially motivated offending). Conversely a series of disconnected previous convictions were to be discounted in the CJA 1991 sentencing arrangements. Undoubtedly this focus on relevance could prove problematic in some cases. For example, in a domestic burglary, a guilty plea might negate a full investigation into motive—the offender possibly keen to avoid such an investigation. That motive could have been sexual but a quick guilty plea to an 'ordinary' theft would avoid any wider discussion and perhaps lessen the eventual sentence. Even in 1991, the need for full and detailed information on instant and previous offences was becoming important—in assessing potential dangerousness, it is paramount.

A threat of harm

The provision on previous convictions therefore represented a departure from the proportionality principle, and there was another relating to potential danger to the public. Section 1(2)(b) of the Act permitted the imposition of a custodial sentence where 'only such a sentence would be adequate to protect the public from serious harm' from the offender, even if the instant offence did not merit custody. Section 2(2)(b) further empowered the court to depart from proportionality when it was convinced that the offender represented a threat of serious harm to the public. In these cases a longer than desert sentence might be passed up to the maximum for the crime, again, even if the instant offence did not merit this. Courts were therefore in a position to pass longer than deserved sentences for those considered potentially dangerous—meaning that an assessment of dangerousness had to be undertaken. It is also clear that if the court did exercise this discretion, that the sentence was composed of two elements, one dealing with the instant offence and the other looking ahead to *potential* offences. Somewhat in contrast to legislation passed later in the decade, the 1991 Act thus focused on the *actuality* of offending behaviour within particular offence categories, notably sexual and violent crimes, and also the *potential* dangerousness of individuals, when determining the additional detention period for certain offenders. The definition of serious harm was contained in s. 31(3) and would be recognized by many professionals working within public protection, it said, 'protecting the public from death or serious personal injury, whether physical or psychological, occasioned by further such offences committed by the defendant'.

Thus, although these provisions might be criticized as running contrary to the more liberal proportionality ethos of the 1991 Act, they did perhaps adopt a slightly more realistic approach to potentially dangerous behaviour, and at least more realistic than that contained in the Crime (Sentences) Act 1997. That said, the successful application of these provisions were predicated upon an accurate assessment of future behaviour and, as we have already noted in Chapter 5, this is not an easy process. Such provisions also run contrary to a belief that punishment should reflect the seriousness of what has been done, rather than what might be done in the future. Here we see the opposite argument deployed for that supporting the 1991 Act's focus on the instant rather than previous offences. This argument suggested that offenders should not be punished again, in the form of an increased penalty, for crimes that have already been punished. In terms of the dangerousness provisions, the argument was that offenders could be additionally punished for what they might do in the future. As von Hirsch and Ashworth (1996:176) note: 'Since punishment involves censure, its amount should fairly reflect how wrong the conduct is—that is, how serious it is. Proportionate sentences are designed to reflect the conduct's blameworthiness, whereas sentences based on prediction have no such foundation.' Of course, the secondary problem inherent in predictive or preventive sentencing is the risk that the prediction is of simply reoffending, rather than a repetition of very serious harm. This might be regarded as a quantity rather than a quality issue.

The 1991 Act therefore presented a series of paradoxes but did lay the foundation for the way in which dangerousness legislation has been framed since. The unstated intention of the Act was probably to reduce the size of the prison population and thereby the economic costs of the Conservative government's law and order policy. Yet, a Conservative government openly declaring an intention to cut prisoner numbers would have been an anathema to the conservative party faithful. Therefore the more liberal provisions were somewhat masked by those targeted at offenders least likely to evoke any public sympathy, namely sexual and violent offenders. This enabled the government to claim that it was still being tough on crime by targeting those offenders that engendered the greatest public fear and anxiety. The measures against these offenders, it could be argued, represented a determined attempt by the government to influence sentencing in a particular (and notably populist) direction. However, just as the measures in the Act aimed at reducing sentence severity in some cases fell short of judicial control (instead a weaker form of control known as sentencing bands was introduced), then so also did the measures aimed at dangerousness fall short of directing judges to a specific action. This is in contrast to measures that would emerge within a few short years.

The government and judiciary at loggerheads

The voluntary nature of these sentencing provisions meant that courts failed to meet government expectations. A clear reluctance to use them emerged on the part of the judiciary who, it appeared, believed that existing sentencing powers were adequate in the vast majority of cases and resisted attempts to make them do the government's bidding. Two recent studies illustrate the lack of enthusiasm on the part of the judiciary for protective sentencing provisions, the second example showing that outside of the UK there was similar resistance, even when the directions upon them were stricter than in the 1991 Act. In England, Henman (2003) examined 561 cases in a six-month research study of certain qualifying offences, and found only 5 (0.9%) longer than commensurate sentences and 4 (0.7%) automatic life sentences (see below). In Victoria (Australia) Richardson and Freiburg (2004) conducted a similar study over a much longer time span but with a similar number of qualifying cases (553), and found only 11 (1.99%) passed as longer than commensurate for the instant offence—this despite a greater number of restraints placed upon sentencers. This reluctance to follow the government's lead has been described by Freiburg (2000, in Richardson and Freiburg, 2004:88) as 'techniques of resistance' and this was to be a notable feature of an ongoing struggle between the judiciary and populist governments throughout the 1990s and into the twenty first century.

It could be argued that the CJA 1991 brought to prominence the debate about the importance of the offender to sentencing decisions. Their personal, social, and economic circumstances, when considered alongside the circumstances of the actual crime, had long featured in sentencing decisions and lay at the heart of judgments made by sentencers in individual cases. The Act, in reaffirming proportionality as a guiding principle, appeared to have reduced opportunities to consider these unique circumstances, although there remained scope to do so in assessing offence seriousness. Courts were entitled to consider a range of circumstantial factors (aggravating and mitigating) in deciding upon the seriousness of a particular offence, and this in effect still enabled a differential sentence for the same crime. However, as we have noted, the most significant departure from proportionality lay in the measures concerning potential dangerousness. Here, it was very much going to be the unique characteristics of an offender that would trigger the additional punishment at the disposal of the court. Not only was it to be the focus on particular offences that would activate these measures, but also something about the person committing these acts. In many ways this accords with the views of Floud and Young (1981:27) who indicated that any assessment of dangerousness had to be specific to the individual rather than generalized from wider offender (or indeed offence) populations.

As reasonable as this might appear to some, political thinking was evidently already moving towards a more strident policy. Home Officer Minister John Patten had already hinted at future events when he said: 'The protection of the public is so important that it would not be right to let the court's ability to afford the public this protection to hang on whether the offender had previous convictions' (in Henman, 2003:52). Ten years later, Lord Chief Justice Woolf proposed a form of civil detention of dangerous people even if they have not committed a crime (The Guardian, 26 December 2001)—although he backtracked on these ideas within a few days following a hostile reaction from reform and civil liberties groups. Plans to deal with dangerous severe personality disordered offenders would however see legislation that would allow the detention—potentially for life—without the prerequisite of a criminal record.

This scope to depart from proportionality at what would have been the lower ends of offence seriousness was not enthusiastically embraced by judges according to the research of Henman (2003) and Richardson and Freiburg (2004) noted above. At the upper levels of offence seriousness the discretionary life sentence remained a viable option for offenders considered by the court to be likely to offend again or too unstable or dangerous for a fixed term sentence. In other words, it appears as if in many ways judges were content with the disposals they had to hand and resented interference in their professional discretion. The CJA 1991 would, however, only prove to be the beginnings of an ongoing battle between the government and the judiciary.

It is difficult to decide who came out of this initial skirmish in a better position. It would clearly emerge over time that judges were not keen on passing protective sentences and resented interference with their professional discretion. A similar response can be seen in their views of the use of previous convictions introduced in the 1991 Act. Here was a determined attempt in the legislation to remove previous convictions as an aggravating feature of sentencing and thus in their minds prevent the appropriate (ie longer) sentencing of repeat offenders. Sentencers were therefore happy to pass longer or shorter sentences than the government wished, provided they could do so unfettered by restrictions within the legislation. The Criminal Justice Act 1993 amended the provisions in respect of the use of previous convictions so at least a mild victory for the judiciary could be recorded, although Brownlee (1998:26) suggested the government's position in the polls on law and order issues was a bigger factor in this particular u-turn than appeasing the judiciary. Aside from interpretations of what should be a guiding principle for sentencing (proportionality, for example), the provisions enabling protective sentences struck at the role of the judiciary from two directions, as summarized by Henman (2003:62):

> Conceptually, longer than commensurate sentences exemplify judges as proactive, bearing the burden of risk assessment and prediction for dangerousness, while mandatory minimums and indeterminate sentences envisage judges as instruments of social regulation, essentially reactive, since they no longer have discretionary power to determine actual sentence.

Tightening up on judges—mandatory penalties

The scene was therefore set for a battle of wills between government and the judiciary. The battlefield was to be the increasingly populist sentencing plans of Conservative and Labour governments and the weapons would be an increase in mandatory, minimum sentencing arrangements for the government, and professional power and discretion for the judiciary. By the mid-1990s this battle had really begun to take shape as the Conservative government, and Home Secretary Michael Howard in particular, appeared to be increasingly attracted to American style legislation, notably that epitomized by the baseball slogan, 'three strikes and your out'. In America a series of well-publicized murders of children, many by people on release from a custodial sentence, had triggered demands not only for widespread community notification of sex offenders (see Chapter 6), but also greater consistency in sentencing and fewer 'chances' for certain types of offender. Mandatory life sentences were introduced for third time felonies, effectively ensuring that the chances would number no more than two. The insidiousness of the American legislation lay in its potential to depart from its intended target group. In one infamous example, a man was sentenced to life imprisonment for theft of pizza, 'California's law defines the first two strikes as violent and serious felonies. The third strike is any felony. In some California counties more than half of the "third strike" cases have involved such non-violent offences as shoplifting and auto burglary, theft of cigarettes and in one Los Angeles case—theft of a pizza' (Skolnick, 1995:5).

Although the provisions for mandatory minimum penalties (including life) in the Crime (Sentences) Act 1997 appeared to be more prescribed than in America, there remained the potential for similar slippage to occur. This is not surprising when populist understandings of dangerousness conflate this problem to include many more offenders than should be considered a real and imminent danger. Indeed, as early as 1993, in a speech outlining the measures to be contained in the Criminal Justice and Public Order Act 1994 (CJPOA 1994), Michael Howard, in typically populist style, completely conflated the issue of seriousness, recidivism, and dangerousness, when he said, 'thousands of dangerous criminals are prevented from attacking the community while they are inside' (The Times, 15 October 2003). The context of this speech was that 'prison works', but the ease with which the concept of dangerousness was used to support greater use of custody for all offenders was very worrying, but an indicator of how dangerousness provisions would become a driver of virtually all criminal justice policy within a decade.

The proposals from the Conservative government (later to be enacted by the New Labour administration in 1997) went one step further than much of the American legislation by introducing 'two strikes and your out'. For a wide range of violent and sexual offences, the second such incidence would trigger a mandatory life sentence. Qualifying offences included:

- Attempt, conspiracy, or incitement to murder
- Offence under s. 4 of the Offences Against the Person Act 1861 (soliciting murder)
- Manslaughter
- Wounding or causing grievous bodily harm with intent
- Rape or attempted rape
- Intercourse with a girl under 13
- Possession of a firearm with intent to injure, or carrying a firearm with criminal intent
- Robbery, using a firearm or an imitation firearm

As we shall see below, the Criminal Justice Act 2003 would see a total of 153 offences qualify for provisions concerning dangerousness—it is a problem that never appears to diminish and indeed is added to at an alarming rate! Michael Howard's proposals would trigger a fierce public exchange with senior members of the judiciary, a situation he relished. Considered opinion appeared to be out of favour compared with populist, electorate-pleasing policies.

These measures were a direct attack on judicial discretion and represented governmental frustration at what they regarded as the intransigence of the judiciary to make full use of their sentencing powers. However, and perhaps more importantly, they were the culmination of a political battle for supremacy between the major parties over the law and order issue. In the discussions and debates preceding the Crime (Sentences) Act 1997 (CSA 1997), leading politicians such as Michael Howard appeared to make capital out of any opposition, especially if it came from the judiciary. Howard saw himself as representing the wishes of the people against out of touch judges. Reflecting the supposed mood of the public was becoming an increasingly important trigger for criminal legislation. In *Protecting the Public* (Home Office, 1996:48), the government made clear its intention to hammer home its message and draw in public support:

> ... too often in the past, those who have shown a propensity to commit serious or violent sexual offences have served their sentences and been released only to offend again ... Too often, victims have paid the price when the offender has repeated the same offences. The government is determined that the public should receive proper protection from persistent violent and sexual offenders.

The emotive tone of this message is clear but it lacks a clear evidence base, instead implying a significant problem that will only worsen if harsher measures are not taken. Yet, fast-forward to 2002 and the measures in the CSA 1997 had clearly not worked enough for the politicians, as another White Paper expressed similar sentiments to those of 1996, 'The public are sick and tired of a sentencing system that does not make sense. They read about dangerous, violent and other serious offenders who get off lightly, or are not in prison long enough ...' (Home Office, 2002:86).

There are several messages in these passages that hint at future developments for potentially dangerous offenders. Paramount among these would become the release of prisoners at the end of their lawful detention if still considered dangerous, an issue discussed in Chapter 6. But perhaps more worrying is the way in which the activities of a very small group of offenders are spoken about in such general terms, as if they are the crime problem itself, rather than the mass of everyday crime that impacts on the lives of many socially disadvantaged people. Dangerousness is presented in such a glib fashion that there is a suggestion that it is as common as other types of offending—this presentation would do nothing to allay public concerns and would foster support for repressive measures.

The reality of very serious crime

It is difficult to understand the reason for the upward punitive shift if criminal statistics are examined. The unreliability of crime measurement is well known and perhaps particularly for sexual and violent crimes. There are numerous reasons why sexual crimes may not be reported, such as the young (or old) age of victim; shame; embarrassment; fear; and people maybe being unaware of even being a victim. A similar list could be compiled for violent crime. And yet, there is some evidence that over the period 1991–2004/5, violent and sexual offending has increased and at a faster rate than for many other offences. Once again, a cautious approach is necessary as reporting behaviour can change, new offences can alter the landscape as can police targeting of certain criminal behaviours. That said, in the period 1995–2004/5, the total number of recorded offences rose from 5.1m to 5.562m (this representing a drop of 400,000 from the previous year), whilst all sexual offences have increased from 30,274 to 60,946 (an increase of just over 100%), although the overall numbers are so comparatively small that they are not used by the British Crime Survey (Nicholas, Povey, Walker, and Kershaw, 2005).

Interrogating these figures a little more closely does however reveal trends that would cause more concern. Recorded rapes on a female increased from 4,986 to 12,867 (nearly 300% increase)—a figure known to be well below the real extent of this offence. Estimating the true extent of rape is extremely problematic (Home Office, 2005:16), with this report citing Painter (1991) as indicating that one in four women had experienced rape or attempted rape in their lifetime. Painter had indicated the majority of perpetrators to be those known to the victim and, worryingly, 91% of victims told no one at the time. In similar vein, recorded rapes on males increased from the baseline 150 in 1995 to 1,135 in 2004/5 (nearly 600%). More serious offences of violence increased from 15,829 to 45,181 (just under 300%) but as noted above, murder increased from 725 to 859 or approximately 17.5%. One of the largest increases in the serious violence category occurred in threat or conspiracy to murder, an increase from 4,712 to 22,232 or just under 500% (all figures from Nicholas et al, 2005).

Can these figures justify the constant changes to sentencing powers in respect of serious offenders or can they be seen as a sign of that legislation's failure? The total figure for all violent crime, including all sexual offending, stood at 1.109m in 2002/3, just under one fifth of all recorded crime. However, further analysis reveals that of these 1.109m offences, 911,902 come under the less serious (violent) offences category. Serious violence and all sexual offences amount to 95,920, or approximately 1.6% of all recorded crime. The same percentage calculated for 1991 shows all serious violence and all sexual offences as 0.86% of recorded crime. In very crude terms therefore, there has been a doubling in the percentage of serious violence and sexual crime since 1991, but these figures remain a very small percentage of all crime.

The question remains therefore if this prevalence and degree of crime merits the responses unleashed by successive governments since 1991, especially as so many of those responses have been deployed against a particular construction of an offender, the percentage of which would be massively smaller than the 1.6% figure just mentioned. As Tonry (2004:134) notes, 'there is nothing in English crime trends to suggest why violence generally, or dangerous offenders, should be regarded as worsening problems'. He further noted that between 1989 and 1999 there was a near doubling of imprisonment for indictable violent crimes (18% of all to 34%) and sexual crimes (35% to 66%) (Tonry, 2004:125). The evidence does not therefore appear to be present to suggest a considerable increase in the numbers of serious offenders or indeed that the courts were becoming softer. Tonry's view may be shared by many when he says, '... the tabloid version of reality is the one in which the government prefers to operate' (2004:124).

The discussions and debates surrounding the introduction of the Crime (Sentences) Act 1997 epitomized the populist drift in thinking and the growing gap between politicians and the judiciary. In a speech to the House of Lords in January 1997 Lord Ackner dissected Michael Howard's proposals:

> In my respectful submission, the Home Secretary is putting forward proposals in a manner which shows a degree of irresponsibility that I would not expect to go with that office. There is a growing belief that he is exploiting for party political gain the misapprehension of the public that judges are too soft on crime, which I accept is a commonly held view ... as the noble and learned Lord, Lord Nolan, pointed out, the Court of Appeal can increase sentences that are excessively lenient. Indeed the Attorney General has a duty to bring these cases to its attention. But the Court of Appeal spends far more time having to reduce sentences when judges have been too severe ... the vast majority of sentences are not appealed against or questioned at all. All this the Home Secretary must know but, as was recently stated in a national newspaper, he has 'an unerring populist streak' which sadly the Opposition seem to wish to emulate. (Hansard, HL, 27 January 1997, col. 1013)

Legal academics joined in the criticism of Howard's proposals, which had been enthusiastically adopted by the Labour opposition,

> The Crime (Sentences) Act represents a low point in the development of English sentencing legislation. It is difficult to think of any legislation in the field of criminal justice enacted during the present century, which has so little to do with the improvement of the administration of criminal justice. It is equally difficult to think of any legislation which has been greeted with such hostility by those who have the responsibility of superintending its operation. (Thomas, 1998:83)

Opposition such as this has not, however, curbed the excesses of either Conservative or Labour politicians and a clear pattern emerges of sentencing being continuously refined and added to, even though the evidence base for new measures is at best insubstantial.

Putting a kick into sentences

Governments during the 1990s were determined to not only restrict sentencers' discretion, but also to develop greater controls on sex offenders at the end of their sentence. In essence this meant that offenders would be supervised to the end of their full sentence, or indeed beyond it. Adding punch to the supervision period would be the power to recall the prisoner at any time. The CJA 1991 (s. 44) set the process in train by allowing sex offenders to be supervised in the community until the end of their full sentence. Therefore a person serving three years could have served half the sentence in custody and one half supervised by the probation service in the community. In other words, punishment was to be extended for the full duration of the original sentence. Any decision to impose this additional supervisory period was at the discretion of the court and had to be stated at the point of sentence. The 1991 Act also provided for extensions in certain community provision for sex offenders. Those sentenced to a probation order could be ordered to spend all of their order in probation centres rather than the customary 60 days. The outcome of these changes was that the caseloads held by probation officers began to show increasing numbers of sex offenders on licence and under supervision. It also began to accelerate a process of change in the nature of a probation officer's work towards a more controlling and containing style that was to unfold with greater speed as the decade moved on.

As discussed earlier in this chapter, governments throughout the decade appeared to be in a hurry to make sure that sentencers did as they were bid. Frustrated by delays and what they regarded as intransigence, discretion was increasingly replaced by requirement. In the case of the extended supervision of sex offenders the shift occurred by the mid-1990s as proposals for the Crime (Sentences) Act 1997 included provisions that an extended period of supervision for sex offenders *would* be imposed unless there were exceptional circumstances. Although these proposals were not enacted, there was only a short delay before measures were introduced in the Crime and Disorder Act 1998. Once again, sex offenders were in the forefront of the new legislation. Courts were now empowered to impose up to ten years of post-release community supervision on sex offenders. A maximum of five years was allowed for violent offenders with a requirement that they had been sentenced to a minimum of four years in custody. These measures are perfect exemplars of the community protection model and continue to demonstrate how long term post-release sex offenders would increasingly skew the workload of the probation service.

Trends elsewhere

Before examining the most recent legislation in England and Wales a few examples from elsewhere in the world can be examined to show that the punitive trends identified in this chapter were becoming increasingly global. Many of the issues raised will touch on issues of rights and constitutionality. In Germany, for example, preventive or protective detention has a history dating back to the 1933 law on habitual criminals, which, because it arose from the Nazi period, remains an issue of national sensitivity. As with the community notification issue in Canada, protective legislation in Germany became something of a battleground between state and federal legislators (Dünkel and van Zyl Smit, 2004). The argument in Germany reflects issues debated in the UK and in America so it is illuminating to detour for a moment.

Dünkel and van Zyl Smit (2004) note that following critical reactions to preventive detention in the 1960s, a series of well-publicized cases of German sexual offences and the horrific case of Dutroux in Belgium, prompted the German Parliament to pass the Law for the Prevention of Sexual Offences and other Dangerous Criminal Acts of 26 January 1988. Subsequent amendments to the penal code allowed for the imposition of preventive detention even where offenders had no previous convictions and, in 2002, a further amendment allowed preventive detention for qualifying offenders if, *after conviction*, they were found to be dangerous, *provided* that this option had been reserved at the time of original sentence. It was this last point that would upset the Conservative opposition and lead several states, particularly those in the conservative south, to interpret the law in a direction that they wanted. Essentially they wished to legislate for provision to impose preventive detention of prisoners even if the option had not been reserved at the original trial. States such as Bavaria, Hesse, and Saxony-Anhalt decided to reinterpret the problem as one of police law, thus enabling the state to amend the law. In February 2004, the German Federal Constitutional Court decided that the states had been wrong to regard preventive detention as a matter of police law and reaffirmed it as criminal law and therefore a federal matter. However, within a month Chancellor Schröder's cabinet proposed legislation that would enable judges to recommend preventive detention even if the dangerousness came to light after sentencing, provided the original sentence was for at least four years and where the lives of the victims had been physically threatened. The trigger for this particular development had been the sentencing of a man for the murder of an 8-year-old girl in 2001 (Deutsche Welle, 2004).

One other issue raised by these German developments throws an interesting light on developments elsewhere, particularly perhaps in America. According to Dünkel and van Zyl Smit (2004) the issue revolved around the guiding standard of resocialization, emerging from the protection of human dignity and commitment to the welfare state (*Sozialstaatsprinzip*). The federal constitutional court argued that preventive detention did not infringe human dignity and was not cruel, inhuman, or degrading punishment, *if there was a guarantee* that the prisoner had a chance of release back into the community. Preventive detention was therefore constitutional if adequate treatment is offered to counteract the detrimental effect of incarceration. This led the federal court to demand that prisons not only conform to the principle of resocialization, but that they produce statistical evidence to prove this. State administrators had to prove that those in preventive detention had a legal and practical possibility of achieving liberty again, and that their detention would include opportunities for treatment, therapy, or work. Compare this with the development of Supermax prisons in the United States.

These super maximum security prisons were originally designed to incarcerate America's 'worst of the worst' prisoners. The prisons would effectively be escape proof, usually built in inaccessible places such as deserts and with fortress-like construction, predominantly consisting of reinforced concrete and steel. Wired perimeters and armed guards ensured that escape was futile. Yet these prisons also aimed to make the custodial experience itself punitive by almost completely eliminating human contact, denying work, treatment, or leisure opportunities, and ensuring inmates spend 23 hours each day in concrete or steel cells. The conditions have regularly been condemned by human rights organizations and the United Nations, yet, rather than limit the growth of these establishments, the numbers have increased. Many states have felt the need to have a Supermax facility to ensure that they are not regarded as soft on criminals. However, the increasing involvement of the private sector has ensured the need for a continuous supply of long term prisoners. A very significant number of three strike prisoners are now located in Supermax facilities—prisoners that would in no way appear to present the level of risk these conditions seek to justify. A more sinister recent development has been uncovered in the research of Lynch (2005). He has found cases where prisoners on death row and being held in Supermax facilities have volunteered to die by abandoning their legal appeals. It appears as if, at least in some cases, death has been preferred to a life in a Supermax facility. To find an ethos further removed from the spirit at least of the German penal code is harder to imagine. An equally sinister development was noted by Gottlieb (2003), who reported that the US Supreme Court upheld a decision in the state of Arkansas that officials had the right to make a convicted murderer take medication to make him sane enough to be executed.

The targeting of sex offenders in particular for special punitive attention has become widespread. In Switzerland, for example, a dispute similar to that in Germany between central and local government has seen 56% of the public in a referendum and the majority of cantons (regions) vote for a law to automatically send sex offenders and those deemed dangerous to prison for life. The government was against the measure, not least due to an absence of high security psychiatric facilities in Switzerland. Prisoners deemed dangerous and incurable would remain in prison until death, unless fresh evidence suggests the possibility of a cure.

Another feature of the ever-changing protection agenda are the restrictions imposed upon those who have reached the end of their lawful detention at the end of a fixed term penalty. In most cases evidence would have emerged during the prison sentence that the prisoner was still dangerous, as for example in the case of convicted paedophiles Sidney Cooke and Robert Oliver (see Chapter 6). However, an emerging trend is to prevent the release of prisoners who have not complied with, or engaged in, prison-based treatment programmes. For example, Australia's High Court ruled in October 2004 that offenders who refused rehabilitation therapy could be detained indefinitely, with the one dissenting judge comparing the ruling to practices in Nazi Germany (Herald, 2 October 2004). Jurisdictions have also used civil procedures in cases of potential dangerousness but where the prisoner has to be released into the community. Sexual Violent Predator Acts in many American states allow for the detention of people convicted of a sexually violent offence and who suffer from a mental abnormality or personality disorder that make the person likely to engage in acts of predatory sexual violence.

These developments, in various forms around the world, show us that sex offenders have been chosen for what is in effect a second time punishment. Having completed their lawful detention they are then subjected to potentially indefinite detention in civil mental health establishments. In essence they are being detained for what they might do in the future, the same rationale for imposing protective sentences in court. These forms of civil detention act almost as a second strike sentence where offenders will be punished again, not for what they have done but for tendencies they show. Perhaps most insidious is the fact that this additional detention will be applied for behavioural characteristics shown during sentence, not essentially as a result of any criminal behaviour. Australia has had two examples of such legislation aimed at individual prisoners in particular. In 1990 the Community Protection Act was passed in Victoria to prevent the release of Garry David, authorizing his detention in a psychiatric facility for up to six months subject to review. Another similar act was passed in New South Wales in 1994 to continue the detention of Gregory Kable, although this Act was later declared invalid because it imposed a sentence of custody without a finding of guilt (Figgis and Simpson, 1997). From failing to differentiate between general offence categories to laws passed against one individual, governments across the world have shown their willingness to develop legislation to tackle potential dangerousness and to appease the fears of an increasingly alarmed public.

Bringing it all together

General provisions aimed at potentially dangerous offenders can be summarized as: longer than proportionate sentences; mandatory minimum sentences; additional supervision in the community at the end of sentence; more rigorous supervision in the community; and continued detention at the end of lawful custody, usually in civil mental health institutions. Many of these provisions coalesce in the Criminal Justice Act 2003, which will now be considered, also the proposals for the detention of dangerous severe personality disordered offenders, which were discussed in Chapter 4.

The Criminal Justice Act 2003 and Protecting the Public

The CJA 2003 appears as if it will continue recent legislative tradition in that it will be implemented piecemeal. For our purposes it contains two important sections, one aimed at setting tariffs for murder and the other establishing new sentences for dangerous offenders, including those specifically for public protection. Undoubtedly the Act continues legislation trends from the 1990s that have sought to offer better public protection at both ends of the criminal process, that is longer initial sentences and greater restriction upon the release arrangements for potentially dangerous offenders. It also undid some of the flagship arrangements that had appeared in the Labour government's first term, namely the automatic life sentence for certain second time offenders. This measure, which had met considerable judicial opposition on its enactment (and indeed comparatively few had been passed as noted above), quietly disappeared in the CJA 2003. As Thomas (2004:702) notes, 'The sound and fury which accompanied the enactment of the Crime (Sentences) Act 1997 forms a strange contrast with the total parliamentary silence which surrounded the removal of this penological aberration from the statute book.'

New sentences for the dangerous offender

The main criticism of the automatic life sentence was that it technically removed the ability of the court to match sentence to crime seriousness, replacing this professional judgement with a bureaucratic formulae based upon offence classifications rather than offence seriousness. What would appear to be the replacement for the automatic life sentence are new sentences for dangerous offenders. Thomas advises that those working in this field will have to master a new set of definitions (2004:707) and these are 'specified offence', 'specified violent offence', 'specified sexual offence', 'serious offence', and 'relevant offence'. The offences are listed in Sch. 15, parts 1 and 2 of the Criminal Justice Act 2003, and number 153 in total (65 violent offences and 88 sexual offences). The lists contain a number of offences that would normally be associated with potential dangerousness (for example, manslaughter, kidnapping, threats to kill, malicious wounding), but also some offences that might cause surprise. Among these might be setting a spring gun, assault with intent to resist arrest, and offences involving threats.

The list of sexual offences contain a similarly diverse range many of which might not be considered dangerous by many, but obviously in themselves remain criminal behaviour that still result in victims and is of course serious to those victims. The issue, however, is whether the very creation of such extensive and inclusive lists of offending continue the upward spiral of seriousness escalation perceived by the public and fostered by governments. An offence in either list becomes 'serious' if it is punishable by life imprisonment or imprisonment for ten years or more. In terms of the life sentence the offence must, as stated, be punishable by life but also be one that convinces the court that there is a significant risk to the public of serious harm. In this instance the court must pass a life sentence.

Offences falling outside of the life sentence qualification (but meeting the other requirements) must result in a sentence of imprisonment for public protection. These sentences are indeterminate and as such fall under similar release arrangements as for life sentence prisoners, that is with release on the direction of the parole board. In both instances the courts are expected to set a minimum period, or tariff, to be served. One obvious point to make here is that some prisoners will remain in custody because the parole board still considers them to present a serious risk of harm to the public and that they may be there long after they have served the maximum sentence for the offence. This provision would address the issues raised by the release of fixed term prisoners such as the paedophiles Cook and Oliver, who were seen to be very dangerous at the end of their sentence but had to be released by law. It is recognition that offenders can be potentially dangerous outside of offence categories that qualify for the discretionary life sentence and indeed these new measures may spell the end of that sentence.

It remains to be seen whether or not judges react to these new sentencing provisions in the way they have with the automatic life sentence for certain second time offenders. Once again this new provision could be taken as an attempt to overcome judicial reluctance to pass longer sentences for certain types of offender. From the other end of sentence, release considerations will be taken increasingly on a wider range of offenders by the parole board, thus offering another check on the original sentence passed. However, much will continue to rest on the court's assessment of potential dangerousness. We know that the criteria to be applied is that the court must be of the view that there is a significant risk of serious harm to the public caused by further specified (but not necessarily serious) offences committed by the offender. We are then back into the realms of prediction, not only of offending, but of a risk of serious harm occasioned by certain offences (but as we have seen, the list is very broad indeed).

The CJA 2003 s. 229 is actually entitled 'the assessment of dangerousness', but it does not move us on much from previous muddled attempts to give guidance to the court. Naturally, previous behaviour in the form of criminal convictions remains important to the assessment process and in this instance the previous convictions must be 'relevant', which in effect means from the list of specified offences. Where no such previous conviction exists, or the offender was under the age of 18 at the time of the offence, the court should (s. 229(2)(a), (b) and (c)):

- take into account all such information as is available to it about the nature and circumstances of the offence;
- may take into account any information which is before it about any pattern of behaviour of which the offence forms part;
- may take into account any information about the offender which is before it.

As Thomas (2004:710) says, 'How else the court could go about this task is difficult to see.' Where there is evidence of a relevant previous conviction, and the offender is over 18, the court *must* assume that there is such a risk *unless*, after taking into account:

- all such information as is available to it about the nature and circumstances of each of the offences;
- where appropriate, any information, which is before it about any pattern of behaviour of which any offences form part, and
- any information about the offender which is before it, the court considers that it would be unreasonable to conclude that there is such a risk (s. 229(2)(a), (b) and (c)).

Although Thomas views these new provisions as a significant improvement on those relating to the automatic life sentence, he remains concerned about the numbers of offences that qualify for them. He hopes that the new provisions '... will not lead to any of the absurdities produced by the automatic life sentence, but the statute book would have been marginally better without them' (2004:711). The Act provides two other significant measures aimed at potentially dangerous offenders. The first involves extended sentences for those convicted of a specified, but not a serious offence (an offence for which the maximum penalty does not exceed ten years) and whom the court considers that there is a risk to members of the public of serious harm occasioned by the commission by the offender of further specified offences. In these cases the court must pass an extended sentence of imprisonment the term of which is equal to the aggregate of:

- the appropriate custodial term, and
- a further period 'the extension period', for which the offender is to be subject to a licence the length of which is set by the court as being necessary to protect the public from serious harm occasioned by the commission of further specified offences.

The appropriate term is explained in s. 153(2) and relates to sentences commensurate with the seriousness of the offence and not exceeding the permitted maximum. The extension period will not exceed five years for a specified violent offence and eight years for a specified sexual offence. The aggregate of custodial term and extended period must not exceed the maximum permitted for the offence. Prisoners subject to extended sentences will serve a minimum of one half of the appropriate custodial term and then remain in custody until their release is authorized by the parole board. They must be released at the end of the custodial period on licence for the extension period. The increased level of sentences imposed on many sexual crimes by the Sexual Offences Act 2003 will undoubtedly lead to a number of offences falling into both the extended sentence category and the public protection arrangements, a potential source of great confusion.

Reworking the life sentence

Finally for our purposes, the CJA 2003 proposes changes to the way in which the minimum term to be served by mandatory life sentence prisoners (the tariff) is to be determined. Under Chapter 7 of Part 12 of the Act, it will be the court, rather than the Home Secretary, who will determine the minimum period to be served. This follows on from decisions made by the House of Lords, the European Court of Human Rights, and application of the European Convention on Human Rights (Thomas, 2004:703). In effect these changes remove the political influence in release decisions, which have caused such controversy over the years. That said, the new arrangements do not give the courts unfettered opportunities to decide upon the length of the minimum term to be served. A new framework imposes relatively rigid guidelines for particular offenders and offences. Despite this limitation, Thomas (2003:703) sees this development as a major advance, 'It is infinitely preferable that judges within the framework of the judicial process should fix the minimum term, even if statutory criteria must be borne in mind, than the minimum term should be fixed privately by a politician, remote from the detailed facts of the case.' He might also have mentioned a distancing from constantly changing and media-dominated political agendas, which are also very remote from the actual facts of the case.

The framework effectively divides murder into three categories for the purposes of determining the minimum term to be served. For the most serious cases, a 'whole life order' should be the starting point. Criteria applicable here are that the offender must be over 21 and the offence is one of 'exceptionally high' seriousness. Schedule 21(4) indicates the type of offending behaviour that may qualify for the exceptional label and this includes the murder of two or more persons, where each murder may involve any of the following:

- a substantial degree of premeditation or planning;
- the abduction of the victim;
- sexual or sadistic conduct;
- the murder of one person if it is a child involving abduction or sexual or sadistic motivation;
- a murder done for the purpose of advancing a political, religious, or ideological cause; or
- a murder by an offender previously convicted of murder.

The second category is one where the seriousness is 'particularly' high and this sets the starting point in determining the minimum term at 30 years. A range of situations are included in this qualifying category, including:

- the murder of a police or prison officer in the course of his duty;
- a murder done for gain (eg in the course of a robbery);
- a murder intended to obstruct or interfere with the course of justice;
- a murder involving sexual or sadistic conduct;
- the murder of two or more persons;
- a murder that is racially or religiously aggravated or aggravated by sexual orientation; or
- a murder falling into the whole life category but committed by a person under the age of 21.

The issue of tariffs, especially whole-life tariffs was brought into stark contrast by the Soham murders of two 10-year-old schoolgirls by Ian Huntley, a caretaker at their school. In passing sentence, the judge recommended a minimum of a 40-year tariff, indicating that he could find no evidence of abduction (it was a chance meeting) and there was no evidence of sexual activity, although he thought that there was a likelihood, which could not be substantiated. However, it would appear that the 2003 Act provisions could well lead to whole-life sentences being imposed on a regular basis, and at least a greater number of long-tariff sentences. One immediate effect of this is likely to be a very significant increase in the life sentence prisoner population.

If the offender was aged under 18 when the offence was committed and the case does not fall into the two categories above, the starting point in determining the minimum term is 15 years. It remains to be seen if the setting of these minimum terms will significantly add to the lifer prison population, although there are a range of aggravating and mitigating factors that may add to or reduce the guideline minima. It is suggested that detailed consideration of these factors could result in a minimum term of any length, whatever the starting point, or indeed in the making of a whole-life order. Aggravating factors are now well established and would include: planning and premeditation; victim vulnerability; mental or physical suffering of the victim before death; abuse of a position of trust; the use of duress or threats against the person to facilitate the offence; the victim being in a position of providing a public service or duty; and concealment, destruction, or dismemberment of the body. Mitigating factors include: a lack of intent to kill; a lack of premeditation; the offender suffering a form of mental disorder or mental disability that lowers the degree of culpability; the offender being provoked by prolonged stress (that would not amount to a defence of provocation); the offender acted to any extent in self-defence; a belief by the offender that the murder was an act of mercy; and the age of the offender.

The CJA 2003 was one of the last pieces of legislation by the second term Labour government and will be implemented by the new third term Blair administration. It has continued many of the trends identified throughout this chapter and in many ways pursues the government's battle with the judiciary to apply the law in ways that reflect its more populist leanings. The failure of the judiciary to do this (at least according to the government) has resulted in further attempts to push them towards sentencing in a particular direction. That said, in many significant areas, a good deal of discretion has been passed back to the judges. How this discretion is used may of course determine how long it remains available to them. The sentencing provisions for dangerous and very serious offenders have attempted to close loopholes, particularly that concerning the release of those still considered to be dangerous at the end of their lawful detention period. The final point to mention before we depart from the CJA 2003 is the new provision for the retrial of certain serious offences in the light of 'compelling' new evidence and if it is in the public interest. The full details are included in Part 10 of the Act, with the list of qualifying offences (29 in number) being listed in Sch. 10, pt. 1. These new provisions have undoubtedly been triggered by high profile and negative media publicity in certain notorious cases such as the murder of Stephen Lawrence. For those who work with the families of victims, this new legislation could have a significant impact.

Summary

This chapter has explored the ways in which governments across the world have introduced a range of legislation aimed at increasing controls over potentially dangerous offenders, and sex offenders in particular. Experiments have been conducted with mandatory minimum sentences in an attempt to reduce judicial discretion, whilst new sentences aim to force judges to deal more severely with certain types of offender. This has not, however, been enough to appease an increasingly alarmed public and electorate so further measures have been devised to restrain offenders at the end of their lawful detention period. Legislation has been issue led, with the issues usually determined by a sensational hungry media. Both those involved in dispensing justice and informed critics have suggested that there has not been an evidence base for measures that have become increasingly populist and punitive. However, this has not stopped successive governments from introducing new measures in a conveyor-belt like fashion and alongside new sentences have been new and more restrictive measures to contain offenders in the community. It is to these that attention will now turn.

7

Legislating for Constraint—Tightening Controls in the Community

Introduction

Chapter 6 highlighted that throughout the 1990s and into the twenty-first century, successive governments had sought to introduce protective and mandatory minimum sentences for sexual and violent offenders. Politically a community protection model had been favoured and has come to dominate the agenda. These recent developments have resulted in a continuing battle ensuing between the legislature and senior judges in particular over judicial independence, and to a lesser extent offender rights. The British government have been equally determined to impose their authority not only in this area but also over the supervision and management of high risk, and potentially dangerous offenders in the community by a number of criminal justice agencies. As a result, a range of legislation has been passed, often in rapid succession as gaps and problems are exposed. Relevant legislation includes the Sex Offenders Act 1997; the Protection from Harassment Act 1997; the Crime and Disorder Act 1998; the Criminal Justice Act 2000; the Sexual Offences Act 2003; and the Criminal Justice Act 2003. Important aspects of these acts will be considered throughout this chapter with a particular effort to identify common themes and trends in respect of offenders posing a high risk of serious harm and potential dangerousness.

Controlling sex offenders in the community— a political battlefield

The Sex Offenders Act 1997 arose out of the same penal and political trends as the Crime (Sentences) Act 1997 (see previous chapter) and reflected the growing American influence in sentencing policy and indeed, the increasingly populist slant of that legislation. Its major achievement was the introduction of the Sex Offenders' Register (SOR), a toned-down version of what had unfolded in America throughout the 1990s. The creation of the register epitomized the political process by which legislation emerged during this period, a process perhaps described best as a bidding war between the two major political parties where both tried to establish 'clear blue water' between each other (Dunbar and Langdon, 1998). Conservative and Labour politicians had vied with each other since Tony Blair emerged as a significant figure in British politics in the early 1990s. The Conservative Party had established law and order as their own since the election of Margaret Thatcher as Prime Minister in 1979. The Labour Party, clinging to an increasingly unpopular welfarist tradition, found itself constantly branded as being the offender's friend, the victim's enemy, and the supporter of scroungers. The new right Conservative governments on the other hand, appealed to populist sentiment as described by Garland (2001:97): 'Hostility towards "tax and spend" government, undeserving welfare recipients, "soft on crime" policies, unelected trade unions who were running the country, the break-up of the family, the breakdown of law and order—these were focal points for a populist politics that commanded widespread support.'

The popularity of policies aimed at these 'problems' endured until the early 1990s when a series of occurrences conspired to shift public sentiment and cast increasing doubt upon the Conservative party's ability to sustain its popularity on law and order issues. It was evident that Labour leader Tony Blair had made a significant impact and much of his success was due to his ability to 'steal the Tories law and order clothes'. Most famously, he declared that Labour would be 'tough on crime and tough on the causes of crime'—a clear attempt to appeal to both Labour traditionalists and the new centrist voters he hoped to entice into the fold. The murder of toddler James Bulger in Liverpool in 1992 by two boys acted not only as a moral catalyst for the country, but also a major trigger for an increase in the punitive direction of political debate. The murder and subsequent public reaction led Prime Minister John Major to call for society to 'understand a little less and condemn a little more', launching in effect a moral crusade. Although the Conservative government might have expected this policy to benefit their standing in the community, it was to have an unforeseen effect as a series of political 'sleaze' scandals saw the party implode. Standing as righteous politicians would blow up in their face and this, combined with major party dissent on European integration, would force law and order to be the sole trump card left to the Conservatives. This would be the battleground leading through to the election of New Labour in 1997, and it would be a battle that the Conservatives would ultimately lose. Unfortunately the political loss would also extend to the loss of a sensible and evidence-led criminal justice policy, being replaced instead by a populist, seemingly knee-jerk and increasingly fear-driven agenda.

As indicated by both Lord Ackner and Thomas (1998) in Chapter 6, there was not to be any brake placed on the legislative excesses originally put forward by Conservatives, and subsequently matched and further developed by Labour. In seeking to shed their 'soft on crime' image, Labour politicians, notably Tony Blair and Jack Straw, would meet everything the Conservatives proposed and in some instances suggested going further. It would become impossible to separate the policies of the two major parties. If the Home Secretary, Michael Howard, had hoped to smoke out the liberals in the Labour Party he failed and, perhaps surprisingly, law and order would fail to become as significant an issue in the 1997 election as might have been expected. Increasing public alarm over the risks posed by predatory paedophiles had marked the mid-1990s in the UK. The emotive and sensitive nature of this issue effectively negated opposition to prevailing arguments over safety and protection, and in its place a punitive consensus emerged, nullifying political debate. Although there was no real evidence that the sexual offending problem had suddenly worsened, there was a coming together of factors, which certainly increased public awareness and concern. These included what had been an acute political battle between Conservative and Labour politicians, the imminent release of a group of notorious paedophiles from prison, a heightened interest from the media in sex offenders and the American way of dealing with them. Part of the problem also appeared to be the growing expectation of living in a risk-free society. Each new case that posed a problem became built into a threat against civilized society; even small issues that would once have been comfortably dealt with by criminal justice professionals became a matter for public and political debate. This has been described by Garland (1996) as a crisis of penal modernism, characterized by the destruction of old certainties including the loss of faith in society's experts. When added to the fears generated by living within the risk society (Beck, 1992) it is not perhaps surprising that people began to blow up every incident into a potential catastrophe, and to seek increasingly punitive, non-rehabilitative measures against offenders. The unease felt within daily life is well illustrated by Holloway and Jefferson (1997:261), 'In other words, because we have no means of being sure where risk and safety lie, nothing can be trusted and anxiety, therefore, potentially finds a location in any area of daily life.'

Side by side with anxiety and fear resides blame and it is one of the notable features of public life throughout this period that all criminal justice agencies received their share of blame, even formerly favoured groups such as the police service. Douglas describes the position as, '... the belief that any misfortune must have a cause, a perpetrator to blame, from whom to exact compensation' (Douglas, 1986:16). All criminal justice agencies operated within this context and this in part might explain why there has been only limited opposition to ever-closer integration between agencies as they work together on risk management and control (see Chapter 8). It might also explain much of the seemingly knee-jerk, loophole filling policy-making of governments in the 1990s and into the twenty-first century. Before considering the British response to this potpourri of problems, it may be useful to reflect upon the American experience to understand more clearly how the agenda unfolded on this side of the Atlantic.

Looking west—lessons from America

Several notorious, well-publicized cases in America during the late 1980s and early 1990s saw the rapid escalation of public and political concern over the threats posed by serious sex offenders in the community. Many of the issues considered, and the measures to deal with the perceived problem, were to surface in the UK a few years later. According to Petrunik (2003) the trigger event was the abduction, sexual assault, and mutilation of a seven-year-old boy by a man, Earl Shriner, who had been released from a fixed prison sentence, imposed for sexual assault. One of the aggravating features of this case was that prior to his release, plans devised by Shriner for torturing and raping children and discovered by the prison authorities, had not prevented his return to the community. Although an early case on the agenda, Shriner's activities raised many of the issues that have been replicated around the world since. These coalesce around the release of fixed sentence prisoners in the face of evidence indicating future serious offending, the ethics of continuing that detention, and the legality of mental health legislation to 'take over' where the criminal justice system 'leaves off', if there is evidence of continuing potential danger. Petrunik (2003) indicates that in the USA, liberal reforms along justice lines to mental health legislation had placed restrictions on the use of involuntary civil commitment and effectively closed that route to those demanding change. Within ten months of Shriner's attack, however, Washington State had passed legislation that offered a range of measures to protect the public, through the Community Protection Act 1990. The Act provided three essential elements that would feature highly in recurrent discussions and debate in the UK in the mid-1990s: post-sentence civil commitment, sex offender registration, and a tiered system of community notification of sex offenders based upon perceived levels of risk.

Two other well-documented cases, the murder of Zachary Snider in Indiana and the sexual abduction and murder of seven-year-old Megan Kanka in New Jersey, saw similar legislation being passed across America. This last case is perhaps the most widely known and appears to have pushed President Clinton, in 1994, into enacting federal legislation requiring states to set up sex offender registries. The carrot, or stick, would be a 10% cut in criminal justice funding earmarked for drug control, if these mechanisms were not established (the Jacob

Wetterling Act). By 1996 further federal legislation, widely known as Megan's Law, required all states to carry out mandatory community notification to federal standards or face similar funding cuts (Petrunik, 2003). President Bill Clinton expressed the emotional intensity surrounding the debate saying that offender rights would be secondary to the public's right to protection, '... there is no right greater than a parent's right to raise a child in safety and love' (CNN Interactive, 22 June 1996). Within six years these terrible cases had led to the creation of a raft of state and federal laws that aimed to curb the activities of sexual offenders. The term *sexually violent predator* entered the everyday lexicon.

A British compromise?

As we have indicated above, the debate over the management of sex offenders in the UK was provoked rather less by a number of serious cases of assault and murder, but more by politicians responding to concerns over the release of sex offenders who might offend again the future. That said, in 1996 the abduction and murder of seven-year-old Sophie Hook in North Wales led to calls for a register by her father when he subsequently learned that the police had been keeping an eye on the offender for a couple of years prior to the attack (Thomas, 2000:107). Despite the perpetrator eventually being told he would serve a minimum of 50 years in prison, extremely unusual in Britain, this case did not reach the levels of notoriety of those in the United States.

It is also fair to say that registration and notification issues were to some extent blurred, although as we note below, the British response was something of a compromise. Notable among the cases provoking debate in the media and the House of Commons were two convicted paedophiles, Sidney Cooke and Robert Oliver. They, with other members of their paedophile 'ring', had brutally raped and murdered a 14-year-old boy, Jason Swift, and having originally been charged with murder were convicted of manslaughter. Their impending release, at the end of their fixed term prison sentences, provoked similar fears to those voiced in America and were quickly picked up by the media. A central issue arose over accommodating the two offenders and plans to house them in hostels around the country met with fierce local resistance, including at one point, attacks on a West Country police station where Cooke was being held temporarily in protective custody. The term NIMBY (not in my back yard) dates from this period and served to demonstrate the potentially hostile and explosive reaction to the presence of sex offenders in the community. In both Oliver and Cooke's case there appeared to be strong signs from their prison behaviour that they had not finished their sexual offending activities but there was no provision to keep them in custody at the end of their sentence. However, the offence of manslaughter does carry a maximum penalty of a discretionary life sentence. Had these two offenders been sentenced to a life sentence then the views concerning their potential dangerousness may have delayed their release. A recurring theme in all legislative debates from this period onwards, would focus more on the need for additional measures rather than considering more efficient use of what was already in the armoury. The singular position of the mandatory death penalty for murder appears to confuse its use for other offenders. Sorting out this confusion may have prevented the increasing politicization of the dangerousness debate since the mid-1990s. In Oliver's case, his release whilst still considered to be a 'sexual deviant with a personality disorder' triggered calls from the Chief Constable of Sussex to make changes to the Mental Health Act 1983 to enable compulsory detention of such prisoners at the end of their sentence (BBC News Online, 13 March 1998). These requests were, of course, to bear fruition in the measures proposed for dangerous severe personality disordered offenders (DSPDOs) discussed earlier in Chapter 4.

A British variant

The Sex Offenders Act 1997, was a very British version of developments that had recently unfolded in America where legislation had been established that effectively abandoned offender rights in favour of community protection. The Act was something of a compromise, and that compromise was over the issue that perhaps was most contentious, that of community notification. The Act did not require any formal system of widespread community notification, and in effect denied the public what in America had become everyone's right, 'the right to know'. It did, however, establish a sex offender register (SOR) to be administered by the police, and held on the police national computer (PNC) but the public were not to have access to this information. In essence, the register would be reactive in the sense that it would enable the police to narrow their enquiries in the event of a sexual crime, as they should know the whereabouts of convicted and registered sex offenders. Crucially, at this early stage of development, there was not an expectation that those on the register would be supervised, either by the police or probation service, although a form of risk assessment and screening was required. It is also worth noting at this point that the establishment of the register began quite a fundamental change to the work of the police service, and their role with sex offenders would be refined and deepened over the next few years.

The list of offences and offenders eligible for registration immediately suggested the probability that the term 'sex offender' would be constructed as all sex offenders, regardless of crime or risk, and that relatively less serious offences—and indeed people convicted of crimes that were no longer against the law—would be included. The list of eligible offences included the following: rape; intercourse with a girl under 13; intercourse with a girl between 13 and 16; incest by a man; buggery; indecency between men; indecent assault on a woman; indecent assault on a man (but not if the victim was over 18); assault with intent to commit buggery; causing or encouraging prostitution; indecent assault on a girl under 16; indecent conduct towards a young child; inciting a girl under 16 to have incestuous intercourse; and taking indecent photographs of children. Undoubtedly this list does contain serious offences and most but not all involve involuntary victims. Yet the rhetoric framing these new measures, in the USA for example the term 'predators' was commonplace and in the UK 'beasts' (Sampson, 1994:124), appears to be some distance from many of the offenders and offences included in the lists for registration. In other words, from day one a major problem of seriousness inflation was underway, a problem that must eventually come home to roost in the allocation of scarce resources.

The number of offenders eligible for immediate registration on 1 September 1997 was 4,524 (by 2003–4 this number had grown to approximately 25,000 with forecasts of an upper limit of 125,000). By December 1997 3,365 had notified the police of their whereabouts—a compliance rate of 88% (Thomas, 2000:117). To the public this number of sex offenders, of whom they had previously been largely unaware, indicated a huge well of risk. There appeared to be have been little attempt to distinguish between types of offender and degrees of potential danger, and as a result the creation of the register did little to reduce or allay public anxiety. One important feature of the registration requirements was that a police caution would qualify. As Thomas (2000:109) notes, this is an issue of concern in that cautions are meant to be for, in many instances, atypical cases, whereas registration implied a typical offence that may well be repeated. In other words, the offence merited either a caution or registration—it should not be both. Gillespie (1998) referred to concerns over people admitting to crimes even if the evidence against them is not strong, with the potential implications for registration that this would imply.

Registration would be for all qualifying sex offenders who were convicted or cautioned after implementation of the Act, or who were in custody, on post-custody licence or under a community penalty supervised by the probation service. Periods of registration would be determined in a fairly crude way by the type and severity of the penalty originally imposed for the sexual offence, as follows:

- a person who has been sentenced to life or for more than 30 months, will be registered for an indefinite period;
- a person who has been admitted to hospital subject to a restriction order, will be registered for an indefinite period;
- a person who has been sentenced to more than six months but less than 30 months, will be registered for a period of ten years beginning with the relevant date;
- a person who has been sentenced to less than six months, will be registered for a period of seven years beginning with that date;
- a person who has been admitted to hospital without being subject to a restriction order, will be registered for a period of seven years beginning with that date;

131

- a person of any other description will be registered for a period of five years beginning with that date.

This last group would include all of those subject to community penalties and indeed the group of offenders cautioned by the police. A period of five years' registration for these offenders who would, one anticipates, be at the lower end of the seriousness spectrum, and be a considerable additional imposition. Failure to comply with the registration requirements could attract a penalty up to a maximum of six months in custody. However, as would prove to be the case with breach of sex offender orders, successive governments would become concerned at the variability in sentencing for breaches of registration requirements and the length of the potential penalty (Home Office, 2001). Breach action for measures passed in the civil courts would increasingly offer severe criminal punishment, a handy back door for governments seeking to take a (veiled) tough line.

Early concerns

As soon as the register became active, and indeed even before that point, concerns were expressed over those offenders not subject to the registration requirements, that is, those 'not in the system' on 1 September 1997. This was another good example of setting a measure and immediately attempting to plug the gaps, to offer the elusive goal of safety. Various calculations were made but perhaps the most authoritative came from the Home Office (1997) which suggested that there were as many as 100,000 sex offenders in the community who would, had the register been retrospective, been subject to registration. In a thoughtful analysis, Soothill and Francis (1997:1325) came to a conclusion that perhaps reflected the tone of debate alluded to above concerning sex offence legislation in the 1990s:

> Any assumption that the scheme 'captures' the most active sexual offenders is untrue . . . there seems no criminological rationale to the determination of the periods of registration. The varying periods under different conditions seems more akin to continuing the punishment of sex offenders rather than representing appropriate measures to protect the public. While it may be a laudable aim to try to keep those most likely to be serious sexual recidivists under surveillance, we suggest that this Act fails to identify such persons in a systematic manner. The public remains equally at risk from those offenders not covered by the provisions of the Sex Offenders Act as well as continuing to be at risk from offenders outside the period of registration. In brief, the Act seems to be a political gesture, which is probably misleading, potentially mischievous and almost certainly mistaken.

In other words, registration (a passive form of community monitoring) relied upon sentence disposition to determine the extent of police involvement, rather than a systematic evaluation of contemporary risk and more, of severity of potential harm. Anyone who has worked with sex offenders knows that a significant degree of risk can emanate from offenders whose offending triggers punishment at the lower ends of the sentencing bands. A mechanistic process had therefore been established to monitor the risks posed by some of the most un-mechanistic of offenders! The concerns expressed over the inadequacies of the registration system would lead to two new approaches. The first would be a considerable strengthening of the registration requirements themselves—a process returned to more than once—and the second a new measure aimed at those not on the register but whose behaviour was apparently causing concern, a measure that itself would lead to automatic registration.

Plugging the gaps

In 1997, the government announced a consultation paper on a proposed 'community protection order' (Home Office, 1997). By the time of its implementation in the Crime and Disorder Act 1998 (CDA 1998), the order had been renamed as a Sex Offender Order (SOO) (which in turn would also be renamed). The discussion document itself posed some of the difficulties being expressed about unsupervised sex offenders but in no way dealt with issues relating to what could amount to additional punishment for those whose offences may have taken place many years previously. The orders would therefore resurrect the debate about punishment for future rather than past crimes. The document summarizes this position very well:

> ... more must be done to protect society from sex offenders who pose a continuing risk. In particular, sex offenders who fall outside the provisions of the Sex Offenders Act 1997, because they were no longer in prison, or under supervision when the Act came into force ... for whatever reason are not subject to adequate supervision in the community, and whose behaviour gives rise to cause for concern are not, at present, subject to safeguards sufficient to protect the community.

This paragraph makes assumptions about the sex offenders' register, namely that it in itself provides protection *through supervision*, a statement that is simply not true. It also talks about safeguarding the protection of the community and this emotive yet unachievable objective was to permeate through much of the government rhetoric during this period. This line was pursued despite warnings from the Association of Chief Officers of Police (ACPO) and the Association of Chief Probation Officers (ACOP) that the public should not rely on the registers for protection, that in effect they were passive rather than proactive devices.

Sex offender orders

Sex offender order requests would come from the police service. The request could be activated by concerns expressed by the public over the behaviour of a person acting in·suspicious circumstances (for example, loitering near schools or children's playgrounds). The offenders needed to have a relevant history of previous criminal sexual behaviour, and to be acting in such a way as to pose a risk of serious harm. However, as noted below, registering concern with the police about even well-known sex offenders is not always a guarantee that action would be taken. Essentially therefore, the Sex Offenders Act 1997 created opportunities for people who were behaving suspiciously to be checked by the police and then potentially made subject to a sex offender order, usually following consultation with other agencies, notably social services departments or the probation service. These and other agencies could also trigger the referral process to the police. The order was to be civil, and requiring a civil standard of proof (later amended to a criminal standard) although, following a ploy used more than once by the new Labour government, any breach would be regarded as a criminal offence punishable with a custodial penalty up to a maximum of five years. Just as with qualification for the sex offenders register, these new orders would also be triggered for those cautioned for qualifying sexual offences. Once again, Gillespie (1998) draws our attention to the fact that these orders could therefore be applied to those who had been cautioned (in other words have not been found guilty in court), a disposal not meant to involve punishment, but could have punishment imposed not for a crime but for a breach of a civil order (itself imposed on a suspicion of future crime). He believed this to be totally against the ethos of cautioning.

The orders themselves would act as a form of restraint and were intended to keep potential offenders away from certain situations where they might offend again. Magistrates were given wide powers to prohibit the defendant from doing anything described in the order. The terms of the order had to be negative; they could not require the offender to do anything such as engage in supervision or treatment. Relevant scenarios might be a paedophile whose previous offending behaviour was to target young children in parks who is seen hanging around children's play areas. He might be made subject to an order preventing him from visiting parks, or certain areas at particular times. Although there may be a certain logic to this, it is easy to spot the possible problems. Policing or monitoring the order would be difficult, unless the person was under near permanent surveillance. Equally, people subject to sex offender orders could simply switch their activities to areas not prohibited by their own particular order. If a paedophile's normal *modus operandi* is to target children in public places, then, unless he is banned from anywhere that children live, it is technically impossible to prevent him offending if he wished to do so. The orders would entail a requirement to register with the police and would thus seek to close one of the loopholes identified above. As with the register itself, it is difficult to escape the conclusion that these orders were another example of a political sop that would likely prove to be more effective for detection purposes than prevention.

The first order was reportedly made in Manchester on a man with a previous conviction for rape after breaking into student bed-sits. The order required him to keep away from much of southern Manchester (a high volume student area) after he was seen peering through bed-sit windows at night before running away (Thomas, 2000:153). Once again, if this man was determined to rape he could do so in other parts of Manchester and, one suspects, could also have found a student victim if that was his preference. The order may have given some comfort to women in the area, but it is vital that these actions do not lead to a false sense of security.

Sex offender orders—intentions and reality

Shute (2004:422) noted that at the time of their creation, considerable concern was expressed over the potential scope of Sex Offender Orders, a concern replicated over Anti-Social Behaviour Orders (ASBOs) (Ward, 2005). One area of concern was the fact that the triggering acts might be non-criminal activities and the other was that the prohibitions contained in the order could be drafted in very wide terms. Shute (2004:422–3) highlights a case from the Avon and Somerset Constabulary to indicate the potential breadth of SOO conditions. In this case the order stated that the offender must not seek contact with any child or young person under 16; not associate with or befriend a child or young person under 16; not reside in any private dwelling where a child or young person under 16 is present; and not to undertake any activity (paid, voluntary, or recreational), which, by its nature, is likely to result in contact with a child under 16. Shute notes that an appeal against these conditions by Cherie Booth QC based on a breach of the defendant's human rights was dismissed in the High Court. In making his judgment, Lord Bingham indicated the philosophy behind SOOs:

> There is no room for doubt about the mischief against which this legislation is directed, which is the risk of re-offending by sex offenders who have shown a continuing propensity to offend. Parliament might have decided to wait until, if at all, the offender did offend again and then appropriate charges could be laid on the basis of that further offending. Before 1998 there was effectively no choice but to act in that way. But the obvious disadvantage was that, by the time the offender had offended again, some victim had suffered. The rationale of section 2 was, by means of an injunctive order, to seek to avoid the contingency of any further suffering by any further victim. It would also of course be to the advantage of a defendant if he were to be saved from further offending. (in Shute 2004:423)

There is a clear rationale in this judgment that a SOO will actively prevent further crime, 'any further suffering . . . by any further victim', yet, logic tells us that this is an impossible claim. It says nothing about the enforceability of such all-inclusive measures. At the same time, where conditions are drawn so widely it could be inferred that the offender is bound to fail, as by going about anything like a normal life, he will breach his conditions.

A Police Research Series Paper (Knock, Schlesinger, Boyle, and Magor, 2002) suggests that there were early problems in implementing sex offender orders, not least among these perhaps being the relatively small number made. Between inception on 1 December 1998 and 31 March 2001, 92 orders had been made in England and Wales. The authors suggest reasons for the low take up but, before examining these, it is perhaps worthy of general comment first. The proposals for the original community protection orders had come about over concerns for the estimated 100,000 sex offenders who were unregistered in the community. The inference was that these people represented a substantial risk to the public and nothing could be done with them until they actually offended. Yet, within a period of 16 months only 92 orders were made, suggesting that the risks were substantially lower than made out by both government and media, or possibly, suggestive of problems with the orders themselves. There was a high rate of success for applications (94%), but nearly a half (46%) resulted in breach action before the court. The study identified four possible reasons for the low take-up, which were: a general lack of understanding of the SOO process, confusion around legislation and guidance, concerns about inadequate resources, and cautious force solicitors. In many cases police officers used the orders as a means to intervene in patterns of behaviour before it amounted to a criminal offence. Several officers also admitted that orders were applied for in the hope of eventual breach action, which would result in a criminal conviction—a classic first strike ploy. Nevertheless, despite these reported difficulties, these figures do suggest that the vast majority of registered and/or convicted sex offenders were not behaving in such a way as to provoke sufficient concern to warrant the request for a sex offender order, that the pool of risk was nothing like as deep as suggested by the thinking behind the establishment of the sex offender measures initially.

As noted above, sex offender orders, along with periodic changes to the registration process and requirements, could be regarded as attempts to placate an increasingly anxious public. Piecemeal developments continued throughout this period, for example in 2001 the government enacted Restraining Orders (ROs) in the Criminal Justice and Court Services Act 2000. These measures were modelled on provisions in the Protection from Harassment Act 1997 and became available where the Crown Court imposed a sentence of imprisonment (or a hospital order or guardianship order) for a relevant sex offence. Again the measures had to be triggered by a risk to the public of serious harm from the offender and could prohibit the offender doing anything described in the order. Breach of the order would render the offender liable on conviction on indictment, to a prison sentence not exceeding five years. These measures did not, however, provide the 'missing link' demanded by many, that of community notification. Although not a full part of the legislation described in this chapter—there did exist provision for limited notification—public and media demands for notification continued and this in many ways increasingly influenced the response of the government. Due to the reluctance to accede to demands for community notification, it appears as if the British government wanted to increase the severity of its other penalties as something of a deflective manoeuvre. Thus community notification set the agenda even in its own absence.

In America, sex offender registration and community notification rapidly became almost one and the same thing. Federal law demanded community notification, the degree and extent of which was determined by the perceived level of risk posed by the offender. It was the desire to have a similar scheme here that lay behind the protests over the release from custody of Cooke and Oliver noted above. It was not only that these offenders were to be released (a problem in itself for many), but also that their release arrangements were being made without consulting the local communities in which they might be located. Before considering the debate as it unfolded it is relevant to consider briefly the American experience.

The right to know—US style

It is clear that, in making demands to know the whereabouts and identity of sex offenders in the community, these offenders are being seen by the public as qualitatively different to other offenders. Despite the extremely low rate of sex offending (approximately 5% of all violent crime and 0.9% of all police-recorded crime, Home Office, 2004), and of its repetition, the risk to the public, particularly the vulnerable, is perceived as very much greater. Although the public is at much greater risk of burglary, or theft of vehicles, or minor assaults on the street, or in the case of sex offending, in their own homes, calls to be notified of these other offenders are not made. It is the singular risks that are perceived to emanate from one small group of offenders that have fuelled these claims and, as indicated above, framed much of the contemporary sex offender policy and legislation. That said, in an area where policy has become exceedingly populist, sex offender notification remains one area where the British government has (perhaps surprisingly) refused to accede to popular sentiment. In America this has not even been an issue for debate since the federal Megan's Law required states to enact notification procedures in 1996.

Two recent studies, Thomas (2003) and Lovell (2001), have attempted to evaluate the impact and effectiveness of community notification strategies in America—the former study involving observation and interviews with the actors involved. Although the federal law requires notification procedures it is clear that each state has a certain amount of discretion to determine the level of notification according to risk, with level 1 (low) through to level 3 (high) becoming more or less the standard. In effect, the higher the risk is perceived to be, the more people will get to hear about the offender and the more informa-tion they can learn about him/her. Thomas gives examples of Internet commu-nications, posters in windows, placards in gardens, marks on drivers' licences, a particular style of clothing, posters in public buildings, and letters from the offender to residents in the area where he hopes to settle (2003:223–4). Clearly these levels of notification severely impact upon the rights and freedoms of the offender although in many cases as we have seen, offender rights tend to lose out to those of the public to be protected. However, as Thomas notes, there is a due process issue in the allocation of a risk category and he cites the Min-nesota example of prisoners having the right to an attorney and if the risk is set at level 2 or 3, the right to be present and to have proceedings tape-recorded. This situation is somewhat in contrast to that in Britain, where the attendance of the offender at MAPP conferences has been the exception rather than the rule, although Mikulski (2004) does report an experiment with offend-ers being present. However, the most recent MAPP guidance (Home Office, 2005), strongly suggests that it is unlikely that offenders will routinely be present at MAPPs but they must be involved in the decisions and plans directed towards them.

Once the risk category is decided the notification process is underway and may well involve notification meetings. These include educative elements about the general risks posed by a range of sex offenders, discussions on vigilantism and the effects of driving offenders away before moving into spe-cific information about the offender. This process is regarded as taking the sting out of any hostile response and has no doubt contributed to the low levels of vigilante attacks in America. It is this type of approach to community notific-ation that leads experts such as Kemshall and Maguire (2003:113–19) to ask if the government cannot engage more imaginatively with communities over this issue. As already noted above, the government in the UK have been remarkably firm in resisting the notification pressure despite its apparent symmetry with many other populist agendas. Kemshall and Maguire cite a breakdown in trust between the public and government and its officials over the issue of managing sex offenders in the community. It is interesting to note that during a period in which governments have increasingly chosen to ignore experts (practitioners and academic) in developing its criminal justice policy (Savage and Nash 1994, Nash and Savage 2001, Garland 1996), in this one area it appears to cling to professional opinion. Senior police and probation managers have maintained that by opening up the sex offenders' register to the public, the offenders would go underground or missing and monitoring of them would become impossible. The high compliance rate with registration of 97% in the UK is frequently con-trasted with an American figure more than 10–40% lower. These figures would appear to support the British government's position, even if it does not exactly accord with the public mood.

Lovell's (2001) evaluation of community notification laws in the United States came to the conclusion that there was insufficient evidence to evaluate the many claims (both for and against) made on behalf of these measures. These included whether or not notification reduced stranger attacks; whether the laws actually empower parents; how if at all parents and children change their behaviour as a result of notification information; whether or not incidents of vigilantism increase; whether sex offenders do indeed go underground; whether the laws reduce reoffending; and the impact of financial and personnel costs. All of these questions need answers and many have been raised in respect of the notification debate in the UK. Clearly the notification debate needs to move away from the emotive to the empirical but the emotional hold of 'dealing with' sex offenders tends to displace support for rational evidence gathering.

An interesting take on some of these issues was explored by Elbogen, Patry, and Scalora (2003) who examined US laws in an attempt to discover whether there was an impact on sex offender treatment attitudes. Their findings revealed that many sex offenders did not understand the full implications of notifications and they believed that many might inadvertently violate the law through ignorance. They also discovered that a number of offenders perceived the notification laws to be unfair and were concerned as to the impact this might have on any treatment programmes. It was felt that public humiliation might engender anger and resistance or relapse. Equally many offenders felt shame at the release of their personal information and believed that this acted as a strong deterrent to future offending. Both Lovell (2001) and Elbogen, Patry, and Scalora (2003) raise important questions over the effectiveness of notification laws and call for extended research into this field—the type of research needed to inform debates in the UK.

The right to know and public protest— a local example

The issue of community notification was to be brought into sharp relief by the abduction and murder of eight-year-old Sarah Payne in July 2000. What was already a terrible case was made worse when it was revealed that the murderer, a man named Roy Whiting, was on the sex offenders' register and known to local MAPPA. It was further revealed that during an earlier sentence for sexual assault, Whiting had not completed any sex offender treatment programmes. It was incidents such as this that appeared to exaggerate the break in trust between society's appointed experts and the public (Kemshall and Maguire, 2003:102–3). The message was simple in that the public now wanted to protect themselves and to do this they needed to be notified about sex offenders in their communities. The fall-out from the murder of Sarah Payne is well documented in Silverman and Wilson (2002), most notably the outbreak of serious crowd disorder over several days in Paulsgrove, near Portsmouth. The trigger for the disturbances appears to have been a decision taken by the editor of the News of the World, Rebecca Wade, to name and shame a list of hundreds of paedophiles. However, Silverman and Wilson (2003) and Williams and Thompson (2004a and b), suggest that trouble may have been brewing on the Paulsgrove estate for some time before the News of the World named and shamed local resident paedophiles (or not as in some cases). Wade declared that the newspaper would continue to do this every week until the government acceded to its (and Sarah's parents) demands for community notification of sex offenders. The newspaper launched a 'For Sarah' campaign, and demanded a Sarah's Law, an equivalent to the federal Megan's Law in the United States, and indeed harsher measures. The results of a poll conducted by the newspaper, calling for responses to a range of extremely populist measures, were predictably overwhelmingly in favour. Over two thirds of respondents agreed that those convicted of offences against children should never be released from prison. If released, 76% demanded the right to know if a convicted sex offender was to be located in their neighbourhood and nearly 60% agreed with the newspaper that sex offenders should be publicly named. The poll also claimed that 82% of respondents supported increasing the penalty for non-compliance with registration requirements from six months to five years—a measure adopted in the Criminal Justice and Court Services Act 2000. Although full of emotive language such as 'perverts', the poll did have the support of over a million people for a Sarah's Law, a groundswell of opinion that the government would find difficult to ignore.

The disturbances at Paulsgrove resulted in attacks on the homes of suspected paedophiles and on people who were clearly not paedophiles. The levels of violence that broke out sporadically around the country confirmed the views of government ministers and senior criminal justice officials that full disclosure would have a detrimental effect on its efforts to protect the public. The received wisdom being that if sex offenders lost their anonymity they would move on or 'go underground', making the task of monitoring them much more difficult. ACPO, for example, saw disclosure as a direct threat to children's safety:

> I am saddened to see that they have ignored my advice and seen fit to publish without any evidence that by doing so children's safety will be enhanced. Their actions will, I believe, have the opposite effect and put children's lives at risk by driving sex offenders underground. Past evidence suggests that the publication of such information causes serious breaches of child protection. (ACPO press release, 23 July 2000)

As already noted, the British government were also opposed to notification and over two years later were still in that position, as expressed by then Home Secretary David Blunkett, 'We cannot open the sex offenders register to the vigilantes who do not understand the difference between paediatricians and paedophiles' (in Thomas, 2003:218). This incident referred to an attack on a doctor's home when local people confused the two terms. Implicit in this statement is a suggestion that the public cannot be trusted with this information, a reverse of the situation alluded to by Kemshall and Maguire (2003) that the public no longer trusted the experts. A case reported by The Los Angeles Times on 4 September 2005, indicates how public notification can go wrong. Three men, all registered and notified sex offenders, lived in one house in Bellingham, Washington. In August two of the men were killed by a man posing as an FBI agent, the third was at work at the time. Subsequent to the murders a man telephoned a local newspaper and said he would kill all registered level 3 offenders.

The government have, however, stood firm in their intention to resist public and media pressure to open up the register. The News of the World campaign ran for only a few weeks but continues to bubble beneath the surface. The government have made a minor concession in that, following a pilot period, they have enabled lay advisers to become members of MAPPA. It should be noted, however, that their attendance is at a strategic level rather than an involvement in the daily management of offenders in the community—it does not represent a local involvement with local cases.

Williams and Thompson (2004a and b) following a detailed ethnographic study on the Paulsgrove housing estate, come to different conclusions to many commentators on the 'riots' and the response of state agents to residents' concerns. They suggest that the residents had been aware of a paedophile on their estate (indeed a number of them) and had both dealt with it themselves (by warning children and monitoring) but also by requesting the housing department to move them and asking the police to help. The authors note that these requests predated the News of the World campaign by many months and that the 'outing' was not the explicit cause of the disturbances, more the frustration with authorities and their own embarrassment that something had not been done earlier. However, Williams and Thompson perhaps make a more telling point when they discuss the role of the community in relation to sex offender orders. Their view was that Burnett, one of the subjects of the News of World name and shame campaign, was the perfect material for a sex offender order. He met, they say, all the conditions used by the government in its exemplar of those suitable for the orders. The problem was, however, that it was the police or other authorities that needed to come to this decision, rather than the public (who had in any case notified the police of their concerns, thus meeting the criteria exactly). In many ways, Williams and Thompson (2004a and b) agree with Kemshall and Maguire (2003) that the authorities need to be more imaginative and creative in how they work with the public over the issues of high risk offenders. They suggest that the public can be trusted perhaps more than the officials appear to believe—Williams and Thompson (2004:203–4) suggest that there was an 'insatiable thirst for information' and that public education may be a way forward. The lessons from America would suggest that community notification, when attached to community education, could successfully lower the risk of vigilante activity.

It would, however, be wrong to assume that information about offenders in the community is not disclosed where appropriate. In many child protection cases, the regular and routine disclosure of information between agencies has generally been supported by the courts (Power, 2003:76–81). Moreover, disclosure by those agencies to members of the public have also been supported, notably in cases where parents of children have an overriding need to know to protect their children. A landmark case, *R v Chief Constable of North Wales ex p Thorpe and another* [1998] 3 All ER 310, did, however, see disclosure outside of the narrow child protection arena. In this case, the police disclosed information to the owner of a caravan park about a couple living there, revealing their identities and serious sex offending history (Power, 2003:85). The decision was held to be lawful because of a pressing social need to prevent crime, and this overrode the offender's right to privacy. However, despite this judgment, in her review of several cases, Power (2003:86) comes to a conclusion that:

> What is manifestly clear from this examination of the domestic law governing public authorities' powers to disclose sensitive information about sex offenders is that the courts are a long way from lending their support to American-style community notification, not least because of their increasing sensitivity to offenders' privacy rights.

As mentioned earlier in this chapter, the provisions governing the sex offenders' register have been strengthened more than once since implementation in 1997. The Criminal Justice and Court Services Act 2000, made several important changes. These included increasing the penalties for non-compliance to a potential five years in custody, reducing the time required to register from 14 days to 72 hours, and introducing police powers to photograph and fingerprint offenders. Further modifications in the Sexual Offences Act 2003 (SOA 2003) require offenders to update their details (including photographs) in person with the police on an annual basis, and this will include national insurance, driver's licence, and passport details, to increase tracking through cross-referral, especially as these details will now be held on the new national Violent and Sex Offender Register (VISOR), accessible by police and eventually all probation services. This new register will be more than the sum of local police-held registers and will include all information held on dangerous offenders enabling targeted searches to be made (for instance, age or occupation). Additional restrictions in the SOA included reducing the notification period when offenders are spending time away from their main residence from 14 days to 7 days.

Battening down the hatches

It should be clear by now that much of the constraining legislation of the past decade has been about closing gaps and loopholes as they have become public, usually arising from cases that have gained media notoriety. In each instance, what are invariably rare occurrences are blown up into a much wider threat to public safety. An example of such a case was the murder of two schoolgirls,

Holly Wells and Jessica Chapman, by their school caretaker Ian Huntley, in Soham during August 2003. The case raised serious issues over the employment of people potentially posing a risk to children, in this instance a person who had allegedly committed sexual offences against children but had not been convicted of a sexual offence by any court. Linked closely with this issue was concern over the way the police gather, record, and transmit its information. Upon Huntley's conviction for the two murders, the government announced an Inquiry under the chairmanship of Sir Michael Bichard. Of course, underpinning this debate would be that which threads itself throughout the dangerousness discussion, namely that of the offender's human rights versus the public's right to protection. The recommendations of the Bichard Report (discussed below) would also raise another issue of particular relevance to the police service, and that was how to assess dangerousness in those without a previous criminal history of such behaviour.

In his report published in June 2004, Bichard made 31 recommendations all of which have been accepted by the government, admitting that a 'vivid picture of the failures in our vetting system' had been painted. The government, in its progress report on Bichard indicated that 'All parties have been keen to ensure that no loopholes are left in new working structures and processes, and have recognized throughout the central task of protecting the public, and especially children' (again, notice the reference to 'no loopholes'). No one yet it seems has learned the lesson of not guaranteeing complete safety. One of the report's most important recommendations concerned the arrangements for the vetting of those working with children and vulnerable adults, described as representing 'systemic failure'. These arrangements centre on criminal records bureau disclosure at standard or enhanced level, backed by three separate lists operating under different legislation and employing different criteria. These lists are List 99 (under s. 142 of the Education Act 2002), the Protection of Children Act List and the Protection of Vulnerable Adults List. All are reactive, meaning that people are considered for banning after harming or placing at risk of harm a child or vulnerable adult. List 99 additionally includes professional misconduct.

The government's proposals are to simplify the process, to introduce a central scheme, and a single point of reference for people deemed unsuitable and therefore barred from working with children and vulnerable adults. Crucially, and with direct reference to the Soham case, expert judgements on unsuitability would be based not only on conviction and caution information, but also on 'soft' information that would include *allegations and suspicions*. This is a clear human rights issue and one that will undoubtedly tax the minds not only of lawyers but also of police officers. The result of information received and expert judgement would be a decision of being barred, not barred, or under consideration. A change to legislation will mean that all disclosures for work with children and vulnerable adults will be at enhanced level, which will include 'soft' information. The measures would include those who work primarily and directly with children; those in jobs that offer the opportunity for regular contact, such as child-line operators or chat room moderators or whose work places them in a position of trust with children, such as police officers or priests. The new scheme would apply to paid and voluntary workers, including private tutors, sports coaches, and so forth. The government called for responses to the issue of 'thresholds' for evidence and seriousness of offence, pointing out that high thresholds, relying on conviction data, would be quicker and cheaper. A low threshold would include soft data but would apply to many more people and would therefore be slower and more costly. The government's response pointed out that a high threshold would not have barred Ian Huntley from his position of school caretaker, as he did not have relevant previous convictions.

The real issue in the Huntley case was that he had faced a string of allegations over a number of years, for underage sexual intercourse and rape, but none had been taken forward by the police service in Humberside, either due to insufficiency of evidence or the unwillingness of victims to proceed with the matter. This is the type of soft information that the Bichard Report has now said must be made available for all potential employees in work with children and vulnerable adults. Humberside police claimed that they had removed this information from their computer to comply with the demands of the Data Protection Act 1998. The Information Commissioner, in evidence to the Inquiry, denied this interpretation and it seems that early on in the hearing many chief constables supported this view, in effect condemning their own colleague (The Guardian, 19 December 2003). However, a few months later, the Association of Chief Police Officers rounded on the Information Commissioner by claiming that directives from his department to clean up the information held on computers was putting children's lives at risk (The Telegraph, 25 February 2004).

Of course, the really tragic element among the many misjudgments in the Huntley case was that he did have a conviction on the police computer (the judge had ordered it) for burglary, but in another name. Although Huntley had informed them of his real name the cross-reference was not made. The Head of Holly and Jessica's college said that he would not have employed Huntley with a burglary conviction because security was a major part of the post. Aside from discussions about what type of information to store and pass on, there is clearly another around the quality of police work in inputting data in a timely and accurate manner. Interestingly in 2001 the government, in debates about the then newly formed Criminal Records Bureau (CRB), agreed that there were some quality concerns over police information processes but did not feel that they were very great (Grier and Thomas, 2001:459). However, in his interim report on progress towards his 31 recommendations in March 2005, Bichard noted that police inputting practice, '... has not improved significantly or in some respects at all' (The Independent, 15 March 2005). He called for failing forces to be named and shamed. The government's intention to facilitate the ability of courts to input data directly onto the police national computer should go some way to easing these problems by the proposed implementation date at the end of 2006.

As a result of the Soham case, there are unlikely to be substantial objections from many people over the government's plans to increase the amount of information held on individuals and subsequently made available to prospective employers. This is somewhat in contrast to the discussions at the time the CRB was created where it was felt by civil liberties groups, academics, and even a government task force, that the significant increase in the numbers of criminal records disclosures ran the risk of creating a newly excluded group in society, far greater in size than the group it was intended to protect (Grier and Thomas, 2001:465). Clearly concerns over human rights of offenders, social exclusion, and even the commodification of people's criminal records were to take a significant backward step following the tragic events in Soham. It was to trigger a huge change to policy and practice, a heavier workload for police and the CRB, and undoubtedly a series of contentious judgements taken over the soft information available and its significance. Assessing potential dangerousness in the unconvicted therefore raises its head again as society continues to rush towards demands for perfect safety.

Summary

This chapter has described a range of legislation and policy initiatives that have sought to improve the protection of the public from serious harm caused by potentially dangerous problems. There has been little in the way of evidence to suggest that the problems posed by these offenders has considerably worsened, but undoubtedly the public's perception of risk and danger has markedly increased and deepened.

This general feeling of fear and anxiety coalesced most notably around predatory paedophile sex offenders and was a phenomenon noticeable in many countries throughout the 1990s. Measures were introduced worldwide to lengthen sentences for these offenders and to limit their opportunities for release at the end of their lawful custody. Governments would increasingly look to mental health legislation to enable the continued detention of potentially dangerous offenders at the end of their sentence. If released, these offenders would face increasingly intrusive supervision and surveillance with a growing tendency towards modern information technology to track their movements. Registration schemes would not only enable police forces to keep track of sex offenders but by default, absence from the register would also emerge as a form of licence to practise in certain occupations. Media pressure and an increasingly vocal public demanding action, information, and protection have driven what has undoubtedly been a relentless policy agenda. Many governments have sought to plug each new loophole as it has arisen and, by so doing, have colluded with a media construction that paints each incident as a generalized threat to innocent and vulnerable members of the public. By acting in this way they constantly allude to a safer society in which risks are assessed and managed—yet by its very nature dangerousness resists these efforts. In general terms, however, it probably does not represent the degree of threat that these measures appear to be suggesting we all face. This policy response has, however, significantly impacted upon the way in which a range of agencies, not only those within the criminal justice sector, responds to dangerousness. This will now be discussed in the next chapter.

8

Working Together—Many Minds, One Voice?

Introduction

Multi-agency working is now regarded as the only effective way to protect the public from dangerous offenders. In the second half of this chapter the mechanism and process of multi-agency public protection panels (MAPPPs) will be explored. However, before doing so, an earlier example of multi-agency working will be considered. Multi-agency working has long marked child protection systems, and the recently established MAPPPs could undoubtedly learn from a similar set-up. In describing the embryonic public protection panels (Nash, 1999a), a suggestion was made that lessons could be learned from the problems experienced by child protection committees and, were this to happen, they might hit the ground running. However, the history of these committees suggests that the road to working together is not always a smooth one and 'system failure' has been a recurring problem identified in numerous public inquiries into child protection tragedies.

Such failures inevitably lead to demands to improve the system and further tighten the protocols determining working relationships. Sometimes though, it may be other issues that contribute to these tragedies and it is important to remember that any system is only as good as its constituent parts. It would not be surprising to find that several different agencies might struggle to work effectively together, at least in the early days of any collaboration. Differing organizational aims, different recruitment and training patterns, and perhaps most importantly different cultures will inevitably lead to communication problems. This chapter will briefly review some of the history of child protection work in the UK and then focus on issues that have arisen from a number of public inquiries. Issues identified of relevance to MAPPPs will be identified and carried forward into the next section.

A problem shared . . . ?

Child protection and MAPPP systems are not really any different in their aims. Both aim to protect people from serious harm by managing perceived risk and, if they fail, death or serious sexual assault could well be the outcome. However, in many respects, child protection remains in the private or domestic sphere in the public consciousness and this appears to lessen its perceived potential dangerousness. Nonetheless, the basic construction of the child protection system is very similar to multi-agency public protection arrangements (MAPPA) and, with its longer history, could well offer valuable insights arising from previous failures and tragedies. In simple terms, if a child protection case reaches the stage of a public inquiry, then something has gone very badly wrong. It hardly needs an inquiry to confirm the usual findings, namely human error or system failure. This has been a feature of child protection inquiries for a number of years, yet each new one appears to reflect little progress from that which preceded it. What then can be deduced for the recently established and much more public MAPPP system?

What is absolutely fundamental to both child protection and MAPPA work is how difficult the actual work is. Professionals involved in this work have to deal with at times unspeakable horrors and, despite their professional training, will often find themselves ill equipped to deal with what most people would run a mile from. Yet they also know that the minute anything goes wrong in this difficult and demanding field of practice, public condemnation will be total, and indeed may be reciprocated from within their own organization. Living within a blame culture is never easy and could lead to very defensive practice (eg an overestimate of all risk) or the choice not to see what is before your eyes (eg ignoring the warning signs). When human error is given as the cause of human tragedy in child protection (as many as 75% of 43 reports published between 1973 and 1994 (Munro, 2005)), then this human failing has to be placed within the tremendously stressful environment in which practitioners, often held in low professional and public esteem, are operating. It should also be remembered at this point that hindsight is much easier than making decisions in real time, and that what Woods (1996, in Munro, 2005) describes as 'local rationality' (seeing things as they appeared at the time rather than with hindsight) is much more appropriate. In some senses there is a need to ask very basic questions about so-called 'human error'. For example, is the worker adequately trained and adequately resourced? Is their workload not so high as to deny them opportunities to think, reflect, and analyse? Are they able to cope with the feelings generated by extremely difficult and unpleasant cases? Assuming that social workers, police, and probation officers are not super human, are we allowing them to be human in what they do?

Munro (2005) compares the failings of child protection systems with other disasters, such as in engineering. For example, she refers to airline disasters that have led to demands for far greater automation of the process in order to limit the scope for human error. But then subsequent inquiries have revealed that when the systems themselves go wrong, the humans involved are not sufficiently skilled to put the systems right again—they have become deskilled by automation. Now, child protection, or indeed MAPPP processes are not the same as flying an aircraft, but there are parallels in the amount of procedural and protocol growth that has considerably limited the opportunity for professional (human) judgement. Munro cites Hood et al (2000) when they describe 'protocolization', a process that sees more and more formal procedures to guide practice to create a 'correct' way to deal with a case (Munro, 2005:541). The erosion of professional discretion, ostensibly in order to improve the effectiveness of 'the system', may not therefore be as helpful as it is intended to be. Parton (2004:87) concurs with Munro when he argues that the Climbié Inquiry reaffirmed the need for professional discretion. He compares the differences between inquiries rather than seeking similarities and, on professional discretion, makes this point:

> ... whereas the introduction of child protection procedures over the previous 30 years could be seen to have had the explicit intention of trying to circumscribe professional discretion, particularly on the part of social workers, the Climbié Inquiry sees it as important that they should exercise their discretion and, in particular have the ability and authority to challenge other professionals, such as paediatricians, as appropriate and act with a degree of independence.

Professional judgement and skills are therefore regarded as essential attributes to successful public protection systems. In improving systems it is incumbent upon managers to ensure that improvements apply equally to the staff that are, in essence, the system. Reder and Duncan (2004) argue that fundamental improvements are needed in the sophistication and skills acquisition of front line staff, alongside significant improvements to working conditions. They make the point that 'training must impart to all professionals a mindset to think through an assessment and appreciate the psychology of communication' (2004:112). This point is absolutely reaffirmed in the Climbié Inquiry when there are numerous references to front line staff needing to do the basic things well. More importantly perhaps is the reference to inaction in the face of concrete evidence. This may result from the type of fears and anxieties arising from this work and generating a form of paralysis. It might also arise from staff taking shortcuts by believing people, by not being sceptical of all that is said to them and by not being suspicious enough. As summarized by Lord Laming in the Climbié Inquiry:

> ...staff doing this work need a combination of professional skills and personal qualities, not least of which are persistence and courage. Adults who deliberately exploit the vulnerability of children can behave in devious and menacing ways. They will often go to great lengths to hide their activities from those concerned for the wellbeing of the child'. (Laming, 2003:3, in Cooper, 2005)

It is easy to transpose this view of good child protection practice into work with potentially dangerous adults within the MAPPP system. Workers in this area of practice have to both see and hear what is before them, as Cooper (2005) argues, workers must remain connected to the case, even if it is of such magnitude that their natural instinct is to disconnect and seek an easier solution. They say that '... the evidence of the Inquiry Report is that workers involved in Victoria's case both saw and did not see what was in front of their eyes'. It is at this point that public protection work goes to the heart of people's feelings and workers may seek to minimize the pain they feel from their involvement. However, Cooper argues that this is the opposite of what is needed, in fact workers need to remain in touch with their feelings if child protection is to improve, 'If we can stay connected to the feelings which such vulnerability and such cruelty arouse in us, then we have some hope of better protecting children in the future. If we cannot, then I fear that all the policies and procedures we can invent may not carry us much further than we are now' (Cooper, 2005:9). With one in three social workers reporting their own abuse or neglect as a child (King, 2003), it is not surprising that some may have difficulty coping with the work.

There is then a balance to be struck between the needs and training of staff and systems refinement. The latter may be as much about the quality of supervision offered to front line staff, as it is the development of new guidelines and protocols. Yet there has been a history of blame in numerous public inquiries leading to the possible removal of staff and further managerial refinement. A number of professionals in a range of settings have reported feeling useless, guilty, and worthless following a death, feelings often exacerbated by their own colleagues response (King, 2003:263). It has to be assumed that workers will try to give of their best if they operate from a level playing field. That has to mean that the systems are designed to support them rather than constrain and hinder. Johnson and Petrie (2004) argue that it is important to empower front line staff and again make reference to sectors outside of social work. They say that in an aircraft carrier the lowest ranked person on the ship can suspend a flight if they feel there is a need—compare this with some of the bureaucratic hurdles to decision-making in the public sector. They say that in the private sector, a strong safety culture is partly engendered by the continual updating and training of staff. They believe that if it takes an Inquiry to reveal organizational pressure points then the target for change should be the manager rather than front line staff. It is evident from numerous inquiries that the response to the aircraft disasters referred to earlier are similarly reflected in child protection, namely attempt to minimize human error by developing and refining systems with more managers and greater audit. Yet the obvious message here is that more and better-trained front line staff are needed, with time to think, evaluate, and do their job properly rather than more managerial oversight. As Johnson and Petrie (2004) note, '. . . a preoccupation with procedures has been evident in many reports . . . despite little evidence that problems in the cases lay with the policies and procedures themselves.'

By further developing systems of accountability and audit, Parton (2004) argues that trust and morale are undermined. He suggests that rather than resolving problems, managerialism has simply changed their nature, with advances in audit, information technology, and procedural guidance all seen as contributing to increasing complexity for front line staff. Munro (2005:534) very neatly summarizes the outcome of numerous child protection inquiries when she says:

> The cumulative results of 30 years of child abuse inquiries have created the traditional solutions: psychological pressure to avoid mistakes, increasingly detailed procedures and guidelines to strengthen managerial control and ensure compliance, and a steady erosion of the scope for individual professional judgement through the use of standardised protocols, assessment frameworks and decision-making aids.

She further argues, alongside many others, that the basic things need to be done well and that front line staff need assistance to do this rather than compliance control. The basics of good interviewing, listening, communicating, and recording are not necessarily enhanced by greater audit, but they do require human beings who are expert in their field and have the opportunity to develop and refine their expertise. Just as in a range of public sector organizations, performance indicators may be designed around what is measurable (process) rather than outcome quality (how good was an interview, rather than did one occur). No one wants to have a serious incident on their conscience and blame is therefore rife; blame lower grade staff, other agencies, or the system. Munro (2005) argues that some agencies will engage in 'blame prevention engineering' by trying to transfer or dissipate the blame onto others.

Undoubtedly, human error does lie at the heart of many child abuse tragedies, but in acknowledging that, it is important to recognize that the system in which front line staff operate will contribute to their problems. High workloads and inadequate supervision have already been mentioned and these have to be considered alongside constant changes to the bureaucracy that appear to make the actual task of protection more difficult. Inquiries inevitably lead to managerial or system change, but these changes need to be considered in terms of their ability to enhance practice rather than accountability and audit. As Johnson and Petrie note, accountability, which is about ensuring that something is well managed, often becomes transformed into audit, which may not always refer to the performance of an organization (2004:183). They also describe 'restructuring fatigue' in one London borough social services department, indicating that it was dangerous and damaging to service users. They believe that these changes disrupt communication pathways and dissipate expert knowledge.

Breaking down the barriers

However, it is important to remember that child protection, like public protection systems, is not concerned with one agency, but with several working together. Lying at the heart of effective multi-agency working is good communication and trust, and it is clear that both of these qualities have not always been present. Of course, multi-agency working is based not only upon the sharing of information, but also the variety of professional expertise brought to bear upon the problem. In describing what he terms 'inter-agency' working, Crawford (1999) refers to the potential loss of difference as agencies increasingly work to common agendas. This may be less of a problem in child protection but, as indicated in the following section, may be an issue for MAPPPs. Parton (2004) argues that sharing should concern not just factual information but also respective expertise. This particular expertise needs to be mutually understood and worked with in relation to individual cases—attempting to eliminate the potential for organizational conflict should not dilute it. Yet there is considerable evidence of multi-agency conflict. Brandon, Dodsworth, and Rumball (2005) noted that professional insularity was a common barrier to rigorous assessment, epitomized by widespread reluctance to trust other groups. What was described as a baseline of mistrust prevented appropriate sharing and analysis of clues that would and should alarm child protection professionals (2005:171). Furthermore, in studying several serious case reviews, they also noted that on many occasions, probation staff were either absent or reluctant participants in child protection meetings. They argued that they were in possession of information, particularly about those people with long histories of violence, but were reluctant to share this either during the investigation or child protection conference. This may reflect the view mentioned at the start of this chapter, that child protection has not been a high profile part of the brief of the probation service. It would be hoped that a more recent focus on this issue (see Probation Circular 32/2005) will change this perspective.

Child protection is not then dissimilar to public protection. Both processes operate within a prevailing, dominating context of risk and increasingly this risk is seen as something to be managed. Ferguson (1997) argues that risk has become central to everyday life and, following Foucault, that the traditional role of the social worker has shifted from family caseworker to seeking out and working with dangerous parents and children at high risk. Legalism has moved childcare from welfare to protection with social work becoming an intrusive, investigative practice focused on policing and normalization of the child rearing practices of marginalized people. For some people, the modernization of the protection system itself leads to its own hazards, what Beck describes as 'modernization hazards' (Ferguson, 1997:225). By 'colonizing the future' new risks are uncovered which themselves need to be managed. Parton (2004) says this process in turn leads to new uncertainties and complexities, which undermines trust in professionals, impacting upon morale and confidence. This overriding obsession with risk is unfortunately too closely linked with a view that it can be predicted and subsequently managed. Johnson and Petrie (2004) suggest that the Jasmine Beckford report accepted that it was possible and indeed incumbent on social workers to identify and predict child abuse before it happened. However, as a report from the National Children's Home (NCH) indicated, 'There is, as yet, no test that can differentiate the child at risk who will come to serious harm from the child in virtually identical circumstances who won't.' If those already considered to be vulnerable are difficult to predict then protecting those in situations without a history must be nigh on impossible. The same NCH report indicated that most of the children involved in serious review cases had not previously come to the notice of any professional agency. In this context therefore it may not be so surprising that defensive practice, ie an overestimation of risk is carried out. However, there is a danger that this defensiveness becomes so dominant that no decision is taken at all. Playing safe will not eliminate risk and may increase the possibility of an adverse outcome (Johnson and Petrie, 2004:185). Yet, in the light of the enormity of those decisions, and the real fear of getting it wrong, it is possible that people will be tempted by inaction.

It is evident that, with each new tragedy, the child protection system is becoming more professionalized and modernized. However, with this process, the whole system of child protection is further removed from the community. A similar direction can be detected in the public protection systems where the government has continually resisted a broader involvement of the public in the process. Brandon and Dodsworth argue that 'expertise is not the exclusive domain of professionals and should encompass children and their families as experts on their own lives' (2005:161). They suggest that child protection is marked by adults not listening to children—a clear echo with some of the domestic violence cases mentioned in Chapter 4. In a chilling indictment, they describe how children relentlessly described their own abuse as a routine life activity but that this information was conspicuous by its absence from case files. This growing sense of the 'correctness' of professional practice could in part explain why professionals are reluctant to alter first impressions about a family, even when faced with subsequent information that contradicts those impressions. To summarize this section it is enlightening to read the comments of Stevenson (in Parton, 2004), in her minority report on the Maria Colwell report in 1974:

> There are few, if any, situations of the kind in which Maria was involved which are 'black and white' ... there are very few situations in which choices are clear cut and outcomes predictable. Unhappiness in children is something that the ordinary humane person finds very difficult to bear and, in consequence of this, frequently seeks simple solutions or suggests that they are unattainable.

It appears as if three decades or more has not moved the debate on very much at all. There are clear issues for public protection in what has just been said, and it is to these issues that this chapter will now turn.

Learning lessons—the MAPPA

Bringing together a range of different agencies to work effectively on joined-up tasks is not an easy business. The history of multi-agency child protection is littered with cultural and policy differences—even though the intended outcome would be the readily agreed task of protecting vulnerable children. The issue is how to go about this task in a manner that will enhance protection, and that will enable a full sharing of information and agreement over who will do what and when. When more than one agency has involvement, or worse, responsibility, the danger is of either duplication of task or the task not being done at all. Absolute clarity over roles and responsibilities is therefore essential and this in part explains the increased use of agreements, service guidelines, and protocols. At the same time, it is important to retain the heart of multi-agency working, which is to bring a range of experiences and diverse knowledge to bear upon a common problem. In other words, in the push to ensure effective joined-up working, that diversity of experience should not be compromised or diluted. Research into multi-agency child protection indicates some of the problems that can result. For example, in examining the role of the police service in child protection arrangements, researchers found a number of common issues. These included, an uneasy alliance with social workers (Fielding and Conroy, 1994), marked by power differentials (Thomas, 1988), role conflict (Blagg and Stubbs, 1988), and different recruitment patterns (Cornick, 1988). Although this research pre-dates a major impetus towards joined-up working, it would not be surprising to find some of these issues continuing to greater or lesser degree. It is against this background that police and probation collaboration on potentially dangerous offenders must be set.

It would be unsurprising to find many of these issues reprised, not least due to the historic cultural differences between the two organizations. Although both services are part of the criminal justice 'system', their relationship perhaps belied that sense of organized purpose portrayed by the use of that word. For those unfamiliar with the two organizations, for long periods a crude division marked their relationship. The common view was that the police caught criminals (the good guys) and the probation service 'got them off' (the bad guys)—although this very crude stereotype belies a great deal of collaboration between the two over many years. However, it is fair to say that these were not two sides easily brought together. Yet for effective public protection these two agencies needed to harmonize their working relationship far better than history revealed it to be, not least because it would form the bedrock of a much more complex set of multi-agency arrangements emerging at the beginning of the twenty-first century.

Recent history, however, suggested this not to be an easy task and early reviews by Her Majesty's Inspectorate of Probation (HMIP, 1995) indicated some work to be done in joining-up public protection services. By the end of the decade though, partly as a result of massive political pressure and the demands of new legislation, considerable progress had been made and the basis of the MAPPA had been well and truly established. The remainder of this chapter will briefly review that history before considering the development of MAPPA in detail.

Cultural differences

In understanding how two organizations were moved closer, it is important to determine how far apart they started. In many respects, both police and probation officers have always shared a common goal of preventing crime, but it was the means of achieving that goal which differentiated them. For most of its history the probation service had been committed to a social work ethos (see, for example, McWilliams 1985, 1986, and 1992) and its training, much of it shared with social workers, led to a professional social work qualification which many in the police might once have regarded as putting them in the 'do-gooder' camp. Intervention with offenders was essentially based around theories of social casework, itself strongly influenced by psychoanalytic theory and practice. A common and fundamental assumption was that (most) people could change if given the right opportunities, and that second chances should be offered. Probation work was essentially private, office-based and somewhat shrouded in mystery as the service sought to increase its professional credibility. There was limited working with other agencies and, overall, relationships with police were confined to an exchange of information over previous convictions and the nature and circumstances of instant offences. Although ostensibly charged with a major crime prevention role, in many ways the police historically worked towards this objective by detecting offenders and passing them through the criminal justice system rather than working within the community with other agencies. This would change though as the emergence of community safety shifted the agendas of a number of criminal justice and other agencies, and a number of major policy documents and criminal justice Acts sought to integrate law and order agencies ever more closely.

The 1995 HMIP report, 'Dealing with Dangerous People: the Probation Service and Public Protection', perhaps represents the most significant evolutionary point in the public protection process—even though so much time has passed since then. The report was a first in examining the work of probation staff in dealing with dangerous people and, perhaps as important, it made what had been a regular but somewhat quiet aspect of practice much more public. It coincided with, or was prompted by, what was reported as 'a time of considerable public concern at the level of violence in our society' (1995:9). A Home Office Minister, Baroness Blatch, was moved to comment on the report's publication that public protection had become the first priority of the proba-tion service. Such a comment was to signify a clear shift in the offender-focused ethic described above and was to contribute to a much more public role for pro-bation officers. Although this shift was to provide a degree of pay-off in terms of additional resources, it would also make the service much more vulnerable to criticism if cases went seriously wrong. The potential for public approba-tion fuelled the moves towards greater collaboration with the police, a service enjoying relatively high levels of public support and with a longer pedigree of 'protection' (at least in the mind of the public). Over the next few years the police service would also be given additional responsibilities for certain poten-tially dangerous offenders and they in turn would look to others for advice and support—thus common ground between the police and probation services was being established, as much by necessity as policy.

The report found many areas of good practice and quality but enough con-cerns for the Chief Inspector to comment that parts 'would make uncomfortable reading'. Key recommendations indicated:

- that court reports should deal more adequately with public protection issues, including what for many years had been almost a taboo subject, the proposal of a custodial sentence if necessary to protect the public;
- that risk assessment should be carried out in every case—the beginnings of a huge bureaucratic demand on staff;
- that staff must record and respond to indicators of dangerous behaviour;
- that the identification of dangerousness must be a corporate responsibility;
- national standards must be complied with; and
- that information must flow more freely between agencies and organizations who deal with potentially dangerous offenders.

Several key principles were established in the report, such as the probation ser-vice at all times needing to work to reduce the risk of serious harm, that proba-tion officers had a personal responsibility in relation to public protection and, crucially for the service, that confidentiality needed to take second place to pub-lic protection. In establishing what had become a frequent crime prevention message, public protection could not be seen as the responsibility of one agency. There would be a need for joint policies and procedures, regular liaison, open exchange of information, and a case conference style of information sharing to be established.

Protocols were suggested as a means of ensuring that information would be exchanged but trust was also regarded as essential. The 1995 report had noted that police and probation services had witnessed a 'growing appreciation on both sides that they were in the same business' (1995:55). Confidentiality was, however, highlighted as a serious possible impediment to progress, with chief officers in particular very concerned with this issue (1995:57). This should not be surprising when the cultural differences identified above are considered. Around the country embryonic public protection panels began to model themselves on these key principles, with that developed in West Yorkshire offered as best practice at the time. Within a few years it was evident that this new movement had gained significant momentum.

A further report from HMIP in 1998, 'Exercising Constant Vigilance: The Role of the Probation Service in Protecting the Public from Sex Offenders', was to indicate how the public protection agenda had progressed. Even the title reflected a much more up-front protective role for probation staff, and was one that sent out a clear message to the public about the service's priorities. Whereas in 1995 the HMIP report had expressed concerns over the reluctance of probation staff to work closely with the police, by 1998 it could report that 'collaboration was extensive and increasing' (1998:10). It carried on, '. . . close and effective working relationships existed between the probation and police services in many areas. The exchange of sensitive information on individual offenders had led to the development of jointly undertaken strategies to reduce the risk posed by dangerous offenders.' A number of key areas of good practice were identified which demonstrated that issues raised in 1995 were being tackled:

- protection of the public was unambiguously identified as a central purpose for probation practice;
- there was strong focus on the distress and harm suffered by victims;
- a high level of vigilance had been observed by Inspectors;
- a high priority had been allocated to the supervision of sex offenders.

Thus, by the time of the legislation formally establishing multi-agency public protection arrangements (Criminal Justice and Court Services Act 2000), it was apparent that a good deal of progress had already been made. The issue would then become how effective the new measures were to prove and how necessary they were when the actual scale of the dangerousness problem was considered.

Naturally enough there would be concerns concerning the ability of the two key public protection players, police and probation services, to work effectively together. Yet it should be noted that a form of collaboration had existed in various areas for a number of years and in some places more formalized systems had begun to emerge (Nash, 1999a). The issue would therefore be, could the two services overcome their differences sufficiently to be effective partners and, if so, what effect would such a partnership have on working practices and indeed values of the two organizations. Early research (Nash, 1999a, Maguire et al, 2000, Kemshall and Maguire, 2001) indicated a patchy response. It was clear that many of the initial fears over the sharing of information would prove to be unfounded. It might have been expected that probation staff would have been the less willing to share on the grounds that it was their traditional role that was most likely to change. Public protection suggested a management of a case determined by the risk they posed, with that management more likely to concern coercive and intrusive measures than welfare interventions. Yet from an early stage the research indicated that the probation service was willing to share its information, at times to the surprise of the police. For example, slightly pre-dating the development of the public protection agenda, Sampson and Smith (1992:108) reported police as saying, 'We shouldn't have liaison with probation; it would make their job impossible ... Clients wouldn't be able to trust a probation officer who had dealings with the police.' In research also pre-dating the legislative requirements for multi-agency public protection arrangements, the author found a shift in what might be termed the traditional police and probation positions. The following are comments from that research which demonstrate how a shift in culture was evident even before legislation required it (Nash, 1999a:108):

'If we have information that can assist the police then I believe we are duty bound to share it' (Probation staff).

'There was no noticeable holding back in the conferences that I attended. I was extremely impressed by the openness on both sides. I think that we gave them a vast amount of information about how we saw things and I think they were very open with us, both about attitudes and about accessing information ...' (Probation).

'There was a sharing of information which I was heartened by. I was a little concerned that maybe the probation service wouldn't release their intelligence but they did—in fact, quite the contrary, they opened up' (Police service).

'The traditional (police) view is still out there—we catch them and you nurse them ... we're more upfront about public protection now and that has helped.'

It appeared therefore that cultural differences, which were still obviously manifest, would not, however, cause major problems with the embryonic public protection arrangements. The concern with managing high risk and dangerous offenders would override individual agency concerns and facilitate an emerging, unified discourse. Kemshall and Maguire (2001) reported similar findings from their research. For example, in discussing MAPP they noted, '... all reflected an overriding concern with issues of risk, control and exclusion, while references to transformative aims such as "rehabilitation" or "resettlement" were rarely heard, even among probation officers' (2001:248). They further noted a change in probation culture, citing an example that sex offenders were increasingly seen as an intractable problem. It was observed that the probation staff were willing to pass on almost any information to the police and ideological disagreements were rarely in evidence. Kemshall and Maguire further make an extremely interesting observation on the nature of the panels' working relationships, a comment that says much about whether multi-agency working is a combination of differing perspectives, or the development of a homogeneous voice:

> The panel itself operates as more than the sum of its constituent parts, a supra or hybrid institution with its own protocols, rules and procedures. Knowledge production and processing are the key activities of panel work, and the key objective of panel work is the constitution and reproduction of networks of surveillance. (Kemshall and Maguire, 2003:192)

Similar sentiments were expressed by two practitioners, Bryan and Doyle (2003:192), who spoke very enthusiastically of their national perspective on the growth in MAPPA. They noted that, '. . . one of the exciting aspects of public protection development has been the growth in trust and cooperation between the police and probation services, adding enormous value to the way each agency is able to conduct its statutory responsibilities.' They also note that much of the work of MAPPA is some distance from the welfare origins of the probation service and imply that this had to be shifted for public protection arrangements to be effective. They also believe that this process had been ongoing for a number of years. Perhaps the CJA 1991 is the best reference point for the beginnings of this change. A cultural shift was therefore almost certainly underway before the development of public protection arrangements. Strong political pressure was undoubtedly a major factor for the police and probation services to work more closely together. For probation, organizational survival in a period that was increasingly less forgiving towards offenders was a necessity and public protection offered a future. For the police service, under less threat but still needing to perform, new responsibilities would increase the need for partners. Police and probation services would therefore quite quickly become bedfellows in this specific area of practice at least. In observing that, '. . . the balance has shifted, and continues to shift, in favour of greater public protection' (Bryan and Doyle, 2003:194), the authors note that MAPPPs now operate in a totally unrealistic set of expectations. They argue that society has become risk averse and demands the right to be protected from all risks. Because the public would demand harsher sentencing or even the death penalty, the MAPPPs have to operate in such a way as to demonstrate that they can be effective managers of risk. They quote the much over-used phrase that, 'we must ensure that this never happens again', whereas everyone knows that it undoubtedly will and in almost all cases could not have been prevented. The authors quote Kemshall (2003) and her extremely sensible and realistic summary of what effective risk management needs to be about:

> The desirable outcome of MAPPA is effective risk management. However, this should not be understood as 'zero risk' as this position can never be achieved

... Risk management should be understood as harm reduction either through the reduction of the likelihood of a risk occurring or the reduction of its impact should it occur.' (in Bryan and Doyle, 2003:195)

In her excellently titled 'Joined-up worrying', Lieb (2003:212) makes similar points about the context in which MAPPA operate, suggesting that they set very ambitious targets but often with vague descriptions of actions. As she observes, the list of dangerous people is ever growing but the resources to deal with them are not matching that growth—something will have to give.

Embedded collaboration?

From the early and often informal collaboration between police and probation services, multi-agency public protection has evolved into a complex and sophisticated series of relationships. Nearly 200 pages of official guidance detail the workings of what, although often regarded as some sort of entity, is basically a set of administrative arrangements. The sum of these arrangements does, however, make the powers available to MAPPA extremely powerful and coercive with a potentially significant impact upon offender rights, which in turn needs to be balanced with the right of the public to be protected. The remainder of this chapter will consider these arrangements.

MAPPA can essentially be regarded as a formal requirement that certain agencies cooperate to better protect the public. The underlying assumption is that both the assessment and management of certain risks will be more effective when a variety of perspectives, experience, and powers are brought to bear on individual cases. Because of the unique nature of dangerous behaviour it will not be possible to apply plans in a formulaic manner, although the process itself may increasingly follow a series of set procedures. Within these parameters there must remain scope for individual agency expertise to shine through, a point noted in the guidance (Home Office, 2004:72) when it refers to the need for 'co-operation rather than conglomeration' (also see Crawford, 1982). The official guidance draws significantly upon the extensive body of work by Hazel Kemshall and at the front of the document cites four principles developed by her:

• Defensible decisions
• Rigorous risk assessment
• The delivery of risk management plans which match the identified public need
• The evaluation of performance to improve delivery (Kemshall, 2003 in Home Office, 2004:5).

MAPPA have then very important duties, including deciding who is to be included (outside of formally governed inclusion such as registered sex offenders); the level of risk they pose; developing the plan to manage that risk;

monitoring the plan (and the risk); and finally deciding when people might be suitable to leave their arrangements or to remain included even if formal requirements are over. The MAPPA guidance identifies four core functions of the arrangements and these are: the identification of the MAPPA offender; the sharing of relevant information among the agencies involved in the assessment of risk; the assessment of the risk of serious harm; and the management of that risk. On paper these functions may not appear to be too taxing but each masks a number of difficulties and uncertainties that in turn demand more detailed guidelines. For example, the identification of offenders requires both fixed rules and the exercise of professional judgement.

Thus all sex offenders registered under the Sex Offenders Act 1997 will be included in MAPPA, as will a range of qualifying violent and other sexual offenders and a third category of 'other' offenders. The middle category includes offenders sentenced to more than 12 months' imprisonment, as well as those detained under hospital or guardianship orders and also those convicted of certain offences against children. The 'other' category is generally taken to mean offenders convicted of an offence indicating a potential to cause harm, but will not automatically be triggered by a disposal of the court. The professional judgement of the lead responsible agency will be vital for this group of offenders. The 'other' category may also be used to keep certain offenders within MAPPA at the end of their formal period if the panels assess a continuing risk of serious harm.

The assessment of risk is therefore a crucial MAPPA function. It can significantly infringe an offender's human rights or put the public at increased risk of harm. The mechanisms of risk assessment have been discussed earlier, but at the present time it is clear that the Offender Assessment System (OASys or EOASys in electronic form), will be the common and determining tool. What the process will do is to place the offender at one of four levels of potential risk, which are:

- Low—no current, significant current indicator
- Medium—identifiable indicators of risk of harm. The offender has the potential to cause harm but this is unlikely unless there is a significant change in circumstances
- High—identifiable indicators of risk of harm, which could happen at any time
- Very high—an imminent risk of harm with a serious impact, more likely than not to happen

Naturally the level of risk will determine the scale of the intervention and who will be involved in that intervention. A fundamental principle of MAPPA is that the risk management plan should operate at the lowest appropriate level. Once again this decision cannot be governed by strict rules, as the nature of risk is extremely dynamic and therefore risk assessment needs to be an ongoing process. Having established four categories of risk, the guidance has created three levels of risk management. The lowest, level 1, indicates that the risk can be managed by a single agency and will include low and some medium risk cases.

The guidance envisages that the majority of offenders will fall into this group. The next group, level 2, will include those for whom local inter-agency oversight is needed as the risk is slightly greater or more complex. Offenders may move to level 2 from the lowest or the higher level as circumstances change. The highest, level 3, is reserved essentially for those described as 'the critical few'. These offenders will be those presenting high to very high risks that can only be managed by close cooperation of agencies at a senior level. It is also perhaps worthy of note that, in a document that endlessly describes risk, another factor may trigger level 3 oversight. This is where the case is of exceptional media or public interest and requires the highest level to ensure the maintenance of public confidence in the criminal justice system. Here then, risk is secondary to other, essentially political, factors. Such a scenario is redolent of the decisions not to release the life sentence prisoner Myra Hindley, despite repeated parole board assessments that she did not present a significant risk.

As indicated above, the police and probation services were the early core members of MAPPS and were the responsible authorities. However, the Criminal Justice Act 2003 s. 325(1) makes the Prison Service part of the MAPPA 'Responsible Authority', recognizing the crucial role it has in working with high risk offenders. Their key function is to be addressing the potential discontinuity in risk management plans that can occur when offenders go into or leave custody. A range of other agencies can, and in many instances might be expected to be, regular members of MAPPA. These would include:

- Social services departments
- Housing authorities/housing providers
- Youth offending teams
- The relevant health authority, including mental health trusts
- Probation victim contact teams or appropriate victim agencies

Such a variety of experience, perspectives, and powers should ensure the most effective protection available, although even the official MAPPA guidance recognizes that it, 'cannot provide absolute protection', even though this is what people increasingly want. In acknowledging that 32% of first time murderers and 36% of serious sex offenders have no previous convictions (Home Office, 2004:5), the document infers that the public need to understand what risk is really about and that a good deal of serious harm is committed by people with no previous history at all, or a history quite different to what might be expected of a potentially dangerous individual. Figures such as this do of course suggest that a wide variety of information about offenders, and even non-offenders, would contribute to a more informed picture. It is evident that profiling potential danger does require as much information as possible about how people behave in a range of social situations. All contributions should be valued and any information stored, even if it has no immediate use.

Summary: Reacting to incidents—a Scottish example

It is often the case that a serious incident triggers a significant change in public protection arrangements. The murder of a child by a registered sex offender in Scotland during 2004 led to recommendations to incorporate the English system, with additional requirements, north of the border. A review by Professor Irving published in July 2005 for the Scottish Executive, can therefore serve as a useful case study to understand how complex systems can be developed out of rare triggering incidents.

The report emphasized the rapid growth in cases on the sex offenders' register, up from 1,931 in June 2003 to 2,809 two years later (an increase of 50%). In his introduction, Irving also noted that there had been a massive increase in those not required to register statutorily but now being so if they gave significant concern. These cases now outnumbered 'official' register cases.

As in England, the use of VISOR will be a major feature of sex offender management and will become a shared facility between police and social work services (the Scottish equivalent of the probation service). However, VISOR is envisaged as more than a simple database with suggestions that it can become a case management tool, a workload planning system, a contact record, a monitoring device, and a work diary. It is easy to see how such a powerful IT system could quickly facilitate the development of joined-up working between agencies. It will undoubtedly feed a thirst for information and the report suggests that the following should routinely be included:

- Household details—partner, other occupants, children
- Main associates
- Leisure activities
- Employment
- Vehicle and/or access thereto
- Telephone numbers
- Computers—Internet access
- Bank account details
- Passport details
- Provision of DNA sample

Details held on VISOR will therefore represent a significant incursion into people's personal details and circumstances. Again, the issue of real risk is important here. If everyone eligible to be on the register has this much information held on him or her then it becomes a huge exercise. If numbers continue to increase at the rate suggested at the beginning of this section, then it has to be questioned how long such a burgeoning industry could be managed effectively.

Irving's report supported the stance taken south of the border that widespread community notification was not likely to improve community safety. It also made the very important point that even in the most accurate of risk assessments a percentage of mistakes are inevitable. The report also identified the growth in the use of OASys in England and Wales, noting its use of clinical data and its more dynamic nature than standardized clinical judgements. Significantly, owing to the major police role in sex offender assessment, where there is a conflict between OASys and RM2000, the latter will take precedence.

Another significant step taken in Scotland is over the issue of information sharing, said to have been a problem since MAPPA were established. The General Medical Council has now endorsed the formal notification of sex offenders being discharged from hospital to the police, a situation that had been particularly problematic. Further developments have since seen the establishment of a National Concordat in May 2005, and signed up to be a range of key agencies. Also in 2005 a Risk Management Authority has been established as a national centre of excellence in risk assessment and management of sex offenders. It is clear that, as in England and Wales, MAPPA and associated processes are increasingly moving onto a national scale, and, as with concerns in those countries, it is important that the growth of bureaucracy does not leave behind it the vital local knowledge of serious offenders.

In all, Irving's report contains 36 recommendations, some of which are already familiar in England and Wales. What it does, however, is point to a further extension of state powers in relation to certain offenders. For example, it is recommended that police officers be permitted to enter, without permission, the homes of registered offenders to undertake a risk assessment. Irving acknowledged that, in trying to deal with current and future issues he might upset human rights supporters, an argument he dismissed summarily, 'Finally, I accept that some of my recommendations may be open to challenge in terms of Human Rights legislation. I believe, however, that the community right to safety and an individual's right to protection outweigh such considerations.' It is clear that this argument will remain predominant in the immediate future. Yet, even though reports such as this acknowledge that perfect safety cannot be achieved, it remains the case that these incidents spark fundamental reforms to policy and practice. How far this can go, and if it can make people any safer, really is the crucial question.

9

Managing Risk in the Community

Introduction

This is something of a 'doing' chapter. It can occasionally be useful to set academic reading alongside a consideration of real-life cases and issues. This chapter offers a number of case vignettes, which raise a number of issues around risk assessment and risk management. They also cause the reader to think between the cases in terms of relative risks and consider how scarce resources might be deployed when more than one of these offenders is due for release from custody at similar times.

There are a number of issues to consider in the real life management of potentially dangerous offenders. Obviously, the most important has to be the estimation of future harm by the offender—in other words will they do it again? The assessment of future harm will inevitably fall between art and science and perhaps always needs to be a combination of both. However, as already noted in Chapter 5, the quest for increasing certainty is never-ending and this will inevitably lead to over- or underestimation of risk, depending upon issues such as the current climate of fear and the level of resource available at any one time. In other words, media and public interest in a particular case might alter the way in which agencies attempt to manage it in the community. Notoriety may not equate with real risk but this message may fall on deaf public ears, forcing agencies to concentrate resources in one area where there may be greater need elsewhere. The real pressure on criminal justice professionals is to bring certainty into a very uncertain process—they are expected to be able to predict human behaviour in people who may not have previously acted in very predictable ways. Worse perhaps they are expected to guarantee public safety, an absolutely impossible aspiration.

The media's fascination with the spectacular can of course lead to resources being deployed towards media friendly targets—at the expense of more mundane but perhaps equally risky and much more common cases. Public protection professionals therefore do not operate in isolation or in a vacuum, and of course it might be argued that nor should they. However, what is already a difficult job should not be made more difficult by media hype. What may appear to be obvious warning signs may be so obvious that they can be more easily managed, whereas less obvious triggers need careful investigation and management—if the professionals involved are given the time and space to do so. This chapter will consider four cases, three loosely based upon real people, and one taken from a live case at the time of writing in October 2005 (a 'worked' example taken from the MAPPA guidance, 2004 is presented in Annex 5). Readers are asked to consider the assessment and management of the risk posed by these offenders. How serious, likely, and imminent is the risk of serious harm? What factors inform this judgement? Are there any matters in the case that might reduce risk? What should a risk management plan contain? Who should be the lead agency and which others should be involved? Is there a case for community or victim notification? What about offender rights? Most of these issues have been dealt with throughout this book so now is an opportunity to think through the application of a risk management plan to a real-life situation.

Four examples of cases

Case 1

Present circumstances

John is 24-years old and about to be released from prison. He was sentenced to 42 months in custody for indecent assault on two boys, aged 9 and 10. The circumstances of the case were that he encouraged the two boys to masturbate him in his local model boat clubhouse. He has served one half of his sentence and will be on licence to a probation officer up to the two-thirds part of his sentence—a licence of 7 months. He will be liable to recall until the end of the sentence.

Social background

John is an only child. He was raised in a dysfunctional household and witnessed a good deal of physical violence from his father to his mother. He was not physically or sexually abused himself but was regarded as a solitary and introverted individual. He performed moderately well at school and passed four GCSE examinations. He has had numerous jobs in shops and local factories and, at the time of his imprisonment, had been working in a large DIY superstore for two years. He has had two girlfriends with both relationships of only short duration. He has not given any reasons for the ending of these relationships. His main leisure activity is model boat building and sailing. He has been a member of a local club for a number of years and was often known to share his knowledge with younger club members. He will not be welcome back at the club on release from prison. Prior to sentence he had been living at his mother's home. She had divorced her first husband and remarried four years ago. The new relationship continues to be marked by very loud rows but not, as yet, any violence. John is not welcome back at his mother's home and is not able to return to his job at the DIY superstore, although his employment record there was very good.

Criminal history

At the age of 15, John was cautioned for indecently exposing himself to two 11-year-old boys at a local park. At 17 he was fined for theft from a shop and at 20 he was placed on probation for two years. His offence on this occasion was assault occasioning actual bodily harm on a ten-year-old boy. The circumstances of this case were that John and three young boys were playing a game after sailing his boats. The game was to try to smack each other as softly as possible, with John providing sweets for the winner. However, he smacked one child very hard on his bottom. He in turn told his parents and the police were called. Whilst on probation John kept all his appointments and attended a short sex offenders group. His order was discharged early on the grounds of good progress after 11 months. Three months later he was convicted of the indecent assaults.

Custodial history

He was a model prisoner in terms of behaviour. He received few visits whilst inside. He worked in the prison stores section, performing a similar role to that he held in the community. He did not attend a sex offender group on the grounds that he had already completed one in the community. He has no plans for his release other than a desire to return to his home area. He was known to associate with a few of the other sex offenders on his wing and had been subject to the customary prisoner abuse accorded to those with his background.

Managing the risk

Three months prior to John's release, an assessment of the risk he presents will need to be undertaken, as well as arranging the plans for his accommodation and potential employment. The assessment of risk will determine much of what follows in this case. It is not possible to predict what one group of professionals might determine for John's release arrangements—it is not an exact science nor does it fit a common template. Probation officers in one area may see things differently to colleagues in another. As noted above, recent local history, any concerns of the community regarding this or other similar cases, and the availability of appropriate accommodation are just a few of the factors that might influence the nature of this man's release. What follows is a discussion of a number of issues raised by John's case with reference to those covered throughout this book. The reader is asked to consider these issues as if she/he is a member of a criminal justice agency deciding upon the level of risk and consequent risk management plan.

John will be required to register his details on the sex offender register upon his release. The police service will need to undertake an initial assessment of the risk he poses. Without actually completing risk assessment forms, let us consider the issues posed firstly by his criminal history. The latest offence offers a number of indicators. He encouraged two boys to masturbate him and did ejaculate in front of them. The boys had known him for some while, as they were members of his model boat club. He had befriended them, helped them with their own model boats and let them work his more powerful model at the local lake. He told them that racing the boats made him excited and, in the club, showed them his erect penis to demonstrate what he meant. He asked to see their penises and stroked them on a number of occasions to give them the 'racing' excitement. On the day in question he said he was excited by the day's racing but wanted to be more excited and asked the boys to rub his penis, in return he offered to give them one of his older boats. They did so and he gave them the boat. However, in investigating where this had come from, their parents discovered the truth and called the police. John was therefore attracted to young boys and gained his sexual excitement from seeing their bodies and having them touch his penis. He had quite deliberately befriended them with a view to gaining their confidence to sexually abuse them. He was prepared to bribe them and abuse his position of trust as an experienced member of the boat club.

This offence cannot therefore be explained as a 'one off' or as a reaction to tempta-tion or provocation. It was planned and deliberate with the offender knowing that this is how he got his sexual satisfaction. If the last offence is considered alongside his previous offending history it may be that the risk he poses could be considered great-er. There are a number of offence-related factors in his background that might lead to further concern. His incidents of indecent exposure take on a more worrying turn when they appear as a part of a more general offending picture according to Scott (1977). The work of Hanson and Thornton (2000) referred to in Chapter 2 shows John to press a number of alarm buttons. Readers will recall that these authors suggested that moderate predictive accuracy could be obtained by using a limited number of factors. These included the following; the offender never having been married (John was single), stranger victims (John did know the boys but had made it his business to do so—they were unrelated to him), male victims (all of John's victims had been male, including those to whom he exposed himself), being under the age of 25 (John is now 24), non-contact sex offences (indecent exposure), and any violent offences (spanking).

Aside from his criminal record, are there other factors in his background that might offer more clues to the risk he poses? According to the work of Silovsky and Nice (2002), witnessing domestic violence was a factor in 58% of their cases involving chil-dren who went on to sexually abuse. John's childhood was marked by his father's abuse of his mother and, even in her present relationship, loud rows had continued. Carpen-tier, Proulx, and Lussier (2005) also noted social isolation as another factor and John was described as solitary and introverted as a child. He had clearly attempted to have relationships with women but these had failed for reasons he would not reveal. He was now clearly showing that his sexual interest lay in young boys. What level of risk do you think is posed by John? Is he very high risk? Is the harm that may result from his behaviour very serious? What do we understand by this term? Is there a risk of serious physical harm, or death, or very serious sexual assault? Of course we cannot know the answer to these questions. However, the picture outlined above does suggest a significantly more than evens chance that John will reoffend in similar fashion in the future. How far into the future that incident might arise is, of course, difficult to know, and much might depend upon John's response to his sex offender programme and the risk management plan put in place for him. This will, of course, involve a consideration of whether or not he should be subject of some form of sex offender notification.

It would appear to be more than reasonable to assume that John poses a substantial risk of reoffending, although he may respond to his treatment programme. However, the risk he poses does need managing and part of that process would include discussion of who should be informed of his whereabouts and of course any restriction on his movements. His preferred target population is clearly young boys. Is it possible to protect all young boys from him? He could be banned from children's play areas but this is of course difficult to police or monitor. He could of course be tagged and/or curfewed, indicating to the authorities when he moves to certain areas or is out at times he shouldn't be. The problem is of course that young children get to all sorts of places, especially perhaps those that are not traditionally associated with children by adults. Many children will prefer a shopping area to a park for example. Many children truant and may therefore be at risk even during supposedly safe periods when they should be in school. It is then difficult to think of where John could be allowed to go, and at what times, that would not present an opportunity to meet children. Similar issues arise in terms of notifying the community, or parts of it, of his details. The boat club, his major leisure interest, has already banned him. Does this stop him visiting another area and becoming involved? Should all model boat clubs in a given geographical radius be informed of John, a photograph, details of his convictions, and present address etc? Where would this stop? Should schools be informed about him and local youth clubs? What about leisure centres and security staff in shopping precincts?

The real difficulty with this case is that John presents a very general risk to a sizeable section of society. How can this possibly be managed? The simple truth is that all risk cannot be eliminated, but the public continue to believe that it can. John will need to know that he is considered to pose a risk and that people know this. He will need to know that his movements are being monitored and that some people have been advised of his release. He needs to believe that there are external controls in place but at the same time practitioners such as probation officers need to continue trying to build the internal controls. We also need to remember that sex offenders traditionally reveal quite long periods between offences, so John could quite easily get through his seven-month licence period without further cause for alarm—but what happens at the end of that period?

The multi-agency approach to this case will require consideration of John's accommodation needs. It is likely that probation approved premises would be considered, or some other form of hostel or sheltered accommodation. Clearly there is a need for oversight of John's whereabouts, and risks to children in his home would be lowered if he were to be housed in a hostel. As ever with potential dangerousness perhaps the real risk lies at the end of the supervision period or at the end of any hostel accommodation. One of the real problems with risk management systems is that they are invariably finite but the risk itself may well continue, unless a good deal of professional work and support has managed to change the offender's behaviour, as well as managing his risk within the confines of a plan.

Managing the risks posed by serious sex offenders in the community is therefore a very difficult task. As can be seen from this example, not only are there a number of interrelated dynamic risk factors demanding constant reassessment of the case, but also a community response to sex offenders that puts professionals, who would prefer to operate in private, very much in the public spotlight. Violent offending on the other hand appears to excite less public concern. This may be something to do with the likely victims of violence who may present as less deserving than those who fall victim to predatory sex offenders. The following example of a violent offender perhaps poses a number of different issues to case one, readers might like to consider how they would approach this case in terms of its risk assessment and management.

....

Case 2

Present circumstances

Carl is aged 31 and is to be considered for release on parole. He had been sentenced to 12 years in prison (reduced on appeal to nine years) for attempted murder and carrying a firearm. The circumstances of the crime involved a revenge attack by seven individuals on a known drug dealer who had, over time, intimidated many of the group. All seven attacked the victim and severely beat him. Carl carried a sawn-off shotgun and shot the victim causing considerable, but not life-threatening injuries. He handed himself into the police on the day following the attack. The victim was registered with local police as a potentially dangerous offender. Carl claimed self-defence throughout his trial.

Previous offences

Carl has a long history of offending, mostly of theft and related to supporting his drug habit. He has only one previous offence of violence that resulted in a small fine and compensation payment. On previous bouts of supervision (probation or licence) he has a poor compliance record. He has breached all of his community orders over the years.

Drug habit

He is addicted to heroin and, although he has completed drug related programmes during his sentence, he has also had a number of prison adjudications concerning his possession of drugs whilst in custody. It should be anticipated that he would return to drug use and a drug culture upon release. His victim, now fully recovered, remains a key player in the local drug scene. It is known that there remains continuing antagonism between the two and their shared involvement in drugs is likely to bring them together at some point in the future, if Carl returns to his home area.

Accommodation

Carl does not have any specific release plans. He has refused to live in a hostel even if this decision jeopardizes his request for parole. He would prefer to return to his home town (a small provincial town with a sizeable drug problem).

Tendency for violence?

His probation officer does not regard him as a particularly violent individual. She believes him to be vulnerable and easily influenced. However, he did concede that his violent act had done much to enhance his status with his peers, a feeling he very much enjoyed. The case generated a good deal of local media interest.

What are the issues generated by this case? One of the first questions would of course be the decision whether or not to support Carl's parole application. What might be the advantages of releasing him early and how are these balanced by the possibility of further crimes? If parole is not to be supported (and is not granted) what conditions might be requested in his release plan? Should Carl be allowed to return to his home town or be required to live elsewhere and keep out of the town boundaries? If this decision were reached how would it be policed or monitored? Victims have a right to be consulted before the release of offenders committing violent and sexual offences. Would you believe it appropriate to consult Carl's victim—himself a registered dangerous offender? If he is not consulted or advised about Carl's rights, what does this mean for his human rights? Elsewhere in this book it has been argued that the public's right to protection has been elevated (in general) above the offender's rights to privacy, so would you inform the victim or not? Would you wish to include a condition of residence in this offender's licence?

The preceding paragraph poses more questions than it provides answers. It is possible that the reason for this is that the issues are not so clear cut in this case compared with case number one because the potential victims may be regarded as 'less deserving'. Elsewhere in this text, reference has been made to a hierarchy of victims and it is likely that many people will regard the potential victim in this case as not so deserving as others. Many might regard this case as one involving two offenders and should not cause too much public protection interest. However, no matter the thoughts about victim and offender, this case remains one with a high potential for future serious violence. If considered alongside number one, which would you consider to be the most serious and why? Which do you think is most likely to result in further serious harm and how quickly? If both of these cases came before a MAPP meeting on the same day it may be that resources would have to be balanced between them—how would you decide that issue? Imminence of further serious offending might be the telling factor here. We have already considered evidence that many sex offenders have long periods between reconvictions (acknowledging that in many cases this may simply be due to their ability to avoid detection). Yet it is likely that in strictly statistical terms the violent offender is more likely to recidivate earlier than the sex offender. Add to that the likelihood of the victim seeking revenge and the continued involvement of both in the illegal drug market, and it might be argued that this case has a much higher risk of renewed serious crime than the closely monitored sex offender—who may simply be biding his time.

....

Case 3

The third case will be presented in briefer format but will hopefully encourage the reader to think about combinations of criminal behaviour. Take two separate scenarios and consider the risks posed by these offenders. The first scenario is of a young, 19-year-old man who had no previous convictions whatsoever. He lived with his parents and did not have a job. He was a bright young man who had achieved good A level results. He was very musical and hoped to go on to study the subject at university. He was waiting a year before making his applications and had been involved in short term casual jobs for pocket money. His elder brother was also a gifted musician and was a conductor for a well-regarded regional orchestra. This man's crime was that, at 7:45 am one summer's morning, he left his house, walked across a field and strangled to death a woman who was walking her dog. He did not know her although, it later emerged, she always took the same route and he had observed her over a number of weeks. There was no sexual element to the attack at all. His rationale for the murder was that he just felt like strangling a woman.

The second scenario also involved a first time offender. His crime was breaking into the mortuary in his hometown and subsequently having sex with two corpses. The corpses in question were of an 84-year-old woman and a 75-year-old man. If you compare these two offences which do you consider to be the more serious? In many respects this is almost a non-question. At the time of these offences necrophilia was not a crime (now a crime under the Sexual Offences Act 2003 and punishable by a maximum of two years' imprisonment on indictment). This man's offence was therefore one of breaking and entering. The other crime is of a seemingly 'straightforward' murder.

Now put these two cases together and you arrive at the one offender in question. One man committed these two acts. We have already considered how offence perception may be heavily influenced by victim status and any additional (unnecessary) activity perpetrated by the offender at the time (additional violence, sexual interference etc). Thus, although murder will undoubtedly engender feelings of revulsion and horror, there will be graded responses according to the nature and circumstances of the crime. The setting of differential life sentence tariffs has illustrated this point for a number of years. However, the crime involving necrophiliac acts may engender greater revulsion because of its very nature. It may be that many people can envisage themselves taking a person's life in certain circumstances. But how many could envisage having sexual intercourse with a corpse? To what extent do our feelings of revulsion influence our perception of crime seriousness? The issue for this offender might come in his consideration for release from his life sentence at some stage in the future. Should his necrophiliac activity lengthen the tariff he is set? What could be the rationale in this if they are unrelated activities? Regardless of the tariff set, once he reaches it should the two matters be brought together to argue that this man presents an additional risk over and above so-called 'ordinary' or 'standard' murderers? Can this be regarded as an aggravating factor in his more substantive crime of murder even if it is unrelated? Does it cast doubt upon his ability to resettle safely back into the community—and why? Determining offence seriousness, a crucial factor in deciding upon future risk and therefore potential dangerousness, is then a far from easy task.

Case 4

The final case illustrates the changing nature of sexual offending as determined by modern technology. Chapter 3 briefly discussed Internet pornography as an emerging form of criminal behaviour that should cause increasing concern. Developments in technology, for example, the increasingly small scale of cameras available to ordinary customers, also plays a part in changing patterns of sexual crime. A case reported in the Portsmouth News (28 October 2005) reveals the nature of a newer form of crime. The headline ran, 'Peep-hole pervert is facing jail term' and described the case of a 54-year-old man who set up miniature cameras in women's toilets, in his place of work, in disabled toilets in a large department store, and at a railway station. A search of his home revealed more than 50 CD-Roms full of images of women in toilets. The defendant was also found to have drilled a peephole in the ceiling of women's toilets. He had also taken a photograph up a woman's skirt using his mobile phone and had also exposed himself to a woman passenger on a train. The judge, in adjourning the case for reports, remanded him in custody and warned that he faced a custodial sentence. The police were planning to apply for an anti-social behaviour order (ASBO) in respect of the offender, which would prohibit him from entering any women's or unisex toilets in England and Wales and from owning any camera or surveillance equipment, including mobile phones that can take a photograph. Aside from the difficulty of policing and enforcing the terms of this ASBO (if granted), there is a real issue about the future risk posed by this offender. He was described in court by the police as an 'habitual offender'. The maximum penalty for the offence of voyeurism is two years' imprisonment on indictment (the same as for indecent exposure).

Where does this individual sit on the scale of future risk? Does the degree of planning in his offending (and expense with several thousands of pounds worth of equipment) aggravate the seriousness of his crimes? He has not, as yet, actually touched any individual, but has invaded the privacy of hundreds if not thousands of women and children. Does this type of offending, when added to his crime of indecent exposure, add to his risk (Scott, 1977 certainly regards this offence as potentially serious when in combination with other crimes)? An issue is also whether or not the activities he has been involved in until now will be enough for his sexual gratification or whether he is likely to become more involved with a personal form of offending.

A case such as this poses real problems for risk management. There is a diffused range of risk, which in effect includes any women using public toilets. Similarly his chosen means of offending, making use of widely available technology, implies a ready supply of his offending tools. It is not possible to prevent him doing this and certainly, in the absence of any other information, he would appear to pose a serious and imminent risk of further reoffending—the issue might be how seriously his actions are viewed.

Summary—Risk management as a real activity

These four cases demonstrate how complicated the assessment and management of risk can be. Even if agreement can be reached on the seriousness of the harm posed, questions about probability and imminence will be important. Some of the more subjective views in risk management will not be ironed out by an actuarial approach and issues about victim status and deservedness will be important. As the numbers of those subject to MAPP arrangements continues to grow issues will become sharper around the deployment of resources. Offender rights will continue to be balanced against those of the public to be protected but it may be that certain sections of the community are regarded as more deserving recipients of that protection. However, if decisions about degrees of risk and need to be protected are made, then professionals need to be absolutely clear about what has determined that decision. Clearly, seriousness and imminence of serious harm should be the deciding factor and measures should be deployed to manage and if possible reduce that risk. Greater certainty about known potential victims, specific victim typologies, and offenders manoeuvring their life to increase access to their chosen and preferred victims are all essential pieces of information.

These four cases have all been unique and distinctly different. They all require a detailed examination of circumstances, motivation, and attitudes. It is clear that if seriousness were measured by maximum penalties then two of these cases are towards the lower end. Yet, in terms of public revulsion they would move quickly to the top of the list. This may be an argument for actuarial assessment in that the clinical interviewer's subjective attitudes can be removed. Yet, the very uniqueness of these crimes militates against a generalized, aggregated approach. A holistic approach to risk may reveal far riskier situations than that perhaps indicated by the presenting information.

Those involved in everyday risk assessment decisions will of course have access to considerable amounts of information from a variety of agency sources. They may have the results of treatment programmes and they may be able to access actuarial data on offence types. Yet, risk is unique and individual. Its proper assessment, however, stands to be clouded by all-inclusive, offence-generated risk classifications. This process is continuing to expand and it is of concern that real risk of harm will be missed. Practitioners cannot also divorce themselves from their immediate environment, be it public opinion or media reporting of certain cases which go on to shape the agenda. Sentencing decisions in particular, often taken out of context, can do much to shape attitudes. At the same time they can also demonstrate how perceptions of real danger appear to be skewed at times, as said throughout this book, towards certain stereotypes.

On 2 November 2005, the Portsmouth News reported the case of a man being sentenced to four years' imprisonment for causing grievous bodily harm to his neighbour. This may not be regarded as a particularly light or severe sentence and the word 'neighbour' may indicate that this is another domestic case and, in many respects, it was. However, that should not diminish the seriousness or potential dangerousness of behaviour. The reported facts of the case were that the offender visited his neighbour to argue over the neighbour's dog fouling in his garden. A fight ensued and the offender left. However, he later returned (possibly with others) and attacked the victim with a tenon saw (he was a carpenter). In the attack, the victim lost a thumb, had all the tendons in his wrist severed, and was in the process of being scalped by the offender when neighbours called the police. Now, in the absence of all the details it is not possible to comment on the appropriateness of a four-year sentence for this crime, although readers will undoubtedly have a view. The issue is perhaps that there are features to this case that might just tip it over into a much more serious category. One significant point is that the offender chose to return to the scene after the first altercation—he clearly felt that there was unfinished business. He may or may not have returned with others, thus securing his chances of a successful fight. However, and perhaps most significantly, he chose to take a weapon with him and to use it. Not only did he just use it though, he inflicted a huge amount of pain and suffering and clearly went way 'over the top' in what he needed to do to achieve his retribution. This man would tick a number of the potentially dangerous boxes—but will he be considered a potentially dangerous offender (PDO) upon his release?

10

Dangerous Offender Versus the People—What Hope for Offender Rights?

Introduction

At the beginning of the twenty-first century it has become decidedly unfashionable to promote the cause of offender rights. A reasonably long (at least professional) tradition of seeing many offenders as victims themselves has largely dissipated. Most 'ordinary' or everyday offenders are viewed as people who have made a conscious choice to offend. As such they deserve their punishment if caught and dealt with by the criminal justice process. Offenders are regarded increasingly as people who have chosen to live outside of the rules and therefore have forfeited the chance to be treated as everyone else and to enjoy the same rights. The more serious the crime the more they stand to lose for longer periods. It is, in the present climate, more difficult to earn society's forgiveness and be allowed back as a full member of the community. When the offence in question is at the very serious end of the spectrum not only are these rules amplified, but also additional factors kick in, such as the possibility of punishment for future crimes or even punishment for no crime at all. There is a direct correlation between alleged high risk of harm or potential dangerousness and the loss of offender rights. This approach appears to reflect the public mood, especially in the UK and the USA. Politicians appear anxious to appease the tabloid press and sign up to increasingly repressive measures, often without a real examination of the actual evidence and it seems with little thought to the wider ramifications for a 'rights culture'. This chapter will explore the rights issue in relation to potential dangerousness and consider the effect on those professionals working within the public protection field.

Fear, loathing, and rights

Throughout this book, and in almost any style of publication anywhere, it is suggested that offenders who pose a risk of serious harm, or those labelled as potentially dangerous, elicit little if any public or official sympathy. This is unsurprising. These people are not only likely to have committed very serious crimes in the past, but have also been assessed as likely to do so again. Thus not only is there a strong sense of retribution in the way they are dealt with by the courts, but also feelings of fear and revulsion among members of the community. Such emotions are unlikely to encourage a defence of the rights of these offenders, especially when they are weighed against the right of the public, notably the vulnerable public, to be protected. Yet, if the retributive element is removed for a moment, the loss of rights is essentially predicated upon a view that the offender might offend again, in a serious manner, sometime in the future. It is not so much punishment for the crime that is at issue, but additional punishment for the possibility of its recurrence. As already noted elsewhere in this book, this is a very 'iffy' judgement on which to base a loss of rights.

This chapter will consider some of the arguments concerning offender rights in general, and dangerous offender rights in particular. The central issue here is at what point does an offender lose their right to be treated the same as others or indeed other offenders, and how great and likely should the risk be to trip that loss of offender rights? The difficulties of risk assessment and prediction means that judgements about future behaviour are far from certain, yet the loss of rights could be total and very enduring. There are certainly questions to be asked here about what it means to live within a democracy. Added to this complicated cocktail is the issue of blame, with practitioners not only concerned to avoid 'getting it wrong', but also avoiding being 'seen' as having got it wrong—the personal and the public.

The issue of offender rights interfaces with assessment and prediction of serious harm at all stages of the criminal justice process. Again, this may be a largely uncontentious issue in those cases where there is clear evidence of very serious offending. For example, a very severe sentence may be regarded by many as proportionate to the harm done by the offender, and therefore completely justified. However, when that severe sentence is based not upon the severity of the instant offence, but on predictions of future serious harm, the waters become much more muddied. Indefinite detention may occur where no crime has been committed. Here the disposition is entirely related to future risk rather than present harms. In deciding upon the nature of custody (eg maximum security, mental health facility), the length of incarceration, the decision to release and the nature of that release experience, risk of future harm will be a crucially determining factor. At each of these stages, offenders stand to lose some of their civil rights, and potentially find their human rights compromised as well but, at the same time, the public will expect their right to protection to be upheld. It is then a balancing act and its resolution perhaps says much about the state of a country's attitudes to its offenders.

An ethical dilemma?

Issues of risk and dangerousness touch on a number of ethical dilemmas, but the most salient is likely to be that of disregarding the notion of proportionality in punishment, a process started in its modern phase by the Criminal Justice Act 1991 (CJA 1991). Proportionality is seen as fundamental to balancing inequities of power between the state and the offender when punishment is given for a crime. Punishment should reflect the severity of the crime, precluding punishment being imposed for reasons other than the instant offence (which of course may be aggravated or mitigated by a range of other factors, although these should, on the whole, be offence related). We know, of course, that this principle comes under periodic threat. For example, 'persistent' offenders have been variously subject to extended sentences or increased sentences throughout the twentieth century. Examples include the Prevention of Crime Act 1908, which allowed for the post-sentence detention of habitual offenders for between 5 and 10 years. This measure was abolished in 1948 by the Criminal Justice Act, which introduced a single preventative sentence of 5–14 years. Once again, this measure was abolished in 1967 because it was felt not to target dangerous offenders but petty, persistent recidivists. By this period life sentences were beginning to gain in popularity. In 1973 the Powers of the Criminal Courts Act introduced extended sentences aimed at repeat dangerous offenders, but this too was abolished in 1991.

The CJA 1991, as we have seen, enabled a departure from proportionality in certain sexual and violent offences if the offender was deemed to present a risk of future serious harm to the public. The Act also followed the earlier 'persistence' trend in the case of burglary and drug offences by imposing mandatory minimum penalties for certain repeat offenders. It is at this juncture that dilemmas might occur for those involved in assisting the courts in the disposition of these cases. For the additional sentence element in the CJA 1991 the court needed to be persuaded that the offender before them constituted an ongoing risk of serious harm, that he was in effect *potentially dangerous*. Psychiatric, psychological and to a lesser extent, probation service opinion, would help determine this finding. In other words, agencies traditionally not associated with being punitive (although for all this might be contested), were now actively involved in determining the imposition of additional punishment for people who might, or equally might not, offend in a serious way in the future. Aside from the dubious accuracy of risk prediction methods already discussed, this process is beginning to push agencies in a different direction, one that could reposition them in the public mind. This chapter will explore the issue of offender rights and the changing role of agencies in respect of those rights. A barrage of new measures since 1991 have brought this issue into even sharper relief for those involved in the criminal justice process. The issues are perhaps most sharp for the medical profession, but similar issues also arise for probation staff and increasingly, others involved in the burgeoning public protection family.

Helping whom?—The case of the medical profession

There has long been debate in medical circles concerning the efficacy of their involvement in decisions that appear not to reflect the health and welfare of the patient, but the wider interests of an undefined public. The most obvious cases here would concern the imposition of punishment, or additional punishment on offenders, where that decision has at least in part rested upon a psychiatric diagnosis. The problem of course is that when that 'diagnosis' is one that leads to a label of dangerousness, it remains highly contentious and questions are raised about loss of liberty, rights, or even life based upon such a prediction. For many psychiatrists the debate goes to the heart of medical ethics and the Hippocratic oath, which enjoins doctors to 'first do no harm'. The World Medical Association Declaration of Tokyo in 1975 put more flesh on these ethical bones. It was declared that doctors should '. . . not countenance, condone or participate in the practice . . . of cruel, inhuman or degrading procedures whatever the offence of which the victim is suspected, accused or guilty' (White, 2002:97). The same author does, however, acknowledge the dilemmas for a government that wishes to protect citizens from preventable harm or death, whilst respecting individual rights to human and civil liberties.

Parallels are frequently drawn, as a source of justification, between potential harm from offenders and harms from communicable diseases. The Public Health (Control of Diseases) Act 1984 permits several public authorities to detain non-criminals who have major communicable diseases in the interests of public protection. Although this example offers a useful comparison, it does suffer from one major difference. Here the 'offender' actually has a disease; in potential dangerousness it remains just that, a potential or possibility. Would we lock up thousands of people because they *might* contract smallpox? There was an excellent example during the BSE crisis when thousands of healthy cattle were slaughtered because they *might* become infected, many farming experts were convinced this was an 'over-the-top' measure. However, the restoration of consumer confidence was adjudged very important. Public confidence in the criminal justice process over dangerous offenders can be viewed in a similar light and is another example of governments seen to be acting, even if many of the actions appear not to be justified.

The slaughter of healthy animals is a useful parallel for considering the detention of innocent people, or more accurately, those not convicted of an instant offence. Involvement in the sentencing of offenders to longer than desert punishments, or even of those who have not committed a crime, should sit uncomfortably with medical and criminal justice professionals. It is explained and excused by the greater good, with the balance coming down in favour of the majority. The suffering of the few, even if unwarranted, is justified by the protection of the many. Essentially, medical staff and others are placed in this position by the shifting positions of governments on proportionality, and their seeming willingness to react to groups of undesirables. The Unanimous Constitutional Court of South Africa summarized the position very well in a 2001 judgment, 'The concept of proportionality goes to the heart of the inquiry as to whether punishment is cruel, inhuman or degrading, particularly where, as here, it is almost exclusively the length of time for which a offender is sentenced that is in issue' (*S v Dodo* 2001 (3) SA 382 (CC) 303 *per* Ackerman J, in van Zyl Smit and Ashworth (2004:541). Many citizens in South Africa will have long memories of what it is like to be imprisoned for years on 'suspicion' or for being members of unacceptable political groupings.

It is this attention to the 'cruel and unusual' aspect of punishment that has, it appeared, softened in many jurisdictions around the world. In Canada, van Zyl Smit and Ashworth (2004:549) report that longer, preventive sentences would not be cruel and unusual if they were meant to protect the public. Janus and Prentky (2003:2) report waves of litigation in mid-1990s America challenging the constitutional basis of the new protective agenda—without success. Indeed, the British Medical Journal in 2003 reported that the US Supreme Court had upheld a ruling that officials in the state of Arkansas had the right to force a convicted murderer to take drug treatment to make him sane enough to be executed (18 October 2003, 327–9).

No doubt, somewhere in this decision, the involvement of a medical practitioner would have been required. It is just such situations that leads Appelbaum (1990) cited in Verdum-Jones (2000:78) to say that, 'psychiatrists operating in the forensic capacity are outside of a medical role ... the application of that expertise in this context does not amount to the practice of psychiatry in any ethically meaningful sense of the term.' Verdum-Jones believes such practitioners are acting as advocates of justice rather than as practitioners of medicine. There is therefore a duality, or tension, between the ethical duties as physicians towards individual patients and legal duties to the state in terms of the administration of criminal justice. The debate goes to the heart of our perceptions of what a 'justice' system is founded upon, a point remarked upon with some passion by Hudson (2003—see below). This debate quite simply hinges on why society punishes people and the extent of that punishment. They are punished for wrongdoing in terms of the criminal law (or at least that should generally be the basis) and, at least in recent democratic jurisdictions, are punished in proportion to the seriousness of their crime. Duff and Garland (1994:239) summarize the position very well, '... it is wrong, in principle, to punish offenders for their predicted future conduct: they should be punished for what they have done, not in respect of what they will or might do. We should treat individuals (unless they are insane) as moral agents who can choose whether or not to desist from future crimes.'

Of course, although many traditional libertarians might agree with this statement, it has become a deeply unfashionable position. The scenario is now much more that certain people should not even be given the opportunity to make such a decision and preventive measures should be taken. This position is neatly summarized by Morris (1994) when he talks of a 'pre-emptive strike', a position taken from warfare strategy and designed to give first advantage to the attacker. Utilizing this justification, potentially dangerous offenders can be 'taken out' before they do any harm. In other words, those regarded as potentially danger-ous are not to be given the status of free moral agents and will be denied an opportunity to offend again, and equally denied an opportunity to prove that they would not do so. A variety of professionals may become involved in the assessments and judgements used to justify this position, but how many are really convinced that the worst-case scenario will actually happen? The bounds of professional judgement, risk assessment, and notions of professional duty become seriously confused within the dangerousness arena leading to many professionals having to seriously compromise their position.

Compromising professional integrity?

The growth of the public protection agenda has thrown psychiatrists into the spotlight, very often giving them a central position in influencing the punit-ive disposition in high profile cases. Bloche (1993, in Verdum-Jones, 2000:79) argues that this position is unacceptable and should merit non-participation by them. Verdum-Jones suggests almost a degree of trickery involved in the use of psychiatric evidence in these cases. He summarizes this position very well in saying:

> Perhaps the 'moral distance' is not sufficiently great where a psychiatrist, whose medical background may lead the offender to believe that the 'doctor' will provide compassion and understanding, attends a criminal court in order to justify the imposition of a more severe sentence than is normally warranted by the circumstances of the offence.

In other words, the trust in the medical profession held by many people would mean that their role in determining punishment would be unexpected. Psy-chiatrists and others have of course long held very influential positions in the release decisions for long term prisoners or the discharge arrangements for psychiatric patients. Questions for future safety have been important to these discussions and the answers could determine the prolonging of detention, or, punishment. The role then is not an unfamiliar one. However, there is a difference when these professional judgements are used to increase punishments at the sentencing stage, or to justify detention for non-offenders. It shifts a professional role from one of assessing safety to one that helps provide additional punishment. These may be two sides of the same coin but they do indicate a significant shift in the professional role of health and other professionals.

It is then little wonder that many psychiatrists, and their professional associations, question their involvement in these cases. It also explains why for many, the use of actuarial risk assessment is preferred over clinical judgement on the basis that it excludes, largely, the human element from blame. It provides an objective shield behind which to hide accusations of misjudgement. However, such a position does reopen the arguments concerning the relative merits of actuarial versus clinical judgement discussed earlier. The move towards actuarial risk assessment (ARA) appears to offer a cloak of respectability when used to determine punishment because of the purportedly scientific basis of its methodology. Janus and Prentky (2003:3) go so far as to describe it as '... a state of the art technique, and courts insist it be employed as a major instrument of risk assessment'. They compare this with clinical assessment that is insufficiently validated and therefore cannot justify the imposition of the sexual predator laws in the United States. They cite Ewing (1991) who claims that, 'There is good reason to conclude that psychologists and psychiatrists act unethically when they render predictions of dangerousness that provide a legal basis for restricting another person's interests in liberty' (in Janus and Prentky, 2003:22). Medical practitioners are therefore really on the horns of a dilemma. Much of the evidence suggests that clinical predictions are generally little better than chance in terms of their reliability, but the professional status of clinicians depends in large part upon their supposed skill to make these judgements. Withdrawing from these proceedings might prevent legal claims against their evidence, but may also damage the mystique that in many ways shrouds and enhances their professional status.

A further complicating factor is the faith of people such as jurors in the power of clinical judgement (Krauss and Dae Ho Lee, 2003); indeed, they suggest that lay people may be overwhelmed by the detail in complex actuarial evidence. Psychiatrists are therefore 'believed' even though the evidence suggests that their predictions may only be slightly more than 50% accurate, although in some cases they may well exceed this figure. That said, actuarial results that may top out at approximately 70% at best, are not hugely better and remain questionably accurate for the rare offending behaviour that falls within the potentially dangerous category. The debate will therefore swing wildly between the view that, '... reliance solely on clinical judgement (being) improper, and under forensic circumstances, arguably unethical' (Janus and Prentky, 2003:58), and what Tribe (1971) described as 'trial by mathematics' (2003:18). As ever then, something of a compromise is likely to result with actuarial and clinical information being combined. Janus and Prentky (2003:58) in their detailed review conclude that, 'By the same token ... best practice ... would not ... rely exclusively on the results of ARA and would never knowingly exclude potentially critical, risk-relevant information that is not reflected in the ARA.' The development of OASys in England and Wales is clearly meant to address some of these difficulties. By combing actuarial and clinical (dynamic) data it is regarded as offering the most effective solution. It has received criticism for being very time-consuming and the development of the electronic variant, E-OASys, is clearly intended to speed the process. However, all the time that risk categories are enlarged, there appears to be little scope for offering the time that proper risk assessment obviously needs.

Medical staff may find themselves further compromised by their involvement in certain 'therapeutic' dispositions, such as sex offender treatment programmes. This practice highlights the difference between treatment for those already undergoing punishment, for example in prison, and those for whom treatment is implicitly a component of their punishment, or where it is undertaken in the hope of a favourable outcome, such as in parole decisions (Glaser, 2003:144). He suggests that clinicians involved in sex offender programmes are required to resolve ethical dilemmas arising from matters such as client confidentiality and promoting patient autonomy. Indeed they argue that the indicator of a 'good' therapist in this context would be their primary focus on protecting the public rather than their own patient. This position is exacerbated by the confusions between treatment and punishment, '... the boundaries between treatment and punishment has become increasingly blurred, with many treatment programmes having primary aims which are mainly punitive in nature, e.g. protection of the community from the offender.' This confusion of aims is increasingly a feature of the effect of the public protection agenda.

In essence, therefore, medical staff involved in public protection cases are frequently asked to compromise the rights of their patients. They are asked to do this to protect the rights of the public, sacrificing the individual to the greater good. It is a reconfiguration of their role almost by stealth and, despite the power of their position in society, seemingly one that it is difficult to resist. This is a position that is already well established in the criminal justice sector and is now, despite greater opposition, becoming so in the medical world.

Compromising rights to confidentiality

Doctors have long held that their relationship with their patients is confidential, a position also held by others such as probation officers, although perhaps to a lesser extent. Confidentiality is however another area that has suffered from the public protection agenda—the rights of the individual being subsumed beneath those of the public. The basis of multi-agency public protection work is sharing of all information—a denial of confidentiality. At a conference in London (CEP, 2003), representatives from France felt that forms such as OASys were intrusive, and would cause concern in their country as a breach of human rights. They stated that the labelling of offenders was illegal and sharing of information between ministries was forbidden. The UK view was presented as a counterpoint to this in that it was felt that labelling is a part of assessment, and that offenders could not change until they recognized themselves as meeting the label. It is evident therefore that views on confidentiality as an offender or patient right, will in large part be determined by governmental attitudes to risk, described by Carlen (2002) as 'political risk' (in Horsefield, 2003:378). This politicization of 'information' is perhaps no more demonstrated than in the debates concerning sex offender notification schemes, both in the UK and the USA.

Chapter 7 outlined the basics of sex offender notification schemes. In essence, the authorities give out information about certain sex offenders by various means, to diverse members of the public. The perceived level of risk posed by the offender will determine the amount of information given, and the extent of its dissemination. These schemes clearly prioritize the right of the public to be protected over that of the offender to have his privacy protected. The schemes also imply, by default, that the end of a sentence is not a signal for the end of punishment. However, not only are there debates about the very efficacy of these schemes, but also over the numbers of people becoming involved as year-on-year, cumulative numbers increase and the task becomes increasingly onerous.

A number of issues can be identified in the American experience of notification, where various schemes have existed for a number of years, which may have increasing resonance for the UK. In California, for example, registration has been required by law since 1947 and the cumulative numbers are becoming problematic. One of the major problems is in losing the tag of dangerousness once it has been applied. In discussing the sexual predator laws, Janus and Prentky (2003:5) argue that only a small fraction of offenders have met their release burden and by September 2001 only 5% of SVPs had been cleared as 'no longer sexually dangerous'. This suggests reluctance on the part of professionals themselves to take a risk with offenders, and this is replicated in public and official attitudes to information disclosure. It takes little mathematical knowledge to work out how this situation will massively increase the cumulative total of registered offenders. At present in the UK as we have seen, registration periods vary according to the sentence/offence combination. The trend from America is for much longer minimum or indefinite periods of registration, a scenario that it would be unsurprising to see imported into UK law.

Tell one—tell all

As indicated above, assessed risk levels determine the extent of information dissemination. This same measure will dictate the nature of that dissemination and potentially whether or not there is a role for the offender in the process. The American literature distinguishes between 'active' and 'passive' notification

(Irwin et al, 2004). Active notification places an onus on the offender as well as local authorities. In Louisiana, for example, the offender is required to directly contact residents within a specified radius of the registrant's home address. In this active phase of notification, postcards will be mailed to private addresses, parks, schools, churches etc. Advertisements will be taken out in local newspapers, bumper stickers placed on the offender's car, and signs in their garden. In other words, this information is likely to reach the public even if they do not go looking for it. Passive notification on the other hand is where perhaps more information is available, but has to be actively sought out by members of the public—*they* have to be proactive. People can visit post offices, police stations, and online databases to obtain offender details—if they can demonstrate a legitimate interest. They can learn details such as age, height, weight, eye colour, photographs, hair colour, as well as the offender's criminal record.

As mentioned earlier, either active or passive notification processes, the choice of which is usually determined by state authorities, will be dependent on the assessed risk posed by the offender. Those assessed as high or serious risk will be included in notification procedures. In excess of 140,000 sex offenders are released from American correctional facilities each year, and numbers under supervision or notification in the community is therefore growing exponentially. The Internet is increasingly being touted as the medium through which to disseminate sex offender information, not least because of its economies of scale, ease of access and, in some cases, ability to make a profit for database holders. However, such a passive system does not easily enable discrimination between offences and offenders, and it certainly lacks the educational element of many community notification meetings run by relevant authorities. For example, Irwin et al (2004:16) claim that notification can re-victimize those who suffered from incestuous abuse, or others whose victim status can be closely linked with the offender. They also argue that indiscriminate notification unnecessarily alarms everyone and makes it difficult to know which victims to protect from which offenders.

In the United States there are already more than a half million people eligible to be posted on the Internet. Furthermore, a new law, the Children's Safety Act 2005, will require registration for 20 years at a minimum and many for life. There will therefore be very limited possibilities for offenders who may have changed their ways to escape from their past, with all the problems that this entails for moving on. The difficulties noted above posed to offenders trying to lose their SVP status only confirms this. This sheer volume of registration cannot however lead to good risk management. In California, for example, it is estimated than 1 in every 180 men could be posted on the Internet when it becomes law to do so. The law requiring these measures is known as the Protect Act 2003 and requires Internet posting by 2006 in all states. Added to this the US government has set in process *Operation Predator* to track sex offenders internationally. The volume of those to be *included*, and by definition *excluded* in future years, can only be guessed at.

Irwin et al (2004:21) believe that Internet posting might further the distortion of sexual abuse because it will continue to be dominated by stranger, rather than the more prevalent domestic abuse. They recommend that websites should include the broad educational elements that are a feature of community notification meetings and appear to limit community violence. The American system, in contrast to that in the UK, reveals more information, to more people, for longer periods. Its indiscriminate nature has made life miserable for many offenders whose present risk must be considered low and who offended years ago. This is not said in any way to detract from the impact of any crime upon the victim, but to inject some reality into the seemingly inexorable rise in numbers. Another contrast between the US and UK experience is the registration rate, at about 75% in America and as high as 97% in the UK (a figure incidentally regarded as unacceptable by Professor Irving in his 2005 report to the Scottish Executive). Once again this reflects a crucial debate about rights and public protection, where, for once, maintaining offender rights to privacy might just offer greater public protection, at least in terms of registration compliance. Of course many would argue that the more people know, the better they are able to protect themselves. However, even detailed notification schemes in the most advanced nation on earth are not foolproof. Natural risks and disasters can still intervene to potentially increase the harm to the community. As a result of Hurricane Katrina in late August 2005, up to 15,000 registered sex offenders resident in the devastated southern states may have relocated and it remains to be seen how quickly their whereabouts can be traced. It will also be of interest to note if sexual offences increase among this group during the period of their dislocation, and if so, which type of offence occurs more often. Reports of rapes and murders from the Louisiana Superdome certainly indicated the onset of a significant problem.

Probation and the defence of justice

According to Hudson (2003:203), 'Justice has come to be almost synonymous with punishment' and, for those working in criminal justice agencies, this notion will have greater or lesser resonance depending, perhaps, on their history and culture. The probation service might be one agency where a shifting understanding of justice will be keenly felt. Their origins and even recent history show an organization that was committed to upholding the rights of the offender. Although many critics might have regarded this stance as being at the expense of the victim (an unfair generalization), the service did nonetheless seek to protect or work towards the restitution of certain offender rights. The whole concept of rehabilitation is based around helping offenders return to citizenship, and the rights that status carries. Recent practice with potentially dangerous and high risk offenders does however suggest that there may be a drift away from offender rights, and potentially a sharp realignment in probation values.

Hudson (2003:215) explores Ashworth's (2002) analysis of three levels of rights to consider where criminal justice appears to be heading at the present time. Ashworth describes the first tier of rights as non-derogable and these include the right to life, the right not to be tortured or to suffer inhuman or degrading treatment. At the second tier, rights are described as 'strong', and these include the right to a fair trial, to liberty and security of the person. These rights may be rescinded at times, but only in the most pressing circumstances. The third tier might include 'softer' rights such as freedom of expression, thought, religion, assembly, and association. These rights might be suspended at times of national emergency and could thus be regarded as civil rather than human rights. It is not difficult to see that recent developments in the public protection agenda may compromise level 1 and 2 human rights.

However, it is not simply the rights of dangerous offenders that may be compromised because concern with this group has an impact on offender rights generally. Relatively rare behaviour sets the tone and agenda for nearly all offenders and fear and concern gives way to intolerance and denial of humanity. A recent example concerning the rights of prisoners perhaps demonstrates this point. In October 2005, an ex-life sentence prisoner won a case at the European Court of Human Rights (The Times, 10 October 2005), which implied that thousands of UK prisoners would be given the right to vote. The ex-prisoner, Jon Hirst, successfully won a case claiming that the Representation of the People Act 1983 breached the right to free elections in the European Convention on Human Rights. However, the British government, having lost an appeal against the judgment, have indicated that even if prisoners are given the right to vote, only some of them will be able to do so. In response, the Lord Chancellor and head of the department for Constitutional Affairs said that 'there was no question that all prison inmates will be given the right to vote'. He felt that those convicted of lesser offences might be given the right, but not those convicted of serious crimes. This of course reflects a judgement about rights and crime seriousness, evident not only in this matter, but in the way these offenders are dealt with throughout the criminal justice process. How serious will the crime have to be before the right is removed? Will the right be denied if there is a 'likelihood' of a serious crime in the future? In the same newspaper report Mark Leech, editor of the *Prisons Handbook*, said, 'Prisoners lose their liberty, they do not lose their position in the human race nor their position in the society of which this judgement makes clear they are still a part.' Despite these words it does appear that for some offenders this place is under threat, if their access to rights is a measure of that position.

The involvement of criminal justice agents in this process will now be considered, although to be fair, many may not regard their contribution as supporting derogation, as the whole issue has been reconfigured as one of protecting the vulnerable, a very defendable position. It could be argued that the politicization of risk, and indeed crime more generally, has led to a blurring of distinction between level 2 and 3 rights, between the human and the civil. Hudson argues that there has been a further blurring between social problems and national security, with slogans such as the 'war on crime' fuelling the situation. The whole social situation is, however, condemnatory, with limited toleration and almost no forgiveness, unless a very deserving case can be advanced. Hudson passionately argues in defence of a rehabilitative philosophy, one held traditionally by the probation service. She says, 'Defending human rights in the risk society demands challenging dehumanising of anyone. Whatever their crime, no person is devoid of humanity, and labels such as "evil", "animal", and "super-predator", which define people entirely by their wrongdoing, should be contested' (2003:223). This position is one, which in popular penal discourse, earns little support. She goes on to say that the fudged language and harsh political climate produces little opposition to these measures and, perhaps more surprisingly, little professional opposition either. In many respects this is unsurprising. Agencies such as the probation service have seen public protection elevated to a number one position in their priority list. The role itself, although to a certain extent foreign to the service, has enabled it to maintain its position at a time when its more traditional philosophy has become increasingly less popular, with government and the population at large.

The issue that perhaps rubs up against the traditional probation ethos is that of where risk management or control sits with rehabilitation. As already noted in several places in this book, public protection has an essentially exclusionary focus and is very unforgiving in terms of allowing people to demonstrate change and re-enter the community. This has not been the traditional stance of probation officers who, even with serious offenders such as those serving life sentences, have worked wherever possible towards their community reintegration. Hudson (2003:76) writes in very strong terms on this issue and her words are worthy of lengthy quotation:

> Risk classification and risk control are therefore, first and last strategies of inclusion and exclusion, and what is more, they form an impregnable, unchallengeable ordering which leaves some individuals and groups outside of rights, outside of the moral-legal community ... Risk control strategies throw into sharp relief the perennial questions of whose rights matter, who is to adjudicate rights conflicts and on what basis; who is inside the fortress of justice and who is outside in the wilderness of danger?

Implicit in this process of inclusion or exclusion is a move away from viewing offenders as individuals, and instead regarding them as members of groups or as categories or aggregates (Robinson, 2002:6). She regards the outcome of this process as the adoption of limited managerial goals rather than the grand narrative of reformation and rehabilitation. However, the inherent and enduring tension of this position is epitomized by the view that protecting innocent victims eclipses any other role for criminal justice professionals, and as such may be regarded by many as not limited but as hugely important. It is at this point of course that all the issues concerning assessment, prediction, and labelling resurface, but as just noted by Hudson, there appears to be increasingly less professional concern with philosophical issues. Probation officers have traditionally been concerned with working with offenders in their social context, individuals in a given social milieu, as a means of explaining, understanding, and tackling their offending. Horsefield (2003:376) suggests that the language of risk '. . . obscures the individuality and hides the social origins of the behaviour which leads to people being defined as dangerous'. He goes on to argue that risk assessment tools such as OASys may also see a reduction in the professional limits of probation practice, seeing them as, 'essentially passive but nominally expert' (2003:377). Working in this way therefore re-shapes the way in which probation staff work away from what might be regarded as their traditional role. The 'need for modernization argument' would undoubtedly be deployed to justify the change in philosophy and practice. Yet, is the evidence compelling enough to prove that the alternative method was ineffective, or that the new way will be more so? The answer will of course be equivocal and should include an injunction to bring forward the best of the past to sit alongside the best of the new. Abandoning one way for another may not be the answer.

Competing rights—but where's the competition?

It should be clear by now that certain offenders have had their rights compromised or removed. The simple premise for this is that their rights matter less than those of the majority to be protected. In an area where rights might compete with each other, these offenders are deemed less deserving and, by their behaviour, worthy of fewer rights than other citizens or even other 'ordinary' offenders. This issue does not excite much debate academically, publicly, or in the practitioner literature. In a few years, the case for the government, indeed for many governments worldwide, is that certain offenders act beyond the pale and are not to be treated as other people. Yet, repeatedly the same issue resurfaces. Are they put into this position for what they have done, or for what they might do? A quick visit to the dangerousness debate of the 1980s reveals a wider concern with offender rights and the powers of the state than is evident at the beginning of the twenty-first century.

In what has become known as the first dangerousness debate, a number of contributors were concerned about the removal of offender rights based on a probability that something serious might happen in the future. Dworkin, writing in 1996, encapsulated the earlier mood when he described a decline in the culture of liberty. He argued that rights and freedoms should only be abridged '. . . in order to prevent a clear and serious danger—a calamity—and even then only so far as is absolutely necessary to prevent it' (1996:60). This simple behest captures much of the dangerousness debate concerning prediction, assessment, probability, and seriousness. In other words, it contains a whole series of relative imponderables. As the climate of fear increases (perhaps still relatively embryonic in the early 1980s), the right to protection eclipses all other competing rights. Pratt (1997:158) summarizes this point when he says, 'Indeed, it is as if the increasing crime fears and insecurities generated by their neo-liberal programme of government are turned back on the state itself, as the right to protection from ungovernable risks, such as those posed by the dangerous offenders of this period, is claimed as one of those inalienable rights of modern society ...'

Pratt argues that dangerousness laws enable the government to be seen as doing something and, 'appearing to guarantee these rights'. Yet we all know that there are no guarantees to the public, short of never releasing any prisoner ever again—and even this doesn't make allowance for all those first time, supposedly out-of-the-blue offenders. This position appears to represent something of a trade-off, with the public prepared to accept a broad incursion into human and civil rights by the government, provided that the attack is targeted at 'the other' and not them. This had been termed the 'just distribution of risks' by Floud and Young (1981), where they argued that some people, because of their behaviour, had forfeited the right to be presumed harmless. This meant that the state was morally in the right to remove their rights. Floud and Young suggested that society needed to make choices between competing claims, although in some respects their arguments sidestepped the issue of probability. They claimed:

> We have to make a moral choice between competing claims: the claim of a known individual offender, not to be unnecessarily deprived of his liberty; and the claim of an innocent (unconvicted), unknown person (or persons), not to be deprived of the right to go about their business without risk of grave harm at the hands of an aggressor. (1981:219)

Justification for this measure came about through the reality of the risk and the seriousness of its nature. As a result, a diffused risk (unknown victims warranting communal or collective claims to protection) is acceptable in permitting protective sentences. This stance does, however, permit certain latitude in dangerousness provision. Generalized risk populations make notions of certainty, or even Dworkin's 'clear and serious danger', much less obvious, questioning the plausibility of evidence deployed against these offenders. Instead the loss of rights here appears more determined by previous behaviour rather than future conduct, in which case the punishment should fit the crime, not anticipated harms.

Rights and wrongs—does anyone care?

Should we really be that bothered if a few potentially dangerous offenders are treated differently to everyone else? They have (in general) already committed at least one very serious crime and have been adjudged capable of doing so again.

For most people one instance is one too many and therefore any hint of repetition is enough to render talk of their rights null and void. This is a position that many people will sympathize with and actively support. It is widespread in the community and is a position fuelled and fanned by the media and government ministers. It is therefore unsurprising that criminal justice professionals find themselves in a difficult position if they begin advocating rights for this group of offenders. Unfortunately though there is, it appears, an insidious seepage of the rights of many people, not just dangerous offenders. The focus on dangerousness, wrapped in a cloak of scientifically assessed risk, masks a whole series of intrusions. We noted above Carlen's (2002) description of the 'politicization of risk', and in many regards, this has become entwined with the reaction to terrorist attacks in the USA and the UK—less so to those occurring elsewhere in the world sadly. Crime and politics, terror and difference escalate the climate of fear and widen the gap of difference between them and us. Few argue against this position, although Morris (2002, in Nellis and Gelsthorpe, 2003:237) expresses the view of perhaps a small minority when he said:

> ... we didn't say that we would support the government undermining our liberty, our freedom and our democracy, and we didn't say that we would declare war on Islam. There's a creeping totalitarianism which is emerging here and the rights of citizens are being incrementally taken away.

In other words, accepting one thing does not necessarily mean agreeing to another. Many criminal justice and other agencies are signing up to agreements and protocols that demand evermore of them and may increasingly take them away from their traditional roots. They do need to be alert to these possibilities.

Rights discourse has then been turned on its head it could be argued. It is used to support exemplary punishment, disproportionate punishment, and indefinite punishment. It supports breaches of confidentiality, intrusive surveillance and supervision, instant recalls to prison, or even the immediate rearrest of those released at the end of their lawful detention. It is now clearly supporting one set of rights over another and, even if risks are not certain and absolute no matter. The potential risk is enough. Rights discourse therefore supports organizations in declaring their decisions to be defensible (or likely to stand up to legal and moral challenge) and may be regarded as spreading a veneer of legitimacy over a good deal of uncertainty. The following extract from the National Probation Service (NPS) resource pack on the Human Rights Act illustrates how rights can be used to justify particular aspects of practice (that might previously have been regarded as suspect):

> Importantly ... the Act strengthens the position of the public authorities in many respects, in that it gives public authorities a duty to protect the rights of individuals and balance the rights of one individual or group against of those of another individual or group. An obvious area of work where that helps the probation service to carry out its public protection duties is that it enables us to take action to disclose—in a proportionate way—information about people

who present a risk to others. Whilst this may interfere with their rights under Article 8 of the Convention, provided the Service can show that it is acting in accordance with its duty in a manner that falls within the exceptions set out in Article 8.2, a challenge to its actions is unlikely to be successful. It is the duty of a public authority to balance conflicting demands that gives us a new and invigorating authority to carry out our work' (NPS, 2001, in Nellis and Gelsthorpe, 2003:233–4)

Although in many respects a very straight statement it does contain possibilities for value judgements, but infers that generally speaking these will be beyond challenge. The statement refers to balance but this could be a euphemism for choice or preference. Risk is the all-embracing justification but there is no reference to its problematic nature. The guidance infers certainties but, even if these are challenged, practitioners will be OK because they are protecting the public good. Defending the rights of those who would do us harm is a thankless task and likely to lead to the award of a bleeding heart. Yet this position is all too frequently misconstrued as excusing crime, or being soft and on the offender's side at the expense of the victim. No one is likely to condone serious crime and, when there is really good evidence that it might recur, few would dispute the continued detention of these offenders. The real problem arises though when all the parameters to this position soften and blur, when people are incarcerated without offending and when they are disproportionately punished for what they might do in the future. It is this pervasive climate that weakens the rights arguments and compromises the traditional practice of probation officers and medical staff.

Summary: Everyone has a right—but do they?

The term 'public protection' is pervasive. It has become a favourite of Prime Minister Tony Blair, who in late 2005, made constant references to it. In his view, public protection was the justification for a series of measures, predominantly aimed at terrorists or those suspected of terrorism, which appeared to carve a deep incursion into peoples' human and civil rights. However, it was not only suspected terrorists that would be on the receiving end of new powers, but also others such as young offenders involved in anti-social behaviour. Here they would not be subject to extreme measures but would find themselves receiving police-dispensed justice, rather than justice through the courts. Their rights would undoubtedly be eroded, not least because within a due process context in court they were regarded as too slow and posed too many obstacles to stopping that behaviour. In other words peoples' rights were getting in the way and needed to be lessened as a more extreme form of summary justice began to emerge. The supremacy of risk has done much to lessen or remove the rights of many and it is difficult, in the present political climate, to see very much changing. The words of Michael Ignatieff eloquently summarize virtually all of the issues raised throughout this chapter and are fitting to be used at its conclusion:

Yet we need to think of rights as something more than a dry enumeration of entitlements in constitutional codes, as more than a set of instruments that individuals use to defend themselves. Rights create and sustain culture and by culture we mean habits of the heart. Rights create community. They do so because once we believe in equal rights, we are committed to the idea that rights are indivisible. Defending your own rights means being committed to defending the rights of others' (Ignatieff, 2000:125, in Nellis and Gelsthorpe, 2003:235)

11

Conclusion—Where Next for Public Protection?

Police and probation

The changes in the public protection business since *Police, Probation and Protecting the Public* was written in 1999 effectively meant that a second edition was out of the question. These changes have been so extensive and profound, and so many other texts published, that another approach has been necessary. In 1999 it was a case of presenting what was an emerging agenda for criminal justice agencies, one that was still largely confined to the police and probation services. In the late 1990s these two services were moving slowly towards agreeing protocols, ostensibly concerned with the sharing of information previously regarded as confidential. This was not the only change however. The embryonic language of public protection hinted that there would also have to be changes to the way in which agencies worked with each other, with an increasing likelihood of shared tasks. Early research (Nash, 1999a and Kemshall and Maguire, 2001) indicated, however, that there was a way to go to break through some of the cultural attitudes that might block greater cooperation. In many respects it was perhaps the probation service that was expected to engage with the greatest amount of change to its role, values, and culture. It was in a number of ways, expected to move closer to the police service, rather than the other way around. Resistance might have been expected to be fierce from an organization with nearly a century's experience of attempting to work towards the integration of offenders back into the community and to reduce the possibility of future offending through a range of therapeutic interventions. Yet Nash (1999a and b) found this resistance not to be so great, and indeed considerable evidence of a willingness to adopt a new language and new roles.

The reasons that police and probation services might have moved together more easily than expected are probably quite complex but may be simplified to perhaps two major issues. One clear issue can be dated to the passing of the Sex Offenders Act in 1997. This Act had been a result of both the aping of American legislation (quite popular in the mid-1990s) and the increasingly politicized nature of the sexual crime problem. Sexual offending had for long been seen as a minority crime that was not really openly discussed, one that was almost too unseemly to bring into the public consciousness. Yet during the 1990s a number of high profile incidents, predominantly related to paedophile offenders, made huge headlines on both sides of the Atlantic. Terms such as *sexual predator* entered the everyday lexicon, and public fear and anxiety increased in direct proportion to the increased media and political attention given to these offenders.

The Sex Offenders Act reconfigured the work of the police service almost at a stroke. Not only was it the agency chosen to be the keeper of the sex offenders' register, it was also charged with assessing the risks posed by those on the register. The police service was to be the lead agency dealing with sex offender risks. This would be new territory, and would require a substantial revision in the way that the police service viewed its relationship with offenders—it would be less reactive in the future. Essentially, responsibilities that were formerly held by the probation service were to be moved across to the police service. What had been a fairly private activity in a relatively secretive probation service was suddenly to become almost public property. The police therefore needed assistance and the probation service were the most appropriate partners, having the greatest amount of community-based experience of working with and managing high risk offenders.

For its part the probation service also needed allies and was also in need of a new and more publicly and politically acceptable role. Somewhat surprisingly perhaps, the service had survived four successive Conservative governments, still largely delivering their traditional services and based upon their historic values. This was a quite remarkable achievement when the values which had spawned an essentially welfare approach to crime had become deeply unfashionable. However, a closer look at their history does suggest that during the 1980s and 1990s the service had already undergone considerable transformation in organization, practice, and even perhaps its values.

Perhaps the most important development was that which saw community-based disposals such as probation orders, move from a notion of help to one of punishment. The CJA 1991 had been established upon principles of proportionality and restriction of liberty. The work of probation officers would increasingly become involved in that notion of restriction, and alongside it compliance and enforcement would become important factors in everyday practice. Words such as punishment, restriction, enforcement, and breach would become more common than advise, assist, and befriend (although to be fair this had been drifting for some time). Yet, this semantic change did not appear to be enough, perhaps because a major cultural and practice shift lagged behind a little.

The election of a Labour government in 1997 led many probation stalwarts to believe that there might be a quick return to traditional practice and beliefs. This hope was, however, totally unfounded. The new administration quickly proved itself to be as tough as its predecessors on law and order issues, and indeed soon moved the agenda forward at a rapid rate. Legislation establishing sex offender orders, mandatory life sentences for second time offenders, and by 2000 *requiring* that formal multi-agency public protection arrangements be established, left little doubt where policy was heading. If the probation service were to have a place in the modern criminal justice sector, that place would have to be closely tied to public protection. Indeed, of more concern would be the future of probation itself. As noted in the Introduction to this book, perhaps the skills required for effective public protection work need to be maintained and developed within the probation service if it is to survive in any recognizable form and to maintain its position at the centre of criminal justice delivery.

Alongside, but also absolutely integral to this change process, was a little word that has assumed total dominance of criminal justice practice. That word was, and is, 'risk'. As the media's influence over the law and order agenda grew, so governments and politicians of every hue began to talk in terms of risks. Although risk discussions always contained the caveat that 'all risks cannot be eliminated', there was an increasing message that risks could be assessed, quantified and wherever possible, managed to improve public safety. That risk management process might involve indefinite detention for those posing the greatest criminal risk, and at lower levels would mean longer prison sentences, restricted release arrangements, and tighter controls in the community.

Risk introduced neutrality into the language used by criminal justice practitioners, especially police and probation officers. It was much less value-laden than that established by two separate and quite distinctive organizations during their respective histories. By utilizing the shared language of risk it was not too great a step to share tasks and blur roles that might once have been seen as on opposite sides of the fence. Common ground had been found between two organizations both under the spotlight for different reasons. Risk management has created a new breed of criminal justice professional; able to step between agencies at all levels, from police and probation staff sharing office accommodation (but often police accommodation Mawby and Worrall, 2004) to secondments of senior police officers to the national probation service. This new hybrid, but for the moment virtual department of public protection, has also been expanded to include a range of other agencies, many of which would once have seen themselves significantly removed from the 'law and order' grouping.

Extending the public protection family

In 1999 it was not inappropriate to focus on police and probation services as the key providers of public protection in the community. The prison service had of course long offered public protection by keeping in lawful custody dangerous offenders until they were required by law to release them. Of course, in the USA even this principle is now under threat as offenders are detained beyond this period if they pose a continuing high risk of serious harm and are moved to the mental health system for continued containment. Considering how greatly US policy has influenced that in the UK, it remains to be seen when similar developments occur on this side of the Atlantic. Traditionally, however, their involvement more or less stopped at the prison gate and, in many instances, their knowledge of the offender remained locked away behind the walls.

The development of the public protection arrangements, however, began to extend the role of the prison service into the community as prison staff brought their 'inside' knowledge of the offender into meetings established to supervise offenders in the community. This role has now been formally recognized with the prison service now recognized as a responsible authority. However, a range of other public services have also now become involved in multi-agency meetings. For example, as public awareness of the accommodation problems of sex offenders grows, so effective risk management has to include serious discussion of housing needs and public vulnerability. Thus local housing authorities, the private and voluntary sector, and hostel managers may all have an important input into MAPPA. Similarly, social services departments will be involved in cases where children may be at risk, or if vulnerable adults may become potential victims. There will be a role for general and mental health specialists as appropriate. Youth and leisure services may need to be represented if offenders target individuals in youth clubs, or swimming pools etc. As risk has become more pervasive, so the awareness of where it may be sited grows and in so doing pulls in an ever-growing number of people.

However, the developing agenda has not only involved a greater number of people but has also moved on from a local to an increasingly regional basis. Strategic management occurs at county levels and, according to a government announcement on 20 October 2005, may increasingly be across probation area boundaries. There is a clearly emerging large-region agenda for criminal justice services into which MAPPA will need to fit. There may well be an emerging national response to dangerous offenders, although it will clearly be important to retain local knowledge and management strategies.

The future for public protection

In many respects public protection is like a gigantic sponge. It has soaked up people, resources, and energy and, at the same time, is a repository for public fears and anxiety. It is difficult to see an end in sight to this process. The growth in the public protection machinery is mirrored by public concerns with risk. However, in true chicken and egg fashion, it is difficult to see which came first. Six years ago a few notorious cases triggered the developments that have now come to fruition. In Nash (1999a) the question was asked if the new developments were absolutely necessary, and if existing powers were not sufficient. Several years on, the evidence of a substantial worsening of the very serious offender problem does not appear to be present. Once again, a few cases have received huge notoriety through the media, but these types of crimes remain rare. Yet legislation and policy deployed against the potentially dangerous has been on a relentlessly upward spiral.

Part of the problem appears to be that governments believe that every case that 'goes wrong' must result in new, tougher legislation and policy. It seems as if when extremely unpredictable behaviour does occur that someone must be blamed and loopholes closed to prevent any further recurrence. This is, of course, an unobtainable goal. Tragedies will continue to happen no matter what systems and legislation are in place.

Summary

It is a reasonable assumption that legislation will become tougher and that civil detention for 'predator' offenders may become an issue in the future *when* rather than *if* a closely supervised MAPPA offender goes on to commit a very serious crime. An independent review has been ordered into Hampshire police and probation service MAPPA following just such an incident in late 2005. In this context practitioners are quite likely to become increasingly cautious and therefore more reluctant to take a chance with their risk assessments, always erring on the side of caution. More people could be assessed as dangerous as the numbers of qualifying offences and behaviours increases. With longer sentences served, more restrictions on release, and if released more rigorous constraints on the offender, the high risk offender population is certain to grow considerably. More and more professionals and resources will be involved and staff may find much of their working week spent in MAPP meetings. An argument may be developed that public protection should become a discrete multi-agency service. There may be a degree of logic to this view but perhaps caution should be exercised.

The strength of the multi-agency arrangements has been just that, a multi-agency approach to a given problem. It is undoubtedly the case that police have learned from probation officers and vice versa. A range of perspectives on the potential harm posed offers a greater opportunity to cover as many angles as possible. Different professions see problems in a different light and with complex and unpredictable behaviour this should be a plus. Yet the trend appears to be towards a uniform, common approach that, although consistent, may miss out on the subtleties that have existed until now. Modernization is probably the hottest ticket in the public sector and creating elaborate management systems appears to fit the bill very well. Undoubtedly efficiency is important, not least to ensure clear lines of communication and to ease information flow. However, at times a less homogeneous approach may be necessary because people will continue to act in very messy ways and do very nasty things. At this point people and professional skills will need to be an essential element in any 'system' and efforts must be made to ensure that these abilities are retained. The future of public protection is contingent upon the people charged with this really difficult job; systems should facilitate rather than constrain their work.

The management of dangerous offenders in the community is a never-ending and constantly changing challenge for the agents of public protection. Not only is there a constant whirl of new legislation and policy but also the guarantee of hostile press responses to every new occurrence of dangerousness in the community. To emphasize this constant movement a joint inspection by Her Majesty's Inspectorates of Probation and Constabulary issued a report in late 2005 covering the management of sex offenders in the community. As one might expect from an inspection, there was evidence of good progress and areas of concern. A very brief summary of this report will follow to perhaps point the way towards the next phase of the dangerousness debate.

As might be expected of a national sample, considerable variations in practice were found with, and equally to be expected, evidence of good practice and matters needing action. What was clear from the inspection was that in the six years since *Police, Probation and Protecting the Public* was written considerable progress has been made. It is clear that police and probation services have developed much closer working relationships in recent years but, that said, there remain discrepancies between them. For example, the report noted that police officers were given little guidance in their work with sex offenders, limited training, and limited managerial oversight. This could be problematic when it was noted that constables carried out most risk assessments. Those police officers questioned were also quick to point out that MAPPPA duties had not attracted any real increase in funding or resources. This in itself was proving increasingly difficult as the workload was growing rapidly (note earlier comments on the forecast growth in numbers on the sex offenders' register to 125,000). There was evidence of more training and supervision for probation officers. As public protection becomes increasingly defined by its multi-agency nature, it is therefore imperative that police officers receive more training, a situation that will undoubtedly apply to the prison service as well.

The report also highlighted a number of gaps between intent and actuality, or perhaps difference between what the public might believe is happening and what the reality of community supervision involves. For example, the report identified 'surveillance' as a strategy in only 1% of cases. Undoubtedly, resources would be a major determining factor in this instance, but it is likely that the public might well believe that there is a higher level of intrusive supervision and surveillance for high risk offenders (which totalled 14% of the sample). Similarly,

199

home visits by police officers (identified as problematic due to an absence of a legal basis for entering the home), most frequently occurred at six-monthly intervals (20% of all cases), with 13% at 12-monthly intervals. In no cases were weekly home visits undertaken. Although the resource issues, coupled with a difficult legal position, no doubt explain this low level of visiting, it may well come as a considerable surprise to many members of the public that the oversight is lower than anticipated. The most common form of oversight was via office supervision at 91%, with monitoring movements and other restrictions in one in two cases.

In many respects, the report is testimony to a significant culture shift between the two primary agencies of public protection, the police and probation services. What had been embryonic in 1999 has undoubtedly become embedded in daily practice, so much so that the report could conclude, '... there was evidence of a strong working relationship between police and probation, with increased engagement from other agencies' and was further able to conclude that, 'the enthusiasm and professional commitment of both police and probation staff for their work and their aspiration to continue to develop and improve their effectiveness to protect the public' was a significant strength. However, the obvious shortage of resources and lack of police training, or more inclusive multi-agency training, is worrying. It is clear that all recent legislative developments will increase workloads and the forecast rise in sex offender registrations, even if the vast majority are of low risk offenders, immediately generates a significant assessment task. However, the report noted that concerns over cooperation did remain, describing the situation as follows:

> There could still be improvements in communication between police and probation staff. For example, information from previous police investigations was not always available to inform risk assessments. Not all probation staff were aware of police expertise and the resources available to police officers. Beat officers were not always aware of curfew conditions. There was also rarely coordination between police and probation concerning home visits. We found just two cases where police and probation staff had adjusted their respective home visits in a coordinated way. (HMIP/HMIC, 2005:53)

Although cultural shifts and greater awareness and coordination will take care of some of these problems, the sheer size of the task will remain a formidable barrier. Public protection will always be fuelled by the next case, especially the 'one that went wrong'. In such instances, legislation and policy will be tightened, public expectations increase, and the demands on professionals become almost unmanageable. Yet all the while, scarce resources will remain locked into cases where the risk of further serious offending is slight and meanwhile 'out of the blue' incidents will continue to unfold. Public protection remains stereotyped around certain types of offender offending in certain situations. Nowhere is this more chillingly revealed than in an article in The Guardian newspaper (10 December 2005) concerning the numbers of women who died at the hands of their partner in one year, a number of murders that the public rarely hear about and it appears is not very concerned about. The article cites research by eminent scholars in the field as follows:

> In a new study, Professors Rebecca and Russell Dobash of Manchester University found that male murderers who used violence against their female partners tended to have more 'conventional' backgrounds than, say, men who murder other men—they tended not to come from difficult homes, or to have fathers who used violence against their wives. However, they were likely to have used violence against previous or current partners—they 'specialised' in violence against women.

Thus whilst the public protection machinery grows, consuming more staff resources and undoubtedly causing anxiety for many people, a significant amount of death, violence, and sexual abuse continues, in the private domestic space of family homes. Stereotyping dangerousness leads us to look too frequently in the wrong places whilst all the time it is right under our noses.

Appendix 1
List of Relevant Legislative Developments in Public Protection

Criminal Justice Act 1991

This Act is important because, in an Act that enshrined the relationship between offence seriousness and sentence severity (proportionality), it allowed for crucial exceptions to this principle.

Section 1(2)(b) allowed for the imposition of a custodial sentence where only such a sentence was necessary to protect the public from serious harm from the offender (even if a lesser sentence was justified by the crime).

Section 2(2)(b) allowed for a longer than proportionate sentence, up to the maximum available, if the offender presented a risk of serious harm to the public.

The 1991 Act also reduced the use of previous convictions in determining sentence for the instant offence, unless a pattern was established that aggravated the seriousness of the present offence. This idea directly supporting the notion of proportionality was abolished in the Criminal Justice Act 1993 following a sustained campaign by sentencers.

Crime (Sentences) Act 1997

A hugely significant Act, which represented a major change in proportionality principles and demonstrating the growing synergy with American legislation. The Act aped the American 'three strikes' measures, by introducing mandatory, minimum penalties for certain crimes. However, in keeping with the climate of the time, 'two strikes and you're out' became the message of the day.

The Act introduced mandatory life sentences for the commission of a number of second time violent and sexual offences. The list included:

- attempted murder, conspiracy to commit murder, incitement to commit murder, soliciting murder, manslaughter,
- wounding or committing grievous bodily harm with intent (s. 18 Offences Against the Person Act 1861),
- rape or attempted rape, sexual intercourse with a girl under 13 years,
- possession of a firearm with intent to injure, carrying a firearm with intent, robbery whilst in possession of a firearm.

If the court decided, in *exceptional circumstances*, not to impose a mandatory life sentence, it had to state its reasons in open court.

The Sex Offenders Act 1997

The importance of this Act is in the signals established for the way in which sex offenders would be dealt with in the next few years. Its main achievement in this respect was the establishment of the Sex Offenders Register, with minimum registration periods set for a range of qualifying sex offenders. Significantly, this Act came under immediate criticism for what it did not do, namely to include all sex offenders in the community on the register. This led to immediate action to plug the loopholes resulting in sections of the Act that follows.

The Crime and Disorder Act 1998

This Act was important for two reasons in the public protection context: it established *sex offender orders* (SOOs) to close the registration loophole; and created *extended sentences* for certain sex and violent offenders.

Section 2 of the Act allowed a chief office of police to request a Magistrate's Court to prevent a sex offender doing anything described in the Order. The Order would last for five years and carry automatic registration requirements as described in the Sex Offenders Act 1997.

Section 58 established extended sentences for certain violent offenders (those sentenced to minimum of four years' imprisonment) and sex offenders. The effect would be to aggregate whatever sentence was deserved with an extension period (supervision in the community). The total term could not exceed the maximum for the offence. The extension period for violent crimes was up to five years and up to ten years for sex offenders.

The Criminal Justice and Court Services Act 2000

For our purposes, this Act had one very significant contribution to the area of public protection. It placed on a statutory footing (s. 67), a requirement that the relevant responsible authorities (police and probation services) establish arrangements for assessing and managing the risks posed by relevant sexual and violent offenders. This would evolve into the MAPPA process, with a formal requirement to produce an annual report. The Act also reduced the sex offender period in which sex offenders were required to register from 14 to 3 days and added a power to the police to take fingerprints and photographs (Sch. 5(1)(2)).

The Sexual Offences Act 2003

This massive Act is hugely significant, representing as it does a complete transformation of the definitions relating to sexual offences, the creation of new offences, and alterations to sentences available for sexual crimes. This Act should be consulted by anyone working with sexual offenders. The Act updates the laws on sexual offences taking note of many points made over the years about child sex offences in particular, the activities of paedophiles, and the use of modern technology to sexually offend.

Sections 80–93 make amendments to notification requirements, again effectively turning the screw more tightly and introducing other measures to close loopholes.

Section 107 introduces Sexual Offence Prevention Orders, replacing Sex Offender Orders, but carrying similar restrictions.

The Criminal Justice Act 2003

Another huge Act that reflects the Labour government's seeming determination to reform as much as possible (and in a short while reform it again). Chapter 5 is dedicated to dangerous offenders and introduces new measures against those regarded as potentially dangerous in the future. The Act made a number of important contributions to the way in which dangerous offenders are dealt with, these include:

- section 225(1)–(3)—Life sentence of imprisonment for public protection for those committing serious offences (where offence qualifies for life) or an indeterminate sentence of imprisonment for public protection when it does not;
- section 227 reduced the extended period for sex offenders from ten to eight years;
- section 269 established minimum tariffs for life sentence prisoners and these are explained in Sch. 21.

Appendix 2
List of Recent Relevant Probation Circulars

PC54/2005 NPS Interim Domestic Abuse Policy and Strategy
http://www.probation.homeoffice.gov.uk/files/pdf/PC54%202005.pdf

PC49/2005 Assessment and Management of Risk of Harm Action Plan
http://www.probation2000.com/pit/circulars/PC49%202005.pdf

PC42/2005 Extension of Victim Contact Scheme to Victims of Mentally Disordered Offenders—The Domestic Violence, Crime and Victims Act 2004
http://www.probation.homeoffice.gov.uk/files/pdf/PC42%202005.pdf

PC40/2005 Dangerous and Severe Personality Disorder (DSPD) Programme
http://www.probation.homeoffice.gov.uk/files/pdf/PC40%202005.pdf

PC39/2005 MAPPA Consultation Paper
http://www.probation.homeoffice.gov.uk/files/pdf/PC39%202005.pdf

PC36/2005 Public Protection: Cognitive Self-change Programme
http://www.probation.homeoffice.gov.uk/files/pdf/PC36%202005.pdf

PC33a/2005 Pre-Sentence Report Guidance for Prolific & Priority Offenders
http://www.probation.homeoffice.gov.uk/files/pdf/PC33A%202005.pdf

PC32/2005 Identification of Individuals who Present a Risk to Children: Interim Guidance
http://www.probation.homeoffice.gov.uk/files/pdf/PC32%202005.pdf

PC20/2005 Implementation of National Sex Offender Strategy
http://www.probation.homeoffice.gov.uk/files/pdf/PC20%202005.pdf

PC18/2005 Criminal Justice Act 2003—new sentences and new report guidance
http://www.probation.homeoffice.gov.uk/files/pdf/PC18%202005.pdf

PC10/2005 Public Protection Framework, Risk of Harm and MAPPA Thresholds
http://www.probation.homeoffice.gov.uk/files/pdf/PC10%202005.pdf

PC05/2005 Investigation of Serious Crimes Involving Offenders under Probation Supervision—Memorandum of Understanding between Police and Probation Services Relating to Victims
http://www.probation.homeoffice.gov.uk/files/pdf/PC05%202005.pdf

PC54/2004 MAPPA Guidance
http://www.probation.homeoffice.gov.uk/files/pdf/PC54.pdf

PC39/2004 Intensive Control & Change Programme (ICCP) and Prolific & Other Priority Offender (POPO) Strategy
http://www.probation.homeoffice.gov.uk/files/pdf/PC39.pdf

PC20/2004 National Scheme for Transfer of Public Protection Cases
http://www.probation.homeoffice.gov.uk/files/pdf/PC20.pdf

PC19/2004b Notification of Critical Public Protection of Cases
http://www.probation.homeoffice.gov.uk/files/pdf/PC19.pdf

PC04/2004 Introduction of Internet Behaviour and Attitudes Questionnaire (IBAQ)
http://www.probation.homeoffice.gov.uk/files/pdf/PC04.pdf

Appendix 3
A Synopsis of MAPPA Guidance

The aim of this annex is to offer a brief summary of the key stages of the MAPP process, with information derived from the MAPPA Consultation Paper (Probation Circular 54/2004). It should be noted that this document was released for consultation and the final version may therefore contain some changes.

1. Numbers involved

40,000 offenders were revealed in MAPPA reports for 2003–4, with 8,000 at level 2 and 2,000 at level 3. It is anticipated that numbers will continue to grow due to changes in the legislation, and the amount of time offenders remain on the register. It is expected that numbers on the Sex Offenders Register will increase from the present 27,000 to 125,000 over the next 20 years.

2. Coordination of responsible authorities to:

- Receive details of all offenders who pose a risk of serious harm and for whom a risk management plan is necessary.
- To make referral of sexual and violent offenders whose risk of serious harm needs managing through level 2 or 3 MAPPs.
- To share information with all relevant agencies on the basis that information will be held securely.
- To help determine which agency is core to the delivery of risk management plans.
- To receive notes of all risk management plans and noted from level 2 and 3 MAPP meetings.

3. Key stages

- To update VISOR when an offender enters MAPPA (stage 1), is referred for multi-agency management (stage 2) or exits MAPPA (stage 3).
- *Stage 1* notifications determined by ss. 325–327 of the CJA 2003, and relate to convictions for sexual and violent crimes and therefore most likely to occur following sentence or prior to release.
- *Stage 2* is the referral of an offender to level 2 or 3 MAPP risk management based on assessed risk of serious harm, requiring multi-agency risk management (predominantly police and probation referrals for category 1 and 2, but all agencies for category 3).
- *Stage 3* refers to exit from MAPPA, determined by end of registration or licence (for category 1 and 2) and when risk of serious harm has diminished (category 3).

4. Timings

- Initial stage 1 notification within three days of sex offender registration or release into the community.
- For referral of those assessed at level 2 or 3, to allow sufficient time before release to convene meetings (stage 2).

5. Actions following stage 1 notification

Following notification to the MAPPA coordinator, all agencies must assess risk of harm in the community and whether a risk management plan is necessary immediately or in the next six months pending release. If it is necessary a stage 2 referral must be made immediately to the coordinator. If no referral is received within five working days of stage 1 notification, it will be assumed that the managing agency is addressing all risk of harm issues through ordinary agency mechanisms.

6. Referral to multi-agency risk management (stage 2)

- The decision to place an offender into level 2 or 3 MAPPA must be made by a senior manager.
- The decision must be based on risk assessed as high or very high and the need for multi-agency risk management.
- Lower risk cases may be referred in exceptional cases (eg local notoriety, threats to the offender).
- Information will include all information regarding likelihood of offending, risk of serious harm and to whom, and imminence.
- The identification of all factors known to be relevant to risk of serious harm.
- The identification of core agency central to the delivery of the risk management plan.

7. Formalized pre-meeting information sharing—a new and important component of risk management which enables:

- All agencies being aware of the referral
- All agencies identify relevant information held by them
- Opportunity to identify themselves as a core agency
- Agencies to search their databases for information on the offender and this should be completed within five days with responses recorded as:
  - if nothing found—no trace/negative reply
  - if irrelevant material found—positive trace/negative reply
  - if positive material found and relevant—positive trace/positive reply and share information with coordinator
  - if material found but unclear relevance—positive trace/further consideration required

8. Initial level 2 and level 3 meetings

- All pre-information will be available.
- Any additional information will be made available, to note risk assessments and agree aspects that are essential to deliver effective risk management plan.

- Design the plan along SMART factors—specific, measurable, achievable, realistic, and timed.
- Specify date for formal review.
- Where elements of the plan cannot be delivered by local agencies, consideration must be given to referral to level 3 MAPP.

9. The organization of attendance at MAPPS

- It is essential that agency time is not wasted by unnecessary attendance.
- Agendas should be organized to maximize the attendance of different agencies and to facilitate their release at the earliest opportunity.

10. Agenda and notes

- Too much time is wasted in telling stories—more time needs to be spent on the specifics of risk assessment and risk management.
- Minutes should be produced in 10 working days and sent under confidential cover.
- In a major change to practice, these notes should no longer be presumed to be secret but regarded as open documents for the offender, unless there are specific elements that should be protected (eg to protect a vulnerable victim or source of information). It is essential to explain what and why certain information is not available to the offender. In some cases it may be appropriate for there to be no disclosure whatsoever.
- It is expected that, over time, the role of the offender in self-management will be more explicitly acknowledged in risk meetings.
- The offender will not generally be invited to level 2 or 3 meetings but there must be a stated mechanism to communicate with him before and after risk meetings.
- There will be regular review meetings.

Appendix 4
A Worked Example of Risk Management
(Source: MAPPA Guidance, Home Office 2004)

Case Study—the Mental Health Dimension

This offender was referred to the MAPPP by the Forensic Mental Health Service prior to release from prison.

Background

- At a low secure Mental Health unit he displayed aggressive, violent behaviour and extreme sexual disinhibition—grossly inappropriate verbal and physical advances towards adult females, staff and fellow patients; he did not appear to hear or accept rejection; allegations of stalking behaviour.
- Involved in violent confrontation with staff at unit, and as a result was sentenced to five months' imprisonment for affray and criminal damage (NB no statutory post-custody licence).
- Subject to Enhanced Care Programme Approach (CPA), but psychological assessments confirmed unlikely to respond to further treatment and scored high on psychopathy checklist. Not suffering from treatable form of mental illness, but diagnosed as suffering from personality disorder. Therefore hospital readmission was not an option and, since rejected by family, he was likely to be homeless on release.

Risk assessment

- High risk of serious sexual assaults on adult females, particularly vulnerable women.
- High risk of physical violence/assault towards staff dealing with him.

Risk management plan

- Housing department agreed to fast track application for council accommodation.
- Case was allocated to high risk outreach team (jointly funded by probation and city council housing department) to support him through application process and during settling into tenancy—liaison with benefits agency, public utilities, etc.
- Social services agreed to expedite social care assessment.
- Psychiatric social worker and community psychiatric nurse allocated to case.
- Risks 'flagged up' on local police criminal intelligence system (CIS) and operational order raised in relation to address, when known. Allocated to police sex and dangerous offenders unit.
- Police reviewed the investigation into alleged indecent assault on psychiatric unit patient.
- To be informed of his MAPPP registered status and implications of this.

- Establishment of core group for operational risk management, chaired by forensic mental health team manager.

Outcome

- In the event offender went to live with a young woman he had known previously and with whom he had been corresponding whilst in prison. This woman had a young child which necessitated the involvement of social services in child protection context.
- The core group also had to consider issues of disclosure to this woman. Offender was persuaded that he needed to disclose his MAPPP registered status (or the authorities would do so) and did so in presence of social worker—to whom he also admitted indecent assaults on patient prior to prison sentence, as a result of which he was charged with this offence. Partner decided to terminate relationship—was assisted to move into independent council accommodation.
- Offender charged with public order offences in relation to threats to ex-partner, and criminal damage to social services office and a taxi, and going equipped for theft. Probation officer who prepared the pre-sentence report alluded to MAPPP registration and explained background to court, who imposed six-month prison sentence. He was still awaiting Crown Court appearance in relation to offence of indecent assault. Also ongoing police investigation in relation to allegations of harassment of a female neighbour.

References

ACPO (23 July 2000) 'The naming of alleged sex offenders', ACPO statement.

Batty, D. (2002) The Guardian, 17 April 2002.

BBC news world edition 22 August 2002 http://news.bbc.co.uk/hi/world/asia-pacific/2209084.stm.

Beck, U. (1992) *Risk Society: Towards a New Modernity*, London: Sage Publications.

Beck, U. (2000) *World Risk Society*, Cambridge: Polity.

Billen, A. (1992) 'The Injudiciary', The Observer, 13 December 1992.

Birmingham, L. (2002) 'Detaining Dangerous People with Mental Disorders', Editorial *British Medical Journal*, 6 July 2002, 325: 2–3.

Blagg, H. and Stubbs, P. (1988) 'A Child-Centred Practice', *Practice*, II, 1, 12–19.

Bottoms, A. E. (1977) 'Reflections on the Renaissance of Dangerousness', *Howard Journal of Criminal Justice*, 16, 70–96.

Bottoms, A. E. (1979) 'A Non-treatment Paradigm for Probation Practice', *British Journal of Social Work*, 9, 159–202.

Bottoms, A. E. (1995) 'The Philosophy and Politics of Punishment and Sentencing' in C. R. V. Clarkson and R. Morgan (Eds.), *The Politics of Sentencing Reform*, Oxford: Clarendon Press.

Bowden, P. (1996a) 'Graham Young; the St Albans poisoner: his life and times', *Criminal Behaviour and Mental Health*, 17–24.

Bowden, P. (1996b), 'Violence and Mental Disorder' in N. Walker (Ed.), *Dangerous People*, London: Blackstone Press.

Brandon, M., Dodsworth, J., and Rumball, D. (2005) 'Serious Case Reviews: Learning to Use Expertise', *Child Abuse Review*, Vol. 14: 160–76.

Brindle, D. (2003) The Guardian, 30 March 2001.

British Medical Journal (Editorial) (2003) 'Should Psychiatrists Protect the Public?' 22 February 2003, 406–7.

Brody, S. R. and Tarling, R. (1980) 'Taking Offenders Out of Circulation', *Home Office Research Study* No. 64, London: HMSO.

Brookman, F. (2005) *Understanding Homicide*, London: Sage Publications.

Brownlee, I. (1998) *Community Punishment: A Critical Introduction*, Harlow: Longman.

Bryan, T. and Doyle, P. (2003) 'Developing Multi-Agency Public Protection Arrangements', in A. Matravers (Ed.), *Sex Offenders in the Community: Managing and Reducing the Risk*, Cullompton: Willan Publishing.

Buchanan, A. (1999) 'Risk and Dangerousness', *Psychological Medicine*, 29, 465–73.

Buchanan, A. and Leese, M. (2001) 'Detention of People with Dangerous Severe Personality Disorders: A Systematic Review', *The Lancet*, Vol. 358, December 8, 2001: 1955–9.

Butler Committee (1975), *Report of the Committee on Mentally Abnormal Offenders*, Cmnd 6244.

Calder, M. C. (Ed.) (2005) *Children and Young People Who Sexually Abuse: New Theory, Research and Practice Developments*, Lyme Regis: Russell House.

Canter, D. and Wentink, N. (2004), 'An Empirical Test of Holmes and Holmes's Serial Murder Typology', *Criminal Justice and Behaviour*, Vol. 31(4), 489–515.

Carpentier, J., Proulx, J., and Lussier, P. (2005) 'Predictors of Criminal Activity in a Sample of Juvenile Sexual Aggressors of Children' in M. C. Calder (Ed.) (59–73), *Children and Young People who Sexually Abuse: New Theory, Research and Practice Developments*, Lyme Regis: Russell House.

CEP Workshop (2003) *The Management of Dangerous Sex Offenders: A European Perspective,* http://www.cep-probation.org, accessed 27 September 2005.

Clear, T. and Cadora, E. (2001) 'Risk and Community Practice', in K. Stenson and R. R. Sullivan (Eds.), *Crime, Risk and Justice: The Politics of Crime Control in Liberal Democracies*, Cullompton: Willan Publishing.

Cleckley, H. (1964) *The Mask of Sanity* (4th ed.) St Louis: C. V. Mosby.

CNN Interactive, 22 June 1996, http://edition.cnn.com/US/9606/22clinton.radio/, retrieved 27 April 2005.

Cobley, C. (1997) 'Keeping Track of Sex Offenders—Part 1 of the Sex Offenders Act 1997', *Modern Law Review*, Vol. 60, 690–9.

Coid, J. and Maden, T. (2003) 'Should Psychiatrists Protect the Public?' *British Medical Journal*, 326: 406–7.

Coker, J. B. and Martin, J. P. (1985) *Licensed to Live*, Oxford: Blackwell.

Cooper, A. (2005) 'Surface and Depth in the Victoria Climbié Inquiry Report', *Child and Family Social Work*, 10, 1–9.

Cornick, B. (1988) 'Proceeding Together', *Community Care*, 17 March, 25–7.

Craig, L. A., Browne, K. D., and Stringer, I. (2004) *International Journal of Offender Therapy and Comparative Criminology*, 48(1), 7–24.

Crawford, A. (1999) *The Local Governance of Crime: Appeals to Community and Partnerships*, Oxford: Oxford University Press.

Critical Psychiatry Network (1999), 'Managing Dangerous People with Severe Personality Disorder: Proposals for Developing DSPD'.

Crow, I. (2001) *The Treatment and Rehabilitation of Offenders,* London: Sage.

Department of Health (1999) 'Reform of the Mental Health Act 1983: Proposals for Consultation', Cm 4480.

Deutsche Welle (11 March 2004), http://www/dwworld.de/dwelle/cda/detail/dwelle.cda.artikel_drucken/0,3820,1, accessed 15 April 2005.

Dodd, T., Nicholas, S., Povey, D., and Walker, A. (2004) *Crime in England and Wales 2003/2004*, Home Office Statistical Bulletin, London: Home Office.

Douglas, M. (1986) *Risk Acceptability According to the Social Sciences,* London: Routledge and Kegan-Paul.

Douglas, M. (1992) *Risk and Blame: An Essay in Cultural Theory*, London: Routledge.

Duff, A. and Garland, D. (Eds.) (1994) *A Reader on Punishment*, Oxford: Oxford University Press.

Dunbar, I. and Langdon, A. (1998) *Tough Justice: Sentencing and Penal Policies in the 1990s*, London: Blackstone Press.

Dunkel, F. and Smit, van Zyl, D. (2004) 'Preventive Detention of Dangerous Offenders: A Comment on two decisions of the German Federal Constitutional Court—Part I/II', *German Law Journal* No. 6 (1 June 2004).

Dworkin, R. (1977) *Taking Rights Seriously*, London: Duckworth.

Dworkin, R. (1996) 'Does Britain Need a Bill of Rights?' in R. Gordon and R. Wilmot-Smith, *Human Rights in the United Kingdom*, Oxford: Clarendon Press.

Elbogen, E. B., Patry, M., and Scalora, M. J. (2003), 'The Impact of Community Notification Laws on Sex Offender Attitudes', *International Journal of Law and Psychiatry*, Vol. 26(2), 207–19.

Farnham, F. R. and James, D. V. (2001) 'Dangerousness and Dangerous Law', *The Lancet*, Vol. 358, 8 December 2001, 1926.

Feeney, A. (2003) 'Dangerous Severe Personality Disorder', *Advances in Psychiatric Treatment* 9: 349–58, The Royal College of Psychiatrists.

Feeney, A. (2004) 'Alcohol and Sexual Violence: Key Findings from the Research', *Findings 215*, London: Home Office.

Ferguson, H. (1997) 'Protecting Children in New Times: Child Protection and the Risk Society', *Child and Family Social Work*, 1997, 2, 221–34.

Fielding, N. F. and Conroy, S. (1994), 'Against the Grain: Co-operation in Child Sexual Abuse Investigations' in S. Stephens and S. Becker (Eds.), *Police Force, Police Service*, Basingstoke: Macmillan Press Ltd.

Figgis, H and Simpson, R. (1997) *Dangerous Offenders Legislation: An Overview,* Briefing Paper 14/97, New South Wales Parliament, http://parliament.nsw.gov.au/prod/parlment/publications.nsf, accessed 15 April 2005.

Floud, J. (1982) 'Dangerousness and Criminal Justice', *The British Journal of Criminology*, Vol. 22(3), 213–28.

Floud, J. and Young, W. (1981) *Dangerousness and Criminal Justice,* London: Heinemann.

Garland, D. (2000) 'The Culture of High Crime Societies: Some Preconditions of Recent "Law and Order" Policies', *British Journal of Criminology*, 40, 347–75.

Garland, D. (2001) *The Culture of Control*, Oxford: Oxford University Press.

Giddens, A. (1990) *The Consequences of Modernity*, Cambridge: Polity.

Gillespie, A. A. (1998) 'Paedophiles and the Crime and Disorder Bill', *Journal of Current Legal Issues,* Issue No. 1.

Glancy, G. D. (2005) 'The Clinical Use of Risk Assessment', *Canadian Journal of Psychiatry*, Vol. 50(1), January 2005.

Glaser, B. (2003) 'Therapeutic Jurisprudence: An Ethical Paradigm for Therapists in Sex Offender Treatment Programmes', *Western Criminology Review*, 4(2), 143–54.

Gottlieb, S. (2003) *British Medical Journal News*, 327: 889 (18 October).

Gray, N., Lang, J., and Noaks, L. (Eds.) (2003), *Criminal Justice, Mental Health and the Politics of Risk*, London: Cavendish.

Gretton, H., McBride, M., Hare, R., O'Shaughnessy, R., and Kumka, G. (2001), 'Psychopathy and Recidivism in Sex Offenders', *Criminal Justice and Behaviour*, Vol. 28(4), 427–49.

Grier, A. and Thomas, T. (2001) 'The Employment of Ex-Offenders and the UK's New Criminal Records Bureau', *European Journal on Criminal Policy and Research*, 9: 459–69.

Grubin, D. (1998) 'Sex Offending Against Children: Understanding the Risk', *Police Research Series Paper 99*, Policing and Reducing Crime Unit, London: Home Office.

Hall, N. (2005a), *Hate Crime*, Cullompton: Willan Publishing.

Hall, N. (2005b) 'Community Responses to Hate Crime', in J. Winstone and F. Pakes, *Community Justice: Issues for Probation and Criminal Justice*, Cullompton: Willan Publishing.

Hanson, K. (2000), 'Will They Do It Again? Predicting Sex-Offense Recidivism', *Current Directions in Psychological Science*, Vol. 9(3), 106–9.

Hanson, R. K. and Thornton, D. (2000) 'Improving Risk Assessments for Sexual Offenders: A Comparison of Three Actuarial Scales', *Law and Human Behaviour*, 119–36.

Hare, R. D. (2003) 'Psychopathy and Risk for Recidivism and Violence', in N. Gray, J. Laing, and L. Noaks (Eds.) *Criminal Justice, Mental Health and the Politics of Risk*, London: Cavendish.

Hart, S., Laws, D. R., and Kropp, R. (2003), 'The Promise and the Devil of Sex Offender Risk Assessment' in T. Ward, D. R. Law, and S. M. Hudson (Eds.), *Sexual Deviance: Issues and Controversies*, Thousand Oaks: Sage Publications.

Hawkins, K. (1983) 'Assessing Evil', *British Journal of Criminology*, 23, 101–27.

Heilbrun, Jr, A. B. (1990) 'The Measurement of Criminal Dangerousness as a Personality Construct: Further Validation of a Research Index', *Journal of Personality Assessment*, 54 (1&2), 141–8.

Henman, R. (1997) 'Protective Sentences: Ethics, Rights and Sentencing Policy', *International Journal of the Sociology of Law*, Vol. 25(1), 45–63.

Henman, R. (2003) 'The Policy and Practice of Protective Sentencing', *Criminal Justice*, Vol. 3(1), 57–82.

Hinsliff, G. (2003) 'Jurors Could See Videos of Rape Victim Interviews', The Observer, 13 April 2003.

HMIP (1995) *Dealing with Dangerous People: The Probation Service and Public Protection, Report of a Thematic Inspection*, London: HMSO.

HMIP (1998) *Exercising Constant Vigilance: The Role of the Probation Service in Protecting the Public from Sex Offenders, Report of a Thematic Inspection*, London: HMSO.

HMIP and HMIC (2005) *Managing Sex Offenders in the Community: A Joint Inspection on Sex Offenders*, London: Home Office.

Holden, A. (1974) *The St Albans Poisoner, the Life and Times of Graham Young*, London: Hodder and Stoughton.

Hollway, W. and Jefferson, T. (1997), 'The Risk Society in an Age of Anxiety: Situating Fear of Crime', *British Journal of Sociology*, Vol. 48(2), 255–66.

Holmes, R. M. and Holmes, S. T. (1996) *Profiling Violent Crimes: An Investigative Tool* (2nd ed.) California: Sage.

Home Office (1996) *Protecting the Public*, Cm 3190, London: HMSO.

Home Office (1997a) 'The Prevalence of Convictions for Sexual Offending in England and Wales', *Home Office Research and Statistics Report*, No. 55.

Home Office (1997b) 'Community Protection Order: A Consultation Paper', November, London.

Home Office (1998) *The Processing of Rape Cases by the Criminal Justice System*, London: HMSO.

Home Office (2002) *Offenders' Risk of Serious Harm: A Literature Review*, RDS Occasional Paper No. 81.

Home Office (2005) 'A Gap or a Chasm? Attrition in Reported Rape Cases', *Home Office Research Study 293*, February 2005, London: Home Office RSD.

Hood, R., Shute, S., Feilzer, M., and Wilcox, A. (2002) 'Reconviction Rates of Serious Sex Offenders and Assessments of their Risk', *Findings 164*, London: Home Office.

Horlick-Jones, T. (2003), 'The Language and Technologies of Risk', in N. Gray, J. Lang, and L. Noaks (Eds.) (2003), *Criminal Justice, Mental Health and the Politics of Risk*, London: Cavendish.

Horsefield, A. (2003), 'Risk Assessment: Who Needs it?', *Probation Journal*, Vol. 50 (4), 374–9.

Houston, S. and Griffiths, H. (2000), 'Reflections on Risk in Child Protection: Is it Time for a Shift in Paradigms?' *Child and Family Social Work*, 5, 1–10.

http://www.nationalcrimesquad.police/uk/printpage.jsp?url=/about/onlinepaedophilia.jsp

http://www.ncis.co.uk/ukta/2003/threat09.asp

http://www.nspcc.org.uk/html/home/informationresources/noplace.htm

Hudson, B. (2001) 'Human Rights, Public Safety and the Probation Service: Defending Justice in the Risk Society', *The Howard Journal*, Vol. 40(2), 103–13.

Hudson, B. (2003) *Justice in the Risk Society*, London: Sage Publications.

Irwin, N., Delson, N., Kokish, R. and Tobin, T. (undated) 'Using the Internet to Provide Passive Community Notification about Registered Sex Offenders', A Resource Paper Prepared for The California Coalition on Sexual Offending.

Janus, E. S. and Prentky, R. A. (2003) 'Forensic Use of Actuarial Risk Assessment with Sex Offenders: Accuracy, Admissibility and Accountability', *40 American Criminal Law Review*, 1443: 1–59.

Jewkes, Y. and Andrews, C. (2005), 'Policing the Filth—the Problems of Investigating Online Child Pornography in England and Wales', *Policing and Society*, Vol. 15(1), 42–62.

Johnson, S. and Petrie, S. (2004) 'Child Protection and Risk Management: The Death of Victoria Climbié', *Journal of Social Policy*, 33(2), 179–202.

Johnson, T. C. and Doonan, R. (2005) 'Children with Sexual Behaviour Problems: What have we Learned in the Last Two Decades?' in M. C. Calder (Ed.) (32–58), *Children and Young People who Sexually Abuse. New Theory, Research and Practice Developments*, Lyme Regis: Russell House.

Kemshall, H. (1998) *Risk in Probation Practice*, Aldershot: Ashgate.

Kemshall, H. (2000) *Risk Assessment and Management of Known Sexual and Violent Offenders: A Review of Current Issues*. London: Home Office, Police Research Unit.

Kemshall, H. (2002) 'Risk, Public Protection and Justice' in D. Ward, J. Scott, and M. Lacey (Eds.), *Probation: Working for Justice*, Oxford: Oxford University Press.

Kemshall, H. and Maguire, M. (2001), 'Public Protection, Partnership and Risk Penality: The Multi-agency Risk Management of Sexual and Violent Offenders', *Punishment and Society*, Vol. 3(2), 237–64.

Kemshall, H. and Maguire, M. (2003) 'Sex Offenders, Risk Penality and the Problem of Disclosure to the Community', in A. Matravers (Ed.), *Sex Offenders in the Community, Managing and Reducing the Risks*, Cullompton: Willan Publishing.

King, S. (2003) 'Managing the Aftermath of Serious Case Reviews', *Child Abuse Review*, 12: 261–9.

Kirkman, C. A. (2002) 'Non-incarcerated Psychopaths: Why we Need to Know More about the Psychopaths who Live among us', *Journal of Mental Health Nursing*, 9(2), 155–60.

Knock, K., Schlesinger, P., Boyle, R., and Magor, M. (2002) 'The Police Perspective on Sex Offender Orders: A Preliminary Review of Policy and Practice', *Police Research Series Paper 155*, London: Home Office.

Krauss, D. A. and Dae Hoe Lee (2003), 'Deliberating on Dangerousness and Death: Jurors' Ability to Differentiate between Expert Actuarial and Clinical Predictions of Dangerousness', *International Journal of Law and Psychiatry*, Vol. 26(2), 113–37.

Laws, D. R. (2003) 'Penile Plethysmography: Will We Ever Get it Right?' in T. Ward, D. R. Laws, and S. M. Hudson (Eds.), *Sexual Deviance: Issues and Controversies*, Thousand Oaks: Sage Publications.

Lees, S. (2000) 'Marital Rape and Marital Murder' (57–73), in J. Hammer and C. Itzin (Eds.), *Home Truths about Domestic Violence—Feminist Influences on Policy and Practice. A Reader*. London: Routledge.

Leung, W-C. (2002), 'Human Rights Act 1998 and Mental Health Legislation: Implications for the Management of Mentally Ill Patients', *Postgraduate Medical Journal*, 78, 178–81.

Lieb, R. (2003) 'Joined-Up Worrying: the Multi Agency Public Protection Panels' in A. Matravers (Ed.), *Sex Offenders in the Community: Managing and Reducing the Risk*, Cullompton: Devon.

Lockwood, R. (undated) 'Factors in the Assessment of Dangerousness in Perpetrators of Animal Cruelty', www.pet-abuse.com, accessed 11 September 2005.

Lovell, E. (2001) *Megan's Law: Does it Protect Children? A Review of Evidence on the Impact of Community Notification as Legislated for through Megan's Law in the United States. Recommendations for Policy Makers in the United Kingdom*. London: NSPCC.

Lynch, M. (2005) 'Supermax Meets Death Row: Legal Struggles around the New Punitiveness in the US', in J. Pratt, D. Brown, M. Brown, S. Hallsworth, and W. Morrison, *The New Punitiveness: Trends, Theories, Perspectives*. Cullompton: Willan Publishing.

Matravers, A. (Ed.) (2003) *Sex Offenders in the Community: Managing and Reducing the Risk*, Cullompton: Willan Publishing.

Mawby, R. C. and Worrall, A. (2004) ' "Polibation" Revisited: Policing, Probation and Prolific Offender Projects', *International Journal of Police Science and Management*, Vol. 6(2), 63–73.

McWilliams, W. (1985) 'The Mission Transformed: Professionalisation of Probation between the Wars', *Howard Journal of Criminal Justice*, 24(4), 257–74.

McWilliams, W. (1986) 'The English Probation System and the Diagnostic Ideal', *Howard Journal of Criminal Justice*, 25(4), 241–60.

McWilliams, W. (1992) 'The Rise and Development of Management Thought in the English System' in R. Statham and P. Whitehead (Eds.), *Managing the Probation Service, Issues for the 1990s*, Harlow: Longman.

Melossi, D. (2000) 'Social Theory and Changing Representations of the Criminal' *British Journal of Criminology*, 40(2), 296–320.

Mikulski, A. (2004) 'Managing the Unmanageable—Dangerous Offenders and the MAPPA Process', Unpublished paper, British Society of Criminology Conference, Portsmouth, 8 July 2004.

MIND (2005) 'Government Rejects Proposals for "Service-based" Bill', www.mind.org.uk.

Moncrieff, J. (2003) 'The Politics of a New Mental Health Act', *The British Journal of Psychiatry*, 183: 89.

Mooney, J. (2000), 'Revealing the Hidden Figure of Domestic Violence', in J. Hammer and C. Itzin (Eds.), *Home Truths About Domestic Violence—Feminist Influences on Policy and Practice. A Reader*, London: Routledge.

Morris, N. (1994) ' "Dangerousness" and Incapacitation', in A. Duff and D. Garland (Eds.), *A Reader on Punishment*. Oxford: Oxford University Press.

Mossman, D. (1994) 'Assessing Predictions of Violence: Being Accurate about Accuracy', *Journal of Consulting and Clinical Psychology*, 62, 783–92.

Mullender, A. (1996) *Rethinking Domestic Violence: The Social Work and Probation Response*, London: Routledge.

Munro, E. (2005) 'A Systems Approach to Investigating Child Abuse Deaths', *British Journal of Social Work*, 35, 531–46.

Myhill, A. and Allen, J. (2002) *Rape and Sexual Assault of Women: The Extent and Nature of the Problem*, Home Office Research Study, No. 237, London: Home Office.

Nash, M. (1999a) *Police, Probation and Protecting the Public*, London: Blackstone Press.

Nash, M. (1999b) 'Enter the Polibation Officer', *International Journal of Police Science and Management* Vol. 1, No. 4, 360–8.

Nash, M. (2004) 'Polibation Revisited—A Reply', *International Journal of Police Science and Management*, Vol. 6(2), 74–6.

Nash, M. and Savage, S. P. (2001) 'Crime and Disorder under Blair', in S. P. Savage and R. Atkinson, *Public Policy under Blair*, Basingstoke: Palgrave.

National Crime Squad (2003) 'NCIS—UK Threat Assessment of Serious and Organised Crime', *Sex Offences Against Children, Including Online Abuse*, accessed at http://www.ncis.gov.uk/ukta/2003/default.asp.

National Probation Service (2004) *The MAPPA Guidance*, London: Home Office.

Nellis, M. and Gelsthorpe, L. (2003) 'Human Rights and the Probation Values Debate', in Chui, W. H. and Nellis, M. (Eds.), *Moving Probation Forward: Evidence, Arguments and Practice*, Harlow: Pearson Education.

NCH, 'Protecting Children from Risk: NCH's View', www.nch.org.uk.

O'Rourke, M. (1999) 'Dangerousness: How Best to Manage the Risk', *The Therapist*, Vol. 6(20), 11–12.

Parton, N. (2004) 'From Maria Colwell to Victoria Climbié: Reflections on Public Inquiries into Child Abuse a Generation Apart', *Child Abuse Review*, Vol. 13: 80–94.

Pearson, G. (1983), *Hooligan: A History of Respectable Fears*, London: Macmillan.

Peay, J. (2002), 'Mentally Disordered Offenders, Mental Health and Crime', in M. Maguire, R. Morgan, and R. Reiner (Eds.), *The Oxford Handbook of Criminology* (3rd ed.), Oxford: Oxford University Press.

Petrunik, M. (2003) 'The Hare and the Tortoise: Dangerous and Sex Offender Policy in the United States and Canada', *Canadian Journal of Criminology and Criminal Justice*, Issue 45: 1 (online).

Power, H. (2003) 'Disclosing Information on Sex Offenders: The Human Rights Implications' in A. Matravers (Ed.), *Sex Offenders in the Community: Managing and Reducing the Risks*, Cullompton: Willan Publishing.

Powis, B. (2002) 'Offender's Risk of Serious Harm: A Literature Review', *RDS Occasional Paper 81*, London: Home Office.

Pratt, J. (1997) *Governing the Dangerousness*, Sydney: Federation Press.

Prins, H. (1986) *Dangerous Behaviour, The Law and Mental Disorder*, London: Tavistock Publications.

Prins, H. (1988) 'Dangerous Clients: Further Observations on the Limitation of Mayhem', *British Journal of Social Work*, 18, 593–609.

Prins, H. (1989) 'The Importance of Previous Convictions in Assessing Criminal Motivation—the Need for Detail', *Medical Science and Law*, Vol. 29(2), 107–8.

Prins, H. (1998) 'Dangerous Offenders: Some Problems of Management', *International Review of Law, Computers and Technology*, Vol. 12(2), 1360–9.

Probation Circular 32/2005, *Identification of Individuals Who Present a Risk to Children: Interim Guidance*, London: National Probation Directorate.

Probation Circular 10/2005, *Public Protection Framework, Risk of Harm and MAPPA Thresholds*, London: National Probation Directorate.

Reder, P. and Duncan, S. (2004), 'Making the Most of the Victoria Climbié Inquiry Report', *Child Abuse Review*, Vol. 13: 95–114.

Richardson, E. and Freiburg, A. (2004), 'Protecting Dangerous Offenders from the Community: The Application of Protective Sentencing Laws in Victoria', *Criminal Justice*, Vol. 4(1): 81–102.

Robinson, G. (2002) 'Exploring Risk Management in Probation Practice: Contemporary Developments in England and Wales', *Punishment and Society*, Vol. 4(1): 5–25.

Robinson, G. (2003) 'Risk and Risk Assessment' in W. C. Chui and M. Nellis (Eds.) *Moving Probation Forward: Evidence, Arguments and Practice*, Harlow: Pearson Education.

The Royal College of Psychiatrists (2004), *Psychiatrists and Multi-Agency Public Protection Arrangements*, www.rcpsych.ac.uk.

Sampson, A. (1994) *Acts of Abuse: Sex Offenders and the Criminal Justice System*, London: Routledge.

Sampson, A. and Smith, D. (1992) 'Probation and Community Crime Prevention', *Howard Journal of Criminal Justice*, 31(2), 105–19.

Saraga, E. (1996) 'Dangerous Places: The Family as a Site of Crime' in J. Muncie and E. McLaughlin (Eds.), *The Problem of Crime*, Sage: London.

Saunders, H. (2005a) 'Twenty-nine Child Homicides: Lessons Still to be Learnt on Domestic Violence and Child Protection', Women's Aid Federation of England, Nalgaro Conference, Children at Risk from their Families (Unpublished paper).

Saunders, H. (2005b) 'Safety and Justice for Children in Families where there is Domestic Violence', Women's Aid Federation of England, Nalgaro Conference, Children at Risk from their Families (Unpublished paper).

Savage, S. P. and Nash, M. (1996) 'Yet Another Agenda for Law and Order: British Criminal Justice Policy Under the Conservatives', *International Criminal Justice Review*, Vol. 4, 37–51.

Scott, P. (1977) 'Assessing Dangerousness in Criminals', *British Journal of Psychiatry*, 131, 127–42.

Scottish Council on Crime (1975), *Crime and the Prevention of Crime*, Edinburgh: HMSO.

Sentencing Guidelines Council (2004) 'Overarching Principles: Seriousness', *Sentencing Guidelines Secretariat*, December 2004.

Sentencing Guidelines Council (2005) 'Manslaughter by Reason of Provocation: Draft Guidelines', *Sentencing Guidelines Secretariat*, May 2005.

Shute, S. (2004) 'The Sexual Offences Act 2003 (4) New Civil Prevention Orders: Sexual Offences Prevention Orders; Foreign Travel Orders; Risk of Sexual Harm Orders', *Criminal Law Review*, 2004, 417–40.

Silverman, J. and Wilson, D. (2002) *Innocence Betrayed: Paedophilia, the Media and Society*, Cambridge: Polity Press.

Skolnick, J. (1995) 'What Not To Do About Crime' *Criminology*, 33, 1–14.

Smit, D van Zyl and Ashworth, A. (2004) 'Disproportionate Sentences as Human Rights Violations', *Modern Law Review*, Vol. 67(4), 54–560.

Soothill, K. (2003) 'Serious Sexual Assault: Using History and Statistics' in A. Matravers (Ed.), *Sex Offenders in the Community: Managing and Reducing the Risks*, Cullompton: Willan Publishing.

Soothill, K. and Francis, B. (1997) 'Sexual Reconvictions and the Sex Offenders Act 1997', *New Law Journal*, 147: 1285–6, 1324–5.

Soothill, K., Francis, B., Sanderson, B., and Ackerley, E. D. (2000), 'Sex Offenders: Specialists, Generalists—Or Both? A 32-year Criminological Study', *British Journal of Criminology*, 40, 50–67.

Soothill, K., Francis, B., Ackerley, E., and Fligelstone, R. (2002) 'Murder and Serious Sexual Assault: What Criminal Histories can Reveal about Future Serious Offending', *Police Research Series Paper* 144, London: Home Office.

Stark, C., Paterson, B., and Devlin, B. (2004) 'Newspaper Coverage of a Violent Assault by a Mentally Ill Person', *Journal of Psychiatric and Mental Health Nursing*, 11(16), 635–43.

Sullivan, J. and Beech, A. (2002), 'Professional Perpetrators: Sex Offenders Who Use Their Employment to Target and Sexually Abuse the Children With Whom They Work', *Child Abuse Review*, Vol. 11, 153–67.

Szmukler, G. (2001) 'A New Mental Health (and Public Protection) Act', Editorial, *British Medical Journal*, 6 January 2001: 322–3.

Taylor, R. (2003) Home Office Findings 210, *An Assessment of Violent Incident Rates in the Dangerous Severe Personality Unit at HMP Whitemoor*, London: Home Office.

Thomas, D. (1998) 'The Crime (Sentences) Act 1977', *Criminal Law Review*, 83–92.

Thomas, D. (2004) 'The Criminal Justice Act 2003: Custodial Sentences', *Criminal Law Review*, 702–11.

Thomas, T. (2003) 'Sex Offender Community Notification: Experiences from America', *The Howard Journal*, Vol. 42 No. 3, 217–28.

Tonry, M. (2004) *Punishment and Politics: Evidence and Emulation in the Making of English Crime Control Policy*, Cullompton: Willan Publishing.

Valier, C. (2003) 'Minimum Terms of Imprisonment in Murder, Just Deserts and the Sentencing Guidelines', *Criminal Law Review*, 326–35.

Vaughan, B. (2000) 'The Civilizing Process and the Janus Face of Modern Punishment', *Theoretical Criminology*, Vol. 4(1), 71–91.

Verdum-Jones, S. N. (2000) *Acta Psychiatr Scand*, 200, 101: 77–82.

Von Hirsch, A. and Ashworth, A. (1996), 'Protective Sentencing under Section 2(2)(b): The Criteria for Dangerousness', *Criminal Law Review*, 175–83.

Walker, N. (Ed.) (1994), *Dangerous People*, London: Blackstone Press.

Ward, L. (2005) 'ASBO Chief Rounds on Liberal Critics', The Guardian, 10 June 2005.

Ward, T., Laws, R., and Hudson, S. M. (Eds.) (2003) *Sexual Deviance: Issues and Controversies*, Thousand Oaks: Sage Publications.

Watts, C. and Zimmerman, C. (2002) 'Violence against Women: Global Scope and Magnitude', *The Lancet*, Vol. 359 Issue 9313: 1232–7.

West, D. (1996) 'Sexual Molesters' in N. Walker (Ed.), *Dangerous People*, London: Blackstone Press.

White, S. M. (2002) 'Preventive Detention must be Resisted by the Medical Profession', *Journal of Medical Ethics*, 28, 95–8.

Wilcox, D. T., Richards, F., and O'Keefe, Z. (2004) 'Resilience and Risk Factors Associated with Experiencing Childhood Sexual Abuse', *Child Abuse Review*, Vol. 13: 338–52.

Williams, A. and Thompson, B. (2004a) 'Vigilance or Vigilantes: The Paulsgrove Riots and Policing Paedophiles in the Community, Part 1: The Long Slow Fuse', *The Police Journal*, Vol. 77, 99–119.

Williams, A. and Thompson, B. (2004b) 'Vigilance or Vigilantes: The Paulsgrove Riots and Policing Paedophiles in the Community, Part 2: The Lessons of Paulsgrove', *The Police Journal*, Vol. 77, 199–205.

Yamey, G. (1999) 'Government Launches Green Paper on Mental Health', *British Medical Journal*, 319: 1322.

Index